PARTNERSHIPS
COALITIONS

PARTNERSHIPS AND COALITIONS

SAMUEL MITCHELL

AuthorHouse™ LLC
1663 Liberty Drive
Bloomington, IN 47403
www.authorhouse.com
Phone: 1-800-839-8640

Published by AuthorHouse   09/17/2013

ISBN: 978-1-4918-1249-5 (sc)
ISBN: 978-1-4918-1248-8 (e)

Library of Congress Control Number: 2013915784

Contents

Dedication ix

Acknowledgments xi

Foreword: Erika Shaker, Editor *Our Schools/Our*
Selves Canadian Centre for Policy Alternatives xiii

**PART I: PERSONAL AND
POLITICAL OPTIONS** 1

Chapter 1:   Forging a Partnership for Survival,
Nancy, MacIntouch, former Inuit
Teacher and Lecturer at Prince
Edward Island University including Inuit 5

Chapter 2:   Coalitions Confronting Opponents,
Amanda Tattersall, Director of the
Sydney Alliance, (Australia) 31

Chapter 3:   University Students Help Urban
Neighbors, Melinda Pollard and Kerry
Kidwell-Slak, former Coordinators for
Washington University 52

PART II: COMMON GROUND 89

Chapter 4:   A Business Teacher Plans for the
Environment Michael Zanibbi,
Former Director, Enviroworks 93

Chapter 5: Credit Union Designs Partners in
Education (PIE), Kari Pepperkorn,
Corporate Citizenship Specialist,
First Calgary 123
Chapter 6: Conducting A Symphonic Partnership,
Roberta Lamb, Associate Professor
of Music, Queen's University 161
Chapter 7: Boundary Spanners,
Lynn Bradshaw, Professor,
East Carolina University 203

PART III: MAKING CONNECTIONS 245

Chapter 8: The Tie That Binds Local and
International Organizing,
Wade Rathke. Founder, Association of
Community Organizations for
Reform Now (ACORN) 249
Chapter 9: Linking Community, Business and Schools,
Rosalyn Black,
Senior Manager, Research and Evaluation,
The Foundation for Young Australians.......273
Chapter 10: Follow Your Star: A Rural Explosion,
Ann Jones, former Superintendent,
Southwest District, Nova Scotia............. 298

Chapter 11: Finding Issue for Urban Organizing,
             Judy Duncan, John Anderson,
             Jill O'Reilly, Josh Stuart,
             Tatiana Jaunzems, and James Wardlaw,
             Association of Community Organizations
             for Reform Now (ACORN) Canada,
             and Heather Marshall, Toronto
             Environmental Alliance 322
Chapter 12: After Partnerships 357

Bibliograpy **363**
Index **405**

Dedication

The highly individualistic people of North America have always had common experiences that united them. From the Boston Commons to Banff National Park, the people in these accounts sought support and renewal in these shared places and events. Ceremonies support partnerships today as they have in the past. The music partnership where the orchestra plays the 1812 Overture and the cannon on the hill in Kingston, Ontario is fired is discussed in Chapter 6. The musical celebrations represent the achievements of a dedicated group maintaining a partnership of musicians and teachers. Other partnerships reach across boundaries to achieve what would never have been expected before founding the new partnerships.

Acknowledgments

This book draws on the efforts of many people who contributed to it as well as the four proceeding volumes on partnership. Bernard Baum, Diana Lauber, Patricia Klinck, and John Burger have all tried to introduce the topic and approach as part of the partnership series (Mitchell, 2000a; Mitchell, 2002; Mitchell, Klinck &Burger, 2004, Mitchell, 2003 & 2005).

A number of people helped find authors for this particular volume: Tim Goddard, Ratna Ghosh, Azis Choudra, and Sharon Cook. The helpful readers include: Ross Campbell, Heather Basaraba, Gabriellle Ems, and Erin Corbett. For this book, Haili Cheng has provided computer and research assistance.

A large selection of photographs has been made available by First Calgary Financial. It is important that those for whom partnerships are created be represented in an account of partners and their advocates.

Family members, Helen Mitchell, Heloise Mitchell, and Charlotte Mitchell, have been both severe critics and unrelenting supporters. Helen's photograph of a statue in an Ottawa park symbolizes the interrelations and complexity of partnerships.

This book also reflects the experience of the editor in Canada, United States and internationally. The authors of individual chapters are drawing upon their direct experience with the organizations about which they are writing. We are all aware of academic writing and the contributions of many others as reflected in the bibliography.

Foreword

Erika Shaker, Editor *Our Schools/Our* Selves Canadian
Centre for Policy Alternatives

I'll be completely honest: the word 'partnership' makes me cringe.

This could have everything to do with the past 20 years I've spent documenting and analyzing the relationships between corporations and schools, relationships that inevitably are described as 'partnerships.' Whether it's Twizzlers providing study guides to students or Coca Cola entering into an exclusive selling agreement with a school board, or members of the community donating to education foundations and school breakfast programs, or WalMart or Indigo Bookstores 'adopting' schools or McDonalds sponsoring an award for 'exemplary' principals or vice principals, or even, in some cases, the more mundane relationships between school boards and the companies they contract with to provide photocopiers or computers, they all seem to be classified as 'partnerships.' Nothing in the label differentiates the blatantly commercial from the decidedly uncreative from the more community-based fundraising activities. And perhaps that's appropriate—not in the use of the partnership label itself, but because the end results in my experience are so similar: they are almost always market-driven (in mindset and in outcomes) and—in spite of some that are based on good intentions—they play a significant role in further dismantling already under-funded and over-stretched public schools.

My discomfort with the outcomes and intentions of many of these arrangements has been reinforced through years of examining blatant displays of commercial manipulation of the school environment— an environment that is particularly effective at "creating future workers and customers," according to at least one education development firm. The classroom provides access to a target market that is required to be there (until the age of 16), an environment that legitimizes the products, messages or entities associated with it, and the use of a respected authority figure (teacher) as a sort of corporate spokesperson. It also has a powerful connection with the community that surrounds the school—a connection that any body associated with the school can benefit enormously from (particularly when trying to mitigate a flagging corporate image, in the case of a number of these business-education relationships). Could that be why so many of these initiatives are referred to as "strategic philanthropy" or cause-related marketing?

But I have also been consistently wary of the terminology itself, of describing these clearly unbalanced arrangements as 'partnerships,' especially given the vulnerabilities of schools in a cost-cutting context that increasingly privileges the private over the public (in spite of recent and catastrophic downturns that one would have thought would shake our faith in the infallibility of the marketplace). How can the school possibly be considered an equal 'partner' when, due to financial insecurity and a series of ideological and rhetorical attacks on the public sector, it is far more dependant on the corporation than the other way around; when successful partnerships are based on the school fulfilling the public relations needs of the private partner? If the continuation of the 'partnership' is to a great extent based on the school becoming a sort of a promotional arm of the corporate entity, is the purpose or even the existence of the school compromised in the process?

Finally, as a strong supporter of local initiatives that serve to create and reinforce healthy, integrated communities, I am very concerned that as governments increasingly get out of the business of governing, more and more of those responsibilities are being taken up by dedicated volunteers. The line between charity and (underfunded and under-supported) public services becomes increasingly blurred, and the understanding of what we collectively own and benefit from becomes further eroded, ironically through the kindness of strangers and the downsizing of government. In an era of cost-cutting it may be a convenient way for elected representatives to get some up-front costs off the books, but it's no way to ensure a decent standard of living or to protect and ensure guaranteed rights for all of us, particularly the most vulnerable. However, in spite of the pitfalls, I'm also fascinated with the potential many of these community-based initiatives (and the impulses that are at their root) has to subvert the hyper-individualized, dog-eat-dog mantra that characterizes many of the market-based reforms imposed on the public sector in general and education in particular.

So given my frame of reference and my professional and personal experience in this area, there's something a deliciously ironic in my writing the foreword to this book.

But once I recovered from my initial discomfort, I realized I was looking forward to the opportunity to really interrogate how such a seemingly positive term—partnership—become, for me, so loaded. I also was particularly interested in a book that examines a variety of self-described partnerships, both inside and outside schools, because in many respects it forced me to revisit a number of my long-held concerns and criticisms in a new, albeit related, context. It also required me to ask several questions:

1. Does each chapter describe a partnership, or is the name simply being applied (appropriately or not) to any integrated relationship?
2. Do the chapters replicate the familiar and unbalanced model of the corporate-driven model of school-business partnerships, or do they speak to a different kind of relationship?
3. What connections can exist or be created between the school and an outside body, and do they interact with each other in a way that actually

reinforces the notion of the neighborhood school, or the school as a community hub?

Some of the chapters only further reinforced my past experience—certainly phrases like "business *is* the classroom," "prepar[ing] young people for the New Economy workplace" and "Partners in Education business benefits primarily revolve around creating awareness and generating positive and unique ways in which to position the organization's brand" do nothing to counter or alleviate the concerns I have with business-education "partnerships". But other chapters evoked a very different, much more nuanced response.

I found myself wondering, for example, if it was appropriate or accurate for a teacher from the South to refer to her experience working in Nunavut as developing a partnership with the community in order to better serve and respond to the needs of students. "My goal was to partner with these people for the sake of their children," she explains. I have no doubt that the author underwent a pivotal experience both as an individual and as a teacher while in the North, and I applaud her wholehearted attempts to understand and connect with the people in the community she was there to serve. I also commend her ability to reevaluate the concept of education and how it resonated—or did not—with the knowledge(s) embedded in that community and the lives of the people within it. But, as with so many other self-described partnerships, the broader context of the real power dynamic is ubiquitous and continues to be reinforced. "It really comes down to power," the author explains. I agree.

But the systemic and unbalanced power structure that is always present in the author's very presence in the community remains unexamined. Perhaps ironically, it is for this reason that I so appreciated reading this chapter—it allowed me the opportunity to parse out the differences between these more personal partnerships and the larger, systemic framework in which they take place; and to determine the ways in which power dynamics work in these relationships which are all, to some extent, about vulnerability and dependence.

Other chapters positioned the school as one player in a network established to create broad systemic change: in advocating for students with special needs; in creating a multi-faceted civic engagement project for students to address community needs and promote awareness and understanding of socio-economic inequities through education and placement of volunteers in agencies driving social change; in creating an interagency partnership designed to model and support the delivery of integrated health, education, and social services to children and their families. These examples appear to be offshoots of the model of the school as a community wheel, where the school's close and integrated relationship with its surrounding community allows it to play a prominent and effective role in social change.

One chapter described an initiative so thoughtful and earnest that I want to end with it because it seemed to me to be as multifaceted and self-reflexive as any good education should be. I found myself thoroughly engaged and inspired by the description of the Kingston Symphony Education Partnership: a unique relationship between the Kingston Symphony Association, Limestone District School Board, Algonquin and Lakeshore Catholic District School Board, and Queen's University School of Music (with participation from the Faculty of Education which is responsible for music teacher certification). I found the constant self-evaluation, the emphasis on education (as opposed to the refrain of "providing a return on investment") and on broad community learning and involvement to be thoughtfully undertaken. But sadly, I understand the program may be ended as Queen's University School of Music is potentially on the chopping block of funding cuts.

I worry that this will be the final irony—that this thoughtful, rich and evocative relationship between public entities may, as a result of the cost-cutting that privileges certain aspects of an education over others, be forced to rely on private largesse to ensure it continues in one form or another as a successful partnership. It's a pattern we've seen repeated time and again; a pattern based on dependence on the kindness of strangers; a pattern that so often evokes my near-automatic response when the terminology of partnerships is broached. I cringe.

Let's hope that, where this initiative is concerned, such a pattern is not inevitable.

PART I

PERSONAL AND POLITICAL OPTIONS

Partnerships can exist particularly in schools that do not touch most of the people in them (Mitchell, 2003). Although not touching most of the people there, the program coordinators and students and teachers, who are involved in the programs, find them meaningful and important. However, partnerships in schools are directed towards students or parents, who are 'problems.' As a result partnerships do not usually change the curriculum or the school as a whole.

Many of the partners may not even know they are linked to the school or other organizations as partners. Particularly, business people may resist making mere donations (Zanibbi, 2001). Business and other leaders may welcome the opportunity to be involved in classes, serve a community need, and solve one of their own business problems. The greater number of groups involved, the more critical it is that a common interest is developed. The most important interest is that of the community and the responsibilities of being a citizen.

Our first selection takes us to the isolation of Canada's North where the teacher, Nancy MacIntouch, finds a partnership with the Natives is essential for her own survival. This partnership with the Inuit allowed her to share her school culture with their traditional ways. Many teachers take the option of remaining in their own white world, but Nancy tries to help her students, understand their parents, and enrich her own life by forming a partnership with them. Partnerships are probably essential for all forms of multi-cultural education.

Emphasizing political options as she initially developed a coalition to protect class sizes and the quality of education, Amanda Tattersall went to the United States and Canada to study strategies that unions and community groups could use to bring about political change there. Among countries there were surprising similarities. In each country for example, she found that small focused coalitions could be more effective than large and diverse ones. She has shown how international views of partnerships can enhance the possibilities of change that they can bring about. Political involvement can be more than personal involvement with a different culture.

Perhaps more involved with diversity than anyone else, college students in Washington, District of Columbia, are expected to connect with their poor urban neighbors. The program at George Washington University is mind shattering in its diversity, but the evidence from student coordinators of the effects the program has had on the students and community is startling. The number of organizations, which the student coordinators, such as Kerry Kidwell-Slak report, is particularly telling in their perception of themselves in this complex project. Outside evaluators may have to prove the effectiveness of this program, but for the participants this program shows relationships being established which will long be a source of pride in the lives of students who came to help their neighbors.

In the accounts of our initial three authors, there is no option for remaining an isolated person in one's own space. The ways in which the personal can become political are further explored to show how institutions connect and individual perspectives change. Conflict between institutions, like businesses, schools, and the arts, are also considered as individual creativity is enhanced or personal alienation is imposed.

Chapter 1
Forging a Partnership for Survival

Nancy, MacIntouch, former Inuit Teacher and Lecturer at
Prince Edward Island University including Inuit

I remember clearly my first week in Auluq, an Inuit community located half way up Baffin Island on the west coast. I remember stepping off the plane and thinking right away how beautiful the mountains were and how warm it was on that August day. I could not believe all the modern amenities that were available. There was a taxi service, a fast food outlet, and a department store. The school was more modern than many I had seen in the south. The building began. We were from various parts of Canada, the majority were from the Maritimes and a handful were from Ontario. There were four teachers out of twenty who were Inuit from the area. We were all in our classrooms working away when my first opportunity to develop a partnership with the community presented itself.

I heard teachers running down the hall yelling, 'Go down to the fiord, there's a beluga whale close to shore.' I was thrilled. I had only seen one of these magnificent animals at Sea World in a glass cage and was very excited to have this opportunity to see one in the wild. I immediately ran to catch up to the other teachers. As I approached the shore, I slowed down in utter horror. The first glimpse I got by the time I reached the gravel by the beach was of a huge crowd gathering out of which I could hear loud popping sounds. I could see the water splashing with every pop and realized with a start that this beluga was being hunted. I began to run again to get closer to the crowd. Everyone was there, construction workers, power company workers, the post mistress, parks people, teachers, nurses, mothers, fathers, kids, police officers and three Inuit men holding guns. The popping continued until a flurry of Inuktitut words flew through the crowd, back and forth. Boats surrounding the whale raced toward shore. Suddenly, out of the crowd, a man brought up to his shoulder a long, pointed harpoon. Slowly and carefully he took aim while the boats maneuvered the whale closer to where the man waited. And then it happened. The harpoon shot from the man's body and the water began to turn red. Great cheers came roaring from the throng and I bowed my head.

I remembered everything people had told me about living in the north. I smiled and nodded at the smiling, nodding faces looking back at me. I watched with my frozen smile as they hoisted the ten-foot, one-year-old male beluga whale onto shore. And I stood frozen as the crowd suddenly lowered their heads and grew silent. All at once I knew. If I did not figure out how to forge a partnership with the people of this small community of 1400, I would be lost. What I set out to do here would not get done. I would not be able to reach my students and I would not be able to communicate properly with their parents. I had to figure out how my journey in Auluq would unfold.

While most partnerships are set up from the perspective of both sides coming together in the context of agreement, the partnership I was about to embark upon was unbalanced before it began. With the killing of the beluga whale, I was experiencing my first glimpse of a cross-cultural community in which I was one of only a few in the minority. I was the outsider, the 'other.' I was the outsider who was invited in to do a job that the government in Ottawa deemed necessary. The people in Auluq were not certain that schooling in the form that white teachers presented was of use to their children or to their community. My goal was to partner with these people for the sake of their children.

As for the whale, once the prayer was said, three men straddled the beast while they held up their huge knives. They dug in and skillfully carved the animal into pieces for all to share. Everyone there (including non-Inuit and Inuit alike) got a piece and most ate right where they stood. People were helping each other get their share of this bounty and I didn't have the heart to refuse the smiling-faced man handing me a rectangle of the blubber and maqtaak for me to eat. I politely held my piece of the whale and walked quickly back to the school. There, in the staff room, were two Inuit teachers eating their share. Lisi, a grade six teacher, noticed that I was nibbling on my piece and began to laugh. She came over to where I was sitting and took the piece from my hand. She grabbed her ulu and skillfully cut the piece into tiny squares—separate on the top, but still attached on the bottom. I learned to scrape the squares of skin off the blubber with my teeth. I had been eating the blubber and dribbling whale fat down my chin. I almost gagged at the taste of the whale skin, but chewed anyway, hoping not to insult the two ladies sharing this feast with me.

In my southern way I saw the Beluga whale as a zoo animal in the wild, never thinking for a minute that any harm would come to it when I ran down toward the crowd at the shore. Instead, I was faced with a food source, 'a gift from God' as the people there were calling it; why else would it have traveled so close to shore? This animal represented to the people that day their very survival. How naïve I was when I think back; and what a rude awakening I got that day.

Many things have changed after that experience. That day on the shore reminded me that I was in the North, in a land so harsh that those living in its midst must band together, must partner with each other, in order to survive . . . a land surprisingly full of warmth traced in the twinkling smiles of its people . . . a land full of mystery and imagination, color and harmony, perspective and dimensions not seen by most people in the world. My journey into this land of community had begun.

Context

The Inuit in Northern Canada present for many people the quintessential example of culture as adaptive response. The Arctic presents for its inhabitants an environment in which very few careless actions can be afforded. Cold temperatures, polar bears, raging blizzards, physical accidents, mechanical failures, and wrong turns on the trail can turn a seemingly natural occurrence like hunting into a fatal tragedy. We have romanticized the Inuit connection with nature, but really, when you are amidst that nature, you need your wits about you at all times. You need to know how to survive. And in order to survive in this environment, you need to create connections with the people.

The Inuit have evolved into a people who reap what they need, do what they need to do and go where they need to go in order to further their race. In my experience, there is very little pretense in Inuit culture. Most of the Inuit people I met while in Auluq told me the truth. Sometimes I did not want to hear what they had to say, but most of the time I really appreciated the candor. The Inuit language is very complex. As Brody (2000) explains:

> . . . words used by the Inuit create the world as well as describe it. A person can explain how a word is used and what it refers to, but the word's meaning depends on knowing a web of contexts and concealed

> related meanings . . . . Therefore, it is held the
> language of the Inuit cannot be translated into
> the language of the Qallunaaq (p. 49).

The term "Inuk-ti-tut" literally translated means "in the manner of an nuk." To learn the language of the Inuit is not just to learn how to verbally express yourself, but which means to learn about "a way of being" (Brody 2000, p. 64). It is sad that the youth are gradually losing this unique "way of being." One of the very unique, and very sad, aspects of the Inuktitut language is that grandparents and teenagers do not have the same words in their vocabularies. So, some of the words for the things teenagers like and do are not in the vocabularies of their grandparents. Communication is limited between generations.

Along with communication difficulties, there is the issue of racism. Before moving to the North, I had what I believed to be a fairly broad understanding of what was meant by the term *racism*. I really had no idea. No matter where I was in the past and no matter what I was doing, I always fought against racism. But the racism I claimed to be fighting never directly affected me. I was really sheltered from the whole meaning of racism in any context.

In the North, there are two forms of racism acting simultaneously. There is the racism that the Inuit have struggled through for many years resulting in some rather horrific stories and scars; and there is the racism that

Qallunaaq (white) people experience when they are in the North delivered by some of the people who live there. It really comes down to power. O'Donoghue (1998) points out:

> . . . collaborative relations of power are based on the belief that power is available to be used positively and ethically in our daily interactions in order to promote practices of freedom, while coercive relations of power are present within institutional structures which tend to promote control and governance through rules, policies.

There are a number of positive situations involving many different people working together but there are also some very negative, very racist situations that occur. I have witnessed both of these, the latter in rather surprising ways. Of course, it was my being naive that clouded my vision about the fact that I might experience racist attitudes toward me. My vision was also clouded regarding the possibility that some of the people with whom I worked exhibited racist behavior toward others. In forging the partnerships with the community, I worked to eliminate as much racism from my time in Auluq as possible. In setting out on a calculated path to learn the language and to attend all community events, whenever they occurred, I was able to become a member of the community to some degree instead of remaining on the outside, as many white teachers experience during their time in the North. I was determined to figure out how I could negotiate with the people there so that we could live together without angst, to the best of our ability. I learned very quickly that much had happened to keep our negotiations tense without me having a full appreciation of what the tenseness encompassed.

I knew that whenever there is racism, there are reasons for the people's fear or anger. And I knew that Auluq was no different. Usually racism involves fear of the unknown—usually the fear of a culture or a race, or of the differences of the people being treated in racist ways. In Nunavut there are many reasons for fearing the unknown including the fact that in the context of Nunavut, Inuit, though they are the majority, still do not hold the power in society. The power structures, in government and private business, though they are changing, still reflect those of a colonial era. Most government bureaucracies and successful businesses are led by Qallunaat. "Qallunaat are economically advantaged, holding most of the wealth in Nunavut communities . . . . [This economic disparity] is visibly evident within most communities, supported by obvious differences in the quality of homes, vehicles and other signs of the economic prosperity" (O'Donoghue, 1998, p. 186).

There are many stories the people told me that caused me to feel a real sense of guilt for being white. I learned of many horrific things that the Inuit had to endure because of the colonization of their land. One memorable story was told to me by an elder couple. The story was about the legendary dog killings that happened in the early 1960s. The Inuit claim that the government was attempting to move the Inuit into communities. To do so, the Inuit claim, the government assigned the R.C.M.P. to have the Inuit come to specific centers for a meeting, Auluq being one of these centers. As Solomonie explained to me:

> My dogs were real fighters as if they knew the polar bears were their enemies. I knew the polar bear wouldn't come at me because of the dogs.

Richard Harrington (1981, p. 106) expounds that "nothing symbolized more the perfect harmony and adaptability of the traditional Inuit way of life than the relationship with their dogs. The hunters and the dogs were completely dependent on each other." Of course the act of killing all the dogs did force the Inuit to move into communities. Solomonie told me that he had to walk well over 26 hours to get to his wife and six children back out on the tundra in order to save them from certain death. He was very angry that his dogs were killed. He and his dogs were the very survival of his family. He had to move his family into Auluq. There were given a house, but as he told me, a house does not replace hunting dogs.

Another significant event that took place during this same time frame was the naming of the people in the North. During this period in the 1960s, officials from the

Canadian Government came to the North and assigned each person with a number. The people were assigned numbers because they did not have last names which were necessary for the government to carry out a census. Solomonie explained what he remembered about that time:

> Back then, we didn't have last names—we had numbers. For example, I was 378. But we don't use them anymore; we started to have last names. Long ago, I remember that we only had the one name. Our last names come from our father's name. The name you got was it; no one had nicknames. (Conversation with Solomonie and Rosie Akpalialuk, May 2, 2002).

During my conversation with Solomonie and Rosie I was struck with how kind they were to me. I could not believe how open and willing to share they were about stories that must have caused them great pain to talk about. So as I was a teacher, teaching their grandchildren, I wanted to know how they felt about Qallunaaq teachers teaching their family. Solomonie explained that he liked Qallunaaq teachers teaching his family because now they can speak both English and Inuktitut. He said:

> I like it also because that's the only way they're going to have jobs in the future.

Before, how we were educated was how to hunt, but nowadays they don't educate them that way anymore. But I like it. I want the kids to know Inuit traditional ways; I want them (the Qallunaaq teachers) to notice because the kids today are not taking the language and the traditions seriously. I want people to know the truth about what it is to be Inuit. (Conversation with Solomonie and Rosie Akpalialuk, May 2, 2002).

The conversation I had with Solomonie and Rosie changed my life. I was forced to change my perspective about things that I had heard about from childhood. I heard about "Eskimo" peoples from Northern Canada, and really thought I had a bit of an understanding about Inuit culture and hunter-gatherer societies. However, as I spoke to Rosie and Solomonie, and listened to their stories, I developed a new understanding about the history of the Inuit in the Baffin region. I asked Solomonie what he wanted me to say to the people who might read this and he simply replied. 'the truth.'

EBB AND FLOW OF PARTNERSHIP

I had a dream that all the people of the world were together in one place. The place was cold. Everyone was shivering. I looked for a fire to warm myself. None was to be found.

Then someone said that in the middle of the gathering of Indians, what was left of the fire had been found. It was a very, very small flame. All the Indians were alerted that the slightest rush of air or the smallest movement could put the fire out and fire would be lost to humankind. All the Indians banded together to protect the flame. They were working to build the fragile feeble flame. They added minuscule shavings from toothpicks to feed it. Suddenly, throughout the other peoples, the whisper was heard. 'The Indians have a fire.' There was a crash of bodies stampeding to the place where the flame was held. I pushed to the edge of the Indian circle to stop those coming to the flame so that it would not be smothered. The other people became hostile saying they were cold too and it was our responsibility to share the flame with them. I replied, 'It is our responsibility to preserve the flame for humanity and at the moment it is too weak to be shared but if we all are still and respect the flame it will grow and thrive in the caring hands of those who hold it. In time we can all warm at the fire. But now we have to nurture the flame or we will all lose the gift.' (King, 1998).

I use this story as a metaphor to explain a little of what my thoughts are about being a southerner in the North. I am one of the people rushing the flame in this story, to warm myself and my family, not to do wrong, but in the interest of self-preservation. Sometimes I feel as though the education system in the North is like this metaphor as well. The Inuit are trying desperately to preserve the 'flame' of their culture and 'the other people' are rushing in to promote their own ways. Often we, who move north, even though we have the best of intentions, almost extinguish the 'flame.' By passing on knowledge through the observation and imitation embedded in daily family and community activities, for the Inuit, immediate personal experience and shared social structure are integrated. The focus is on values and identity, which is developed through the learner's relationship to other persons and to the environment (p. 140). For these people, personal excellence involves being socially adept in any situation. While social involvement and interaction has a very important place in southern schools and communities, personal excellence is paramount. But looking at involvement and interaction in social situations in Auluq, what is acceptable and what is not acceptable is quite different from what I was used to from my experience.

Personal excellence in the "southern" way of thinking is seen as secondary to being socially mature. As Stairs (1995) explains: "Awareness of interpersonal relationships and one's role in the social network is what constitute maturity; this social competence has priority over individual excellence and productivity" (p. 143). So while there are those who seemingly excel in certain areas, when you put all the strengths of all the people together, the whole is stronger than the individual.

In the way I was brought up and schooled, I was only able, for whatever reason, to acknowledge that I knew something once I was told by someone, a parent or a teacher, that I actually knew it. That is not the case in Inuit society. The children learn from older siblings things that are very necessary to the group. So children learn at a very early age that they can contribute something very important to their society. Children in traditional, non-native societies from southern Canada often learn skills that cannot be generalized to anything else or to any other context, but they learn to live with this reality. They learn because they have to, not because they need to. They learn because someone is telling them that they have to cover a certain amount and type of material within a certain amount of time.

In what Stairs (1995) calls *Ilisayaq*, teaching (the type of teaching found in most schools in the south) "involves a high level of abstract verbal mediation in a setting removed from daily life, the skills of a future specialized occupation being the principal goal" (p. 140). In traditional Inuit society, the young learn out of necessity for survival. It becomes apparent relatively early if one is to be a hunter, a great story-teller, or whatever else one seems to be aspiring to, and the society works together so that all the pieces fit together to form a cohesive whole. If one of the pieces is missing or doesn't quite fit in, then there are problems for the survival of the whole.

Prior to the 1960s, there were no social workers, police officers or school officials to deal with these anomalies, so the group itself dealt with problems. There would be the elders and a great deal of pressure from the group for the person to conform. If he or she didn't, there would be very drastic measures taken. There simply was not much tolerance for delinquency. The very survival of the whole depended upon unity.

Today, the way Inuit society works in the midst of a great deal of Southern influence is quite different from how it worked traditionally. Because of so many changes happening so quickly, many problems have emerged. In 2000, an initiative was undertaken to provide answers to the questions surrounding the problems facing Inuit people in today's society. A document was put together by the Nunavut Social Development Council entitled, *On Our Terms, The State of Inuit Culture and Society.* In this document there are very startling statistics and information about education in the Canadian Arctic; for instance, "Education in Nunavut is a serious problem. In 2006, 51% of the Inuit did not have a high school diploma. And only 4% of the adult population had a university degree (www.statscan.gc.ca). There are many possible reasons for this low number of graduates. In my experience, I found that some of the reasons are not what many people might think.

During the time, I was in Auluq, I formed partnerships with mainly the youth in the community. Out of a possible 37 graduates, only 15 students ended up graduating from high school. This number, to me, is quite upsetting, but if we look at the overall statistics in Nunavut, the number of graduates in Auluq was quite a bit higher than in many other communities. What I noticed was there were different categories of possible graduates: students who, if they completed the subjects assigned to them for their grade 12 year, could graduate. Out of this group there were those students who just simply did not have the ability to complete what was required of them. Among these students there were those who had ESL issues, learning problems, or personal issues keeping them from attending school. I could get into a great amount of detail about each of these sub-categories, but I am just providing an idea here about what I noticed during my interactions with the students I taught. I would suggest that another category comprised students who actually were quite capable of graduating but really did not want to because there was nothing for them to do once they did graduate. I felt most sorry for this group of students. They were the ones who were undecided about what they wanted to do when they graduated and usually had financial issues about going to a post secondary institution to further their education. And finally, there were those students who were capable and determined to graduate no matter what they were going to do after graduation.

Out of this last group of students, there was a mixture of ability levels, English language proficiency and aspirations for the future. There were students who wanted to be hunters, nurses, lawyers, and mothers. There were males and females and there were students ranging from 17 to 22 years of age during the time I was involved with teaching grade 12 in Auluq. I worked with these students to fill out application forms for colleges, universities and funding institutions. I worked with the other groups of students in grade 12 as well. The category of students who had the ability to graduate but, for different reasons did not, were the ones I worked with the most. I noticed a trend within this group of students. I would say that out of the 37 possible graduates during the time I was in Auluq, this group comprised 9 students. There were 8 males and 1 female. This group seemed to have a rather defeatist attitude. They often would seemingly give up on tests and other assignments and, for the most part, decided quite early in the grade 12 year that they were not going to graduate.

I met with these students in my home after school and spent a considerable amount of time giving them pep talks in school. Out of the nine students in this group, my extra pushing and motivation worked for only one. I say "worked" because one of these students did graduate and did go to college. He successfully completed his college program and is now an R.C.M.P. officer in Auluq. But it was a constant struggle trying to convince this boy that he could, in fact, graduate and that there was life after high school. In his particular case I had lots of support from his parents. I think, in retrospect, the partnership I forged with his parents was the key factor in his success. In the eight other cases, the parents did not interact at all. I would call the parents to discuss the possibility of their child not graduating and I would be met with a "so what" kind of response. Initially, their responses upset me, until I came to understand that the most important thing in their lives was not the graduation of their son or daughter. There were many other important things and many other successes that they celebrated with their children; these were not necessarily things that I would consider successes until I remembered where I was and in which culture I was living amidst. Again, in spite of my understanding and in spite of the negotiating I had worked on to create the partnerships with the parents and students, two cultures were colliding. I had to constantly remind myself that my ways were not their ways and that I was the outsider, not the people with whom I was interacting.

As mentioned, *Isumaqsayuq* is the term used by Stairs (1995) to describe the traditional method of educating the young in the Arctic. As she explains, *Isumaqsayuq* "validates knowledge on the basis of life experience and community consensus. This knowledge is conveyed holistically and thematically." (p. 144). Also, as mentioned previously, Stairs (1995) uses the term *Illisayuq* to describe the way the young are educated in southern schools and in northern schools most recently in Inuit history. As she explains,

> *Illisayuq* validates knowledge on the basis of objective proof and expert opinion. It conveys knowledge in abstract, universal categories (for instance, insects, fish, mammals, or science, philosophy, art) rather than situational specifics, and it organizes these categories into hierarchies rather than treating each in its own right (p. 145).

I believe that one way to be productive as a teacher in the north is to take both philosophies and marry them somewhat in one's approach to teaching. Putting these completely different philosophies together in any cohesive whole is really a difficult task. I found myself fighting my urge to control and to have students memorize facts *just because*. Instead, I used portfolios and provided marks for the completion of tasks not for the correctness of tasks. In other words, my teaching changed completely. Two philosophies came together. As O'Donoghue (1998) explains:

> It seems reasonable to suggest that teachers are, to some extent, influenced by cultural reproduction, and that changing deeply engrained patterns of behavior requires teachers to critically examine their beliefs and their willingness to maintain and accept the status quo. This kind of critical reflection can shake educators to the core (p. 180).

This coming together of the two philosophies and my unwillingness to maintain and accept the status quo had not gone on without much pain and strain along the way, both personally, in my own teaching and for the whole education system in the north. Hugh Brody (2000), in his book *The Other Side of Eden,* has a strong opinion about the two cultures over education. As he writes:

> The residential school was part of a process of ethnocide. The plan that shaped these schools, and the attitudes that informed their daily regimens, emerged from the agriculturalists' need to get rid of hunter-gatherers. These schools represent a dedicated and ruthless attempt to transform the personalities and circumstances of 'native people' into . . . well, what? Farm workers and industrial labourers? Domestic servants and housewives? All of these, and yet the project is easier to understand as a negative rather than as a positive undertaking. The intention was to stop people being who they were—to ensure that they could no longer live and think and occupy the land as hunter-gatherers. The new and modern nation-states make no room for hunter-gatherers (p. 189).

Even though Brody's words might sound rather harsh, the situation he illuminates still resonates in today's educational facilities in the north. In his experience, Brody explains that "In the history of the 'education' provided [to Arctic peoples], there is no acknowledgment that hunter-gatherers had a right to be on their lands, nor a jot of concern for their skills and knowledge" (p. 189).

What Brody is saying is similar to what Stephen Harris (1990) points out in his book, *Critical Multiculturalism: Rethinking Multicultural and Antiracist Education*:

> Radical theorists have argued that there would appear to be an irreducible gap between the emancipator conception of multicultural education as cultural pluralism, and the realities of school practices (p. 40).

For those going into another culture to teach, there should be culturally based curriculum guides to follow. But, in spite of all the documents supporting a culture-based curriculum, the educational system within which I worked in Auluq still did not fully acknowledge the "right" of the Inuit people to be educated according to who they are. There were pockets of time when cultural activities were taking place, but these were outside the regular curriculum, not part of it. There were no marks given for these activities and there was no acknowledgment of these activities other than the verbal appreciation of the teachers involved. I had to keep my eyes wide open the entire time I was teaching in Auluq. I looked specifically for ways I could develop partnerships with the people there. I also worked hard to bring the culture into my classroom. I looked for opportunities for a teachable moment.

Some of the partnerships that I forged for survival included those I made with my students while slipping on skies in the mountains and flying across the tundra. I worked at these partnerships by opening the gym at lunchtime and during recess so that the students (and I) would not have to go out in the icy cold temperatures. I developed partnerships with my students by visiting them in their homes with their families. And I created partnerships with my students by setting up times during which I could help them with their studies. I had to change my perspective about how I would help each student. My goal moved from promoting academic success to helping each of them succeed on their own terms to help them with their own futures.

One of the most important lessons I learned was from a young Inuit boy named Adam. Adam was 14-years old and a very traditional Inuit person in both his beliefs and his values. His goal in life was to become a sculptor and the few little pieces he shared with me certainly indicated that he was well on his way. It was the end of June. Adam had not been in school for about a week by the time he was supposed to write his final English exam for grade 10. Even though I called his house the night before, Adam did not show up. It was around 4pm when I gave up waiting for him and was leaving the school. From across the half frozen gravel surrounding the school I spied Adam walking out of the glare of the Arctic sun toward me. He was carrying a nap sack very carefully as it hung over the front of his torso.

Adam called to me asking me to wait for him. He jogged the last few meters. I told him that he did not come to his final English exam. He smiled and very earnestly replied that he knew. His smile warmed me; his eyes twinkled. He began to open the flap of his nap sack and then he carefully pulled out a magnificent sculpture. Adam had worked all week at this skillfully carved piece of art; it was his first bigger piece he ever did on his own. The soap stone was now a perfectly shaped polar bear standing on its hind legs. In the polar bear's grasp was a huge, startled-looking walrus, also perfectly shaped. Adam's syllabic initials were carved in the bottom of the foot. I was speechless.

Adam gently moved the statue toward me and told me he wanted me to have it. I didn't know what to say. He told me that this was the first real piece that he did totally by himself. Then I remembered the final English exam that he had missed. I carefully accepted the cold statue Adam was handing to me. His eyes sparkled even more brightly. I explained to Adam that since stories were a major part of the grade 10 academic English that year, he had just passed the course. The story shining in my hands at that moment was perfect with every expertly carved curve. Adam said thanks, gave me one more wonderful smile and headed back across the gravel. I cried as I took the soapstone sculpture home with me.

On that day, all my learning and experience came together. Why are we doing what we do as teachers? Whose culture are we teaching? During my two years in Auluq, my beliefs changed in terms of my teaching! I became more aware of Isumqsayuq, "the way of passing on knowledge through the observation and imitation embedded in daily family and community activities" (Stairs 1995 p. 140). I now believe that no matter where I teach, we must hold on to Isumqsayuq to some degree. School is not the only place that learning takes place; school learning must connect with community education.

I now am flexible in the way I look at both summative and formative assessment practices. I always involve my students in the assessment process as well as their parents (if age appropriate). I ask myself why we are going through these processes and if I have appropriate assessments planned for each of my students.

As a mother of five who did not get my Bachelor of Education until I was 35, I understand the importance of education for each individual according to his or her needs. I have been called a late bloomer, but I know I have been blooming all along. I never want to have my education end—to stop learning would be death for me.

My two years in the North were difficult. I was separated from my family and friends for most of the time. I had always been drawn there since I can remember so when the opportunity presented itself, I gave myself no other choice but to go. Thankfully, I am blessed with a very understanding and helpful family or this wonderful adventure would not have been possible.

Much of what I saw in the North was awesome, but some was heart-wrenching. It was difficult to keep open to all that was happening. But I would not have missed any of it for the world. Through living as a teacher, a coach, a mother, a friend and a community member with the people in Auluq, I learned a whole lifetime of things. Though I still have a great deal to learn, my whole way of thinking has changed. With any change there is resistance and some of the change I went through did not come easily. I learned that while I was no stranger to risk-taking before, risk-taking in Auluq took on a whole new meaning. In my negotiations as I forged partnerships with the people of my adopted community, the way I teach, in fact, the way I live has never been the same. My concept of who I was as a teacher and a person completely transformed since living in the North. I have come to see things from a different perspective. My perspective changed right up until the last moment that I was in the North. Every day I learned something new, something that changed the way I look at things. I will be forever grateful for the lessons I have learned, and for the people I will hold in my heart—their twinkling smiles and warm welcome resonate within me. I am so truly grateful for having had the experience of touching the lives of the youth of Auluq and for the youth of Auluq touching my life. Quanamiq!

EDITOR'S COMMENT

The author believes that the differences in culture involve power, but she does not see how power affects her gift from her prize student. Should she have paid him for the sculpture? Nancy MacIntouch focuses on her students, connects with parents, and follows the words of experts on Natives, but she does not see how personal partnerships fail to change the social and power structure. She needs a vision of change if she is to connect with future students in Aulug. Otherwise, no matter how insightful she becomes, her partnership may reinforce the power difference between her students and herself.

Chapter 2
Coalitions Confronting Opponents

Amanda Tattersall, Director of the Sydney Alliance,
(Australia)

In the late 1990s the New South Wales (NSW) Teachers Federation, one of the largest union locals in Australia, was in crisis. The Murdoch owned tabloid newspaper—the Daily Telegraph—was running a vitriolic attack on the union's contract campaign for increased salaries. One notable front cover headline included a picture of the union's President with a dunce's cap drawn on, with the caption "if the cap fits." The government at the time was resisting a settlement with the union. The union's political influence and industrial strength were at an all time low.

Yet within four years, everything had changed. The union had turned around its public image, the media presented hundreds of positive stories about public education and the union had won a series of policy reforms including a $250 million policy to reduce class sizes for kindergarten to year two children. This change of fortune occurred because the union built a powerful coalition with parents that ran a successful independent inquiry into public education.

The idea of establishing a coalition came from a group of rank-and-file leaders inside the union. They believed that in order to confront the teachers' political isolation, the union needed to form strategic links across the education community. These activists began forming local public education lobby groups in the socially disadvantaged areas of outer Western and South-Western Sydney, where parents, teachers and school principals organized forums and events on public education. The rank-and-file group argued in union forums that it was necessary for teachers to work constructively with school principals—seeing them as partners in improving education instead of seeing them as employers. And, they argued that the union needed to collect dedicated resources to fund a long-term public education campaign. They successfully moved a motion at the union's annual conference to create a new Public Education Fund—a million dollar public education war chest with annual contributions of $17 per member.

These internal reforms put the union in a strategic position to confront a major policy proposal from the state government in 2001. The government had been experimenting with changes to schools, and by 2001 had developed a major policy framework called Building the Future that included closing thirteen inner city schools. Initially, the union simply proclaimed its opposition to these proposals, calling on the government to launch an inquiry. But in a discussion at a union rank-and-file executive meeting, one school teacher remarked "why don't we just do an inquiry ourselves." The idea of an independent public education inquiry was born.

The union knew that it could not run an independent inquiry on its own, so it approached the Federation of Parents and Citizens as a partner to the process. Together they funded the inquiry and drafted the terms of reference. Senior elected officials from each organization became responsible for the day-to-day management of the Inquiry. They approached an Emeritus Professor of Education, Tony Vinson, to be the inquiry's head. He was well-regarded by government, having run previous government initiated inquiries. He set up his own team to commission submissions, visit schools and run hearings around the state.

Over the following 12 months, between 2001 and mid-2002, the Vinson Inquiry (as it became known) received 790 submissions, held almost one hundred hearings and visited several hundred schools. As it traversed the state it provided an organizing opportunity for school parents and teachers, who mobilized people to attend hearings. Moreover, the inquiry process was very open. Hearings asked participants to identify "what they would change to improve the education system", providing a space to talk about people's personal experience in the school. The hearings sought to build new ideas for public education reform based on the experiences of the schoolyard.

The Inquiry process was also consciously planned to coincide with election timelines. The inquiries findings started to be released as public documents in the nine months leading up to the 2003 state election. In total, 96 recommendations were tabled. To turn these broad reform proposals into a winnable political program, the union formed a new coalition—called the Public Education Alliance. This Alliance involved the union, parent groups and school principal groups. They prioritized six united demands, and amongst them agreed that the highest priority was a reduction in class sizes for young children.

Together the Alliance lobbied for these changes. Sometimes they worked in parallel: school principals lobbying the Department of Education, Tony Vinson lobbied Ministers, teachers used their war chest to run advertisements, and teachers and parents held meetings with local elected representatives. They also worked in concert, jointly lobbying the Premier and leader of the Opposition. The Alliance organized a public assembly five weeks before the election where all the political parties were invited and questioned about their support for the six united demands.

The lobbying worked. Two weeks before the election, the New South Wales Labor Party, the same party that had been so hostile in the contract campaign in 1999, announced that they would fund a $250 million policy to reduce class sizes—identical to the policy reform proposed by the Vinson Inquiry. The public education coalition had built and delivered a new agenda for public education while actively engaging union and community members in the process.

Coalitions like the public education coalition are an increasingly important strategy for unions and community organizations. Unions face a difficult economic and political climate is dominated by powerful employers, political parties that are increasingly disengaged from their union allies, and declining participation in unions and community organizations. This context requires the development of new strategies for social action and the revitalization of old ones. Moreover, while state spending is more focused on the needs of economic growth than social welfare, the importance of social power that can proclaim and improve the lives of citizens is even more urgent.

Coalitions between unions and community organizations are not new. In the United States, the idea of working partnerships between unions and community organizations was prominent in the 1930s community organizing, where Saul Alinksy's Back of the Yards brought together the Catholic Church and the Congress of Industrial Organizations. In Canada, coalitions between farmers, unions and the New Democratic Party led to major social reforms like Medicare. In Australia, coalitions between unions and community organizations led diverse social movements—for women's rights, against the Vietnam war, for workplace health and safety and to protect the urban environment (Burgmann 2003).

But today what is missing from coalition strategy is a clear understanding of the elements and principles that make coalitions succeed or fail. Scholarship on coalitions has struggled to assist social movement actors in this regard. Much of the research lauding coalitions as a strategy for union revitalization has acclaimed best practice campaigns rather than identifying what works and what does not (Lopez 2004, 12). But comparative analysis of long-term coalitions across countries reveals clear elements that all coalitions have in common, and lessons about what works to deliver powerful coalitions.

My experience as a union organizer building coalitions exemplified these challenges. I first cut my teeth as a social movement organizer in the student and immigration movements, beginning as a union organizer in 2002. I was employed by Unions New South Wales, the central labor council as their community campaigner, and immediately became part of numerous coalitions on issues like transport, health care, education funding as well as contract campaigns. Yet the success of these ventures was highly uneven. A key moment was the building of the Walk against the War coalition in response to the 2003 war in Iraq. According to popular wisdom, it was an incredibly powerful coalition—over 60 organizations ranging from radical to conservative speaking with one voice. But this diverse coalition was brittle. While it helped organize the largest demonstration in Australia's history on February 16, 2003, it struggled to sustain a consensus across the organizations. All we could agree on was to hold more rallies! Over the following two months, tensions mounted and the coalition tore itself apart in May. However, around the same time, I had the privilege of participating in an event hosted by a very different coalition—an assembly held by the public education coalition (whose campaigns are outlined at the beginning of this chapter). That coalition had deployed vastly different strategies to the peace coalition—it only involved a couple of organizations, it was run by the leaders of each of the organizations and it had a set of very specific proactive issues that it was pursuing. The contrast between the two experiences was very instructive. I learned that not all coalitions were powerful. Instead, there are important strategies and lessons that are likely to lead some coalitions to succeed where others may fail. The book, *Power in Coalition*, is the result of my own quest to uncover some of these lessons by engaging in a comparative analysis of long-term coalitions across three countries. It uncovers clear elements that all coalitions have in common, and lessons about what works to deliver powerful coalitions.

THE ELEMENTS OF COALITIONS

In *Power in Coalition*, I argue that all coalitions have three features that describe how they work (Tattersall 2010). Coalitions occur when two or more organizations come together, to work on something they have in common, to have a social impact in a specific place. The three elements of coalitions are therefore: organizational relationships, common concern, and scale.

These three elements are common to all coalitions, but how they work in practice varies. The way in which organizations relate to each other, the kinds of issues that coalitions work on, and how a coalition seeks to achieve social influence affect the chances of coalition success or failure. When it comes to a coalition's organizational relationships, coalitions may vary according to:

- How are they structured?
- How many organizations are involved and how similar or different are they?
- Is decision-making shared or is it dominated by one partner organizations?
- Are there coalition staff that can help bridge across organizations and support effective decision making?
- Which individuals are involved? Are organizational leaders involved in decision-making? Are there individual bridge builders who have experience across different kinds of organizations (Rose 2000)?
- Does the coalition spend time cultivating strong relationships as well as working on issues?

Using these questions to examine the public education coalition helps us understand what made it powerful but also what made it struggle. That coalition followed a key principle for building strong organizational relationships—"less is more". By only involving a couple of organizations, each of whom had a strong shared interest in public education, the coalition maintained these organizations' active involvement for a two-year period. Yet in other ways, the coalition's organizational relationships were constrained. Coalition decision-making was dominated by the union, which provided most of the financial resources for the public education inquiry and had greatest influence over the decision-making process. There was no independent coalition staff that could help manage tensions between the parties and the coalition focused on action around education rather than building strong trusting relationships between the organizations. These weaknesses left the relationships fragile, and after the class sizes campaign was won, the coalition fell away (Tattersall 2010, 49-52).

Coalitions also vary depending on how they work on issues and the kind of common concern cultivated between the organizations. Common concern may vary from shared commitment to an issue, an event, a broad political agenda, or shared concern for organizational renewal. The extent to which these concerns are short-term or long-term affects the likely length of the coalition. When it comes to building successful common concern, key issues include:

- Whether the coalition's objectives are in the self-interest of the participating organization.
- Whether the coalition's objectives are also in the self-interest and direct experiences of the organizations members.
- Whether or not the common concern is in the mutual self-interest of the partner organizations.
- Whether the common concern connects to the public interest or common good.

- Organizational relationships also affect common concerns; for instance, they shape how the coalition decides to work on issues.

The public education coalition drew strength when its common concern was based on a mutual parent-teacher interest around the broad agenda for improved public education and the specific demands around reduced class sizes. A key strategic goal for both the teachers' union and parents' federation was to promote the importance of public education, a goal aptly served by the public education inquiry. More concretely, a reduction in class sizes was a core concern for each organization's membership. Teachers would benefit from smaller class sizes because it made classrooms easier to manage, reducing teacher workload. Parents equally supported smaller class sizes but for a different reason; it improved the quality of their children's education.

The success of the coalition's common concern was enhanced because it not only engaged the interests of the organizations leaders but also its members. There was a high degree of parent and teacher participation in the public education inquiry hearings. The hearings were run in a highly inclusive way. Instead of telling teachers and parents what the issues were, the hearings asked parents and teachers to identify specific challenges that they faced and nominate specific solutions they would like to see adopted. The immediate needs and day-to-day experiences of parents and teachers were central to the work of the coalition.

Moreover, by working on an issue that was in the mutual interest of multiple constituencies in the public education community, the coalition's core demands connected to the public interest. The union's vulnerability in its 1990s salaries campaign came about because it was stigmatized as acting only for its "vested" interests for increased pay. The media backlash that confronted this narrow agenda motivated union activists to demand that the union open up how it expressed itself in the public arena. It shifted its language to talk about the importance of public education, not just teacher salaries. Then, in order to build a long-term relationship with parents, the union worked on new issues like class sizes to supplement its work on contract bargaining.

Finally, coalitions take social action in particular places—the neighborhood, across a city, a state or country. A coalition's ability to influence decision makers depends on the scale of the coalition and the geographic dimensions—or scale—of the employers or political representatives they are challenging. When it comes to influencing public policy, coalitions frequently need to be able to contest for power at multiple scales. Political representatives that sit in a city council or provincial government are simultaneously representatives of the city as well as specific wards or electoral districts. Creating popular pressure frequently requires organizing amongst local voters as well as influencing public debate more broadly. The scale of a coalition varies:

- Is the coalition organized at a single scale (such as organizations based across a city or state) or is it multi-scaled (operating simultaneously through local coalitions in neighborhoods or towns as well as across the city or state)?
- Is the coalition taking advantage of political opportunities like electoral or legislative timelines?
- Is the coalition able to develop a long-term plan for how it exercises public power?

The multi-scaled activity of the public education coalition was critical to its success. The coalition operated at the local scale as well as across the state of New South Wales. The public education inquiry hearings generated dozens of opportunities for local organizing by teachers and parents, as well as supportive media for public education. These local actions made an impact across the scale of the state because the hearings moved from town to town over a fifteen month period. Before the Inquiry began, the teachers' union had already encouraged the establishment of local coalitions between parents and teachers, building public education lobbies in electoral districts across Sydney that organized public education forums and visited political representatives. The coalition had a plan to consciously escalate public pressure in advance of political opportunities—the public education inquiry released its findings in three reports nine months before the 2003 state election. Then, the coalition escalated public activity to build popular and political support in lead up to the state election. Taking action in advance of the election helped the coalition win its class sizes policy.

LESSONS ABOUT SUCCESSFUL COALITIONS

In *Power in Coalition*, I contrast the strategies of the public education coalition with two other long-term coalitions, the Ontario Health Coalition in Canada and the Grassroots Collaborative campaign for living wages in Chicago (Tattersall 2010). This international comparison identified a series of lessons for building successful ties that bind unions and community organizations. Four important, and frequently undervalued, principles for strong coalitions are:

Coalition success is more than just winning policy victories

We need to have a more sophisticated understanding of what coalition success actually means. Scholars and organizers often assume that coalitions are successful if they win public policy victories, or fail when they don't. While "wins" are important, I found they were an insufficient measure of what it takes to build a powerful, long-term coalition.

We must understand coalition success in more sophisticated terms. In addition to "winning outcomes", another measure of coalition success is the extent to which a coalition helps shift the political climate. For instance, in Chicago the Grassroots Collaborative briefly won a living wage ordinance for big box retail stores that would have significantly increased the wages of retail workers (like Walmart employees). But the Mayor vetoed the ordinance. Yet in years following there was a significant shift in the political climate in Chicago. Mayor Daley supported an increase in the state's minimum wage, with Illinois's minimum wage becoming the second highest in the country. And, in 2010 when Walmart wanted to build a second store in Chicago, for the first time ever in the United States, Walmart negotiated a wages agreement with local labor unions that paid retail workers above the minimum wage. While the living wages campaign lost its ordinance, its public campaign changed the political climate around living wages.

Coalition success is not only about social change

Coalitions are successful if they can also enhance the strength of the organizations that are working in coalition. This can be measured in two ways: whether the coalition helps sustain relationships between organizations over time, and if the coalition helps develop the leadership skills and capacity of the members and staff of the partner organizations.

Taking the public education coalition as an example, one of its strengths was it developed the leadership capacity of union and community organization members while one of its weaknesses was that it struggled to sustain relationships between the partner organizations. At the conclusion of the class sizes campaign, the union struggled to maintain a working relationship with the parents' organization. In part this was because the union shifted its focus to work on salaries, but it was also because the union did not have a strong relationship with the newly elected leadership team in the parents' organization. In contrast, the coalition was effective on the question of rank-and-file leadership development. Its public education lobbies and the public education inquiry's local hearings provided opportunities for teachers and parents to work together and develop public policy solutions based on their own experiences.

These four different measures of coalition success are outlined in Table 1.

Table 1: Measures of coalition success

Coalition Success			
Social change		Organizational strength	
Wins/ Policy outcomes	Shifting political climate	Sustaining organizational relationships	Developing leadership— members and staff

FEWER MEMBERS ARE MORE EFFECTIVE

Coalitions are more successful when organizational membership is restricted and there are fewer groups making decisions and sharing resources. Instead of long lists of partners, long-term coalitions are likely to be stronger if they trade breadth for depth and build a narrower agenda that more deeply engages the commitment of their members and leaders.

A "less is more" approach can help coalitions avoid lowest common denominator demands and campaigns where coalitions end up a "mile wide and an inch deep" and tend to be able to agree only on what they are against rather than what they are for. The power of the public education coalition was that it developed and won new policy reforms that enhanced public education based on the coalition's vision for how the education system should be fixed, rather than just being "against" the Government's Building the Future report.

But the principle of "less is more" runs counter to typical coalition practice. Too often "coalition power" is thought to be created by the number of organizations that can be squeezed on to a letterhead or press release. But across the case studies in *Power in Coalition*, it was only when the coalitions restricted membership that they built sufficient trust to keep organizations at the table working together.

Less is more requires coalition organizers to be strategic with 'the less.' There is a need to identify partners that have the right mix of power, interest, and, potentially, unpredictability. Power must not be defined narrowly. Power here is not only about whether organizations can produce "organized numbers or organized money," but also the diversity of organizations at the table. After all, a coalition's legitimacy relies on its ability to stand for the whole of the constituency it claims to represent (Tattersall 2010, 171).

With less people around the table there is then an incentive to do 'more' together. Coalitions with a restricted membership have an incentive to invest in building close, respectful public relationships between the individuals involved. Coalitions may invest in leadership development training for leaders and members, or be more likely to develop long-term campaigns that require organizations to invest time and resources (Dean and Reynolds 2009; Tattersall 2010; Warren 2001).

Powerful coalitions set an agenda

Powerful coalitions, like the public education coalition, develop positive campaign agendas that advocate for new reforms rather than just reacting to government or employer initiatives with defensive 'no' campaigns. The breakthrough in the public education campaign was that the inquiry helped the union and parent organizations identify reforms to public education that were in its interests. By promoting solutions to the problems faced by the public education system, the coalition was able to substitute the government's vision for school closures with an alternative policy agenda.

In contrast, in *Power in Coalition*, I document two campaigns that initially struggled to challenge powerful political adversaries because they were mounted as defensive campaigns. In Canada, the Ontario Health Coalition's "no public-private partnerships in hospital" campaign found it difficult to present an alternative agenda for funding hospitals. While it was able to build public awareness around the negative impact of public-private partnerships, it struggled to articulate a clear reform agenda to remedy the funding challenges in the hospital system. Similarly, the "No Walmart" campaign in Chicago struggled to build public support amongst low income communities that supported Walmart because of its 'bargain prices.' The living wage campaign that followed was far more successful at building popular support because, instead of resisting Walmart, it argued that all retail stores, including Walmart, should be required to pay a living wage.

Powerful coalitions are not controlled by unions

Coalitions are frequently dominated by one organization, and often this is a union. Much of the union revitalization scholarship that embraces coalitions as a union strategy narrowly construes that the purpose of coalitions is to serve union goals (such as win a contract bargaining campaign or help grow unions). As important as coalitions such as these may be, I found that unions need to think differently about how they work in coalition if they want to reap the benefits of long-term coalition work. The most powerful coalitions between unions and community organizations occurred when the union and community partners were open to working together— building power with each other. This involved each of the organizations being open to how they could win and what they could work on together.

This was evident in Sydney's public education coalition. While the teachers union had more resources than its alliance partners, the union chose to work in coalition on a set of issues that were in their shared interests and they sought to harness the strengths of each of the partner organizations in running the class sizes campaign. Consequently, the union let the school principals lead negotiations with the Department of Education rather than running these themselves, as principals had a far better relationship with these public servants. Working on a shared issue agenda ensured that parents and school principals had a strategic interest in maintaining their relationship with the teachers union throughout this campaign, and meant they were willing to share their powerful relationships with the Department of Education to help achieve a policy victory.

CONCLUSION

Coalitions between unions and community organizations can be a critical strategy for transformative social change and reinvigorating our civil society organizations. But not all coalitions are made equal. There are specific lessons and strategies that are likely to lead to more successful coalition practice.

Many of these lessons fly in the face of popular wisdom about coalitions. Where many community coalitions are an exercise in assembling the largest number of organizations possible, I found that smaller, more strategic "less is more" partnerships create a stronger basis for collaborative action. Where many coalitions come together to resist specific policy changes, collaboration is likely to be more powerful if the coalition commits to building a proactive agenda. And, while many labor-community coalitions are built to serve union goals, coalitions that can develop a shared agenda based on mutual self-interest are more likely to engage the commitment and the strengths of all the coalition partners, as opposed to just the union.

Understanding these lessons is important. The difficult social and political environment means that no one organization can achieve wide-scale social change on its own. Organizations need to develop powerful ties, and these lessons seek to guide organizers in thinking through how this can be possible.

EDITOR'S COMMENT

The study of coalitions complements research on partnerships because it shows how conflict can support cooperation. Single interests, such as the unions, require a broader justification. Similarly, companies need support from the broader community in order to realize their aims, such as membership support in credit unions or future customers among students and their families. On the other hand, cooperation can just reinforce existing policies such as large class size or higher patient loads for health care professionals. There are broader issues including the environment and the arts where community goals complement special interests. These broader issues can mobilize many more constituents than a few limited objectives can for a limited number of organizations.

Chapter 3

University Students Help Urban Neighbors

Melinda Pollard and Kerry Kidwell-Slak, former
Coordinators for Washington University

Since 1993, the Neighbors Project, a student-led
service program in the Office of Community Service at
The George Washington University (GW) in Washington,
District of Columbia (DC) has provided meaningful
volunteer and service-learning opportunities for thousands
of students and many community agencies. Our work has
been guided by partnerships with students, campus staff,
faculty, and employees at non-profit organizations within
DC. The services provided to the community constitute
one of the most extensive student projects in the United
States. Neighbors Project adopts a reciprocal approach in
which students gain as much as they give. Over the years,
the Project has taken many forms but what has remained
constant is the willingness of the university community
and the broader Washington, DC social service
community to work together to identify the strengths of
each and determine how resources might best be utilized
to further the goal of social justice for all.

Since the original publication, the Neighbors Project
has continued to evolve in its goals and challenges
(Mitchell 2002). These changes have impacted the way we

accomplish our mission as a university office by providing institutional support through the supervising student staff, obtaining funding, and identifying new places for collaboration, both internal and external to the university. The experience of two coordinators, together with that of the students and residents in our surrounding community is the primary basis of this report, which includes other documentation from project reports and accounts of previous community projects (Neighbors Project, 2000).

The Neighbors Project partners with community organizations including public schools, health clinics, community development corporations, day care centers, and senior service providers. From 1997 to 2003, the Neighbors Project operated in collaboration with a sister program at Howard University, one of the United States' most prominent historically Black institutions. While good relations still exist between the two schools, the formal partnership was discontinued due to divergent priorities of the two schools.

The Neighbors Project deeply values reciprocity in all of our work. The essential theme that runs throughout our program is the understanding that while the GW community has much to contribute, there is also much to learn. No individual or organization is simply a server, and no individual simply receives service from another. The Neighbors Project aims to build lasting relationships and understanding, and, through reciprocity, make social change happen.

HISTORY

The George Washington University (GW) is located in the Foggy Bottom neighborhood of downtown Washington, DC, surrounded by the White House, National Mall, fashionable Georgetown neighborhood, and homes of DC's high powered businesses and lobbying firms. There is another side to the city. Washington, DC's city government has a notorious history of mismanagement, moving from local to congressional control and back on several occasions. Plagued with poverty and issues that surround life in the inner city, D.C.'s government and its citizens have historically faced an uphill battle in providing quality education, adequate housing, job opportunities, health care, and other social services to a large, predominantly Black population. In the last ten years, the city has also experienced a booming housing market and increasing gentrification resulting in a veritable crisis in affordable housing. Further, the city's rates of infection for HIV/AIDS continue to exceed those of many comparable urban areas. Many students enter GW, a private non-profit university, having seen the side of Washington, DC represented by the marble architecture and tourist attractions. It is our hope that through the Neighbors Project they will understand the experience of Washington, DC as it is lived out by its residents. Through our work we believe it is possible to empower students to develop insight and experience regarding their role in bringing about positive social change.

Prior to 1993, GW students worked independently throughout the city to address D.C.'s social concerns. With rising numbers of students involved in community service and service-learning, a small group began to ponder the possibility of creating a network which would focus GW's service efforts on one neighborhood. The intention was to relate different community projects in order to create change in the community over time. With the support of GW's Human Services Program, a university major that prepares students to assume leadership roles in non-profit organizations, the Neighbors Project was born. The Project was originally awarded funding through the federally-based Corporation for National Service and became a Service-Learning Corps focused on serving the under-resourced Shaw community of northwest Washington. Since that time, the Project has expanded its outreach program to address needs throughout all eight wards of Washington through funding from private foundations. This expansion has resulted in an increase of more than one hundred percent in the number of students involved in volunteer service.

MISSION

The Neighbors Project seeks to promote awareness and understanding of social and economic inequalities throughout Washington, DC by the education and placement of volunteers in agencies that drive social change. Accordingly, the students and staff who guide the

Neighbors Project work closely with community agencies to ensure that the needs of the community are heard and addressed through the students' service. The Neighbors Project is guided by the voice of the community through its ongoing partnerships with schools, community centers, health clinics, and social service agencies.

In addition to working toward community impact, the Neighbors Project serves as a valuable co-curricular learning experience for the hundreds of students who are involved as leaders and volunteers. The Neighbors Project provides orientation and ongoing opportunities to reflect and learn throughout the service experience, both of which are significant for the quality of the service experience. Educating students about race, class, and poverty are part of this mission in the inner-city. Further, student leaders of the Neighbors Project work closely with faculty members to develop service opportunities that are connected to students' classroom work and thus encourage the expansion of the service-learning pedagogy throughout the campus.

GOALS OF THE NEIGHBORS PROJECT

The Neighbors Project is committed to addressing short and long-term community needs identified by our community partners. In the short-term, we work with community partners to meet the immediate needs of the poor and underprivileged, such as food, shelter, and basic healthcare. In the long-term, the Neighbors Project works with community partners to change the systems that perpetuate poverty and inequality.

While meeting the needs of community, the Neighbors Project works closely with thirty-seven local organizations that serve individuals and families throughout Washington. These organizations are grouped into seven issue areas based on their mission. Issue areas include Hunger, Homelessness and Poverty; Community Development and the Environment; Health, Aging, and Disability Services; Pre-K and Elementary Education; Secondary Education; Intervention Services and Adult Education; and Social Action and Advocacy. Each issue area includes three to seven different agencies. Seven Neighbors Project undergraduate student leaders, known as Service Coordinators, are employed by the GW Office of Community Service to serve as liaisons between the university and the organizations within their assigned issue area. Additionally, the student leaders serve as advocates and educators on campus concerning the social issues being addressed by their community partners. In this regard, students are able to raise the awareness levels of their peers, prompting students to apply their education toward addressing social change. Students work to deliver university resources to the community organizations to foster a sense of trust between parties that have experienced mistrust and differences in priorities. The most valuable resource that student leaders bring is the volunteer efforts of their fellow students. Currently, approximately 1500 GW students volunteer throughout the city in a range of capacities.

The Neighbors Project's community partners include:

Pre-K and Elementary Education

- *Bright Beginnings* is a Head-Start program for children who are homeless or living in transitional housing. *Bright Beginnings* currently serves nearly 100 infants and preschool age children, providing full day care, education through a creative curriculum, and emotional support.

- *Northwest Settlement House* is a community center with infant, preschool, after-school enrichment, and senior service programs. *Northwest Settlement House* serves children, families, and senior citizens through a year-round infant care center and preschool, a school-year enrichment center, and full day summer camp, and weekly programs which engage senior citizens in community activities.

- *New Community for Children* offers an after-school program for children and teens focusing on literacy and school achievement in order to help students excel and pursue higher education. *New Community* serves children aged five through seventeen and supports them academically and artistically throughout their development.

Children attending *New Community* show high levels of achievement in school and many of them continue to volunteer with the organization as they become adults.

- *CentroNia* (formerly the Calvary Bilingual Multi-cultural Learning Center) is a community center with preschool, high tech after-school, and a wide range of culturally focused programs for children and families. *CentroNia* focuses on serving a diverse community and is a leader in service as well as advocacy. *CentroNia* is a large organization and continues to expand as the needs of DC's Latino community develop.

- *Seaton Elementary* is in the Shaw neighborhood, *Seaton Elementary School* strives to help its students become self-disciplined, creative, technologically literate, and able to communicate through oral and written expression. They seek to create a school climate that will offer every student the opportunity to become engaged in their education. Their motto is "Together, we achieve the extraordinary."

- *School for Arts in Learning (SAIL)* is a Kindergarten through 5th grade public charter school that seeks to address the needs of students with learning differences by providing creative learning environments. *SAIL* has developed a specialized curriculum using the arts to help children learn in ways that match their personal styles, paying special attention to individual learning styles and specific need. *SAIL's* focus is on developing the whole child, intellectually, emotionally, physically, and socially. Volunteers serve in the classroom or as after-school tutors and mentors.

- *Hermanos y Hermanas* is a Big Brothers Big Sisters Latino outreach initiative in the National Capital Area. It provides District of Columbia children, many of whom are Latino, with positive role models who understand their culture. The one-on-one mentoring relationship a child has with his or her Big Brother or Sister helps them realize their strengths and get the most out of life.

Secondary Education

- *Metro Teen AIDS is* an organization dedicated to the improvement of the quality of life for the youth of DC. The organization was founded in 1988 with the initial mission of preventing new HIV infections among the youth of DC. The organization has evolved since then and has committed itself to the improvement of the quality of life of DC youth affected by or infected with HIV. Volunteers serve as tutors, mentors and educators for DC youth.
- *Bell Multicultural High School* is committed to multicultural and multilingual academic and

career education. Located in NW DC, Bell views education as a lifelong process and believes that everyone has the ability to achieve and excel regardless of their background. Bell strives to create a nurturing atmosphere that promotes creativity and self-expression. Bell views language development as a cornerstone of a curriculum which develops necessary skills in communication, interpersonal relationships, career development, health, problem solving, mathematics, science, and technology. Bell's ultimate mission is that every student develops marketable skills which will lead to success in the world of work and post-secondary education.

- *Thurgood Marshall Academy* is founded upon the belief articulated by Supreme Court Justice Thurgood Marshall that all children have the right to a first-class education and the opportunity to reach their full potential. Students learn substantive information about law, human rights, conflict resolution and democracy. The faculty employs teaching strategies that promote engaged participation, fair and cooperative learning, respect for diverse perspectives, critical thinking, experiential learning and, activism for positive change.

- *School Without Walls Senior High School* was established in 1971 to offer an alternative to conventional instructional programs, where students could develop "methods of learning outside the traditional classroom." The history of tapping community resources to enrich and expand upon textbook learning has remained a tradition at School Without Walls.

- *Time Dollar Youth Court* is authorized by the Superior Court of the District of Columbia to work with the courts in a 'partnership for the purpose of jointly developing a diversion program that provides a meaningful alternative to the traditional adjudication format in juvenile cases.' Youth court is a way for youth to avoid the juvenile system. An individual is sentenced by a jury of their peers (all of whom have been through the same youth court system). Through this, the program seeks to keep kids out of trouble and instead focus their energy in new and positive ways. Volunteers serve as judges and advisors through the judicial process.

Intervention Services and Adult Education

- *Academy of Hope* (AOH) provides educational empowerment to DC adults. Students earn high school credentials, improve their math and reading skills, and learn how to use and apply computer technologies. AOH strives to give students an environment of compassion, acceptance, and encouragement so their hopes and dreams become reality. Volunteers tutor students at *AOH* in a one-on-one setting.

- *DC Rape Crisis Center's* services include: a 24-hour hotline, group and individual counseling services for rape and incest survivors and their families and friends, a companion program to accompany survivors to hospitals, courts and police proceedings, and a wide array of community education programs including "Staying Safe" classes for children of all ages within the DC public school system. Volunteers are trained to answer crisis hotline calls as well as accompany survivors to hospitals and advocate on their behalf.

- *My Sister's Place* was established in 1979 by the Women's Legal Defense Fund. My Sister's Place (MSP) is a nonprofit shelter for battered women and their children. Committed to eradicating domestic violence, MSP provides shelter, and offers counseling and educational programs.

- *Ronald McDonald House* provides a 'home away from home' for families of seriously ill children receiving treatment at nearby hospitals. More than 10 million families around the world have benefited from the comfort provided by a Ronald McDonald House. At the DC house, volunteers are needed for checking families in and out of the home and other administrative tasks.

- *Safe Shores—DC Children's Advocacy Center* is a direct service nonprofit organization dedicated to supporting and working directly with child victims of sexual and physical abuse in the District of Columbia. Through its child-friendly facility and multidisciplinary team approach, Safe Shores coordinates the work of medical and mental health providers, social services professionals, victim advocates, law enforcement, and prosecution officials to reduce trauma and promote healing for child victims of abuse. Volunteers play with children, assist caretakers with paperwork and lead fundraising efforts.

- *Rape, Abuse and Incest National Network (RAINN)* is the nation's largest sexual assault hotline providing both telephone and online access to victims of sexual assault. GW volunteers participate in the pilot of the online hotline providing 'instant messenger'-style assistance to those seeking help.

Social Action and Advocacy

- *National Student Partnerships* is the nation's only year-round, student-led volunteer service organization that links people in need with the resources and opportunities necessary to become self-sufficient. It is a national network of 14 drop-in centers, each staffed by student volunteers from area colleges and universities. Students work one-on-one with clients to provide immediate research and problem-solving services to community residents in need of access to sustainable employment opportunities, social services, and/or educational opportunities.

- *So Others Might Eat* (SOME) is a community-based organization that exists to help the poor and homeless of D.C. The services that SOME provides to poor, homeless individuals aim not only to meet the immediate daily needs of the people, such as food, clothing, and health care, but also to break the cycle of homelessness by offering such services as affordable housing, job training, and addiction treatment. SOME is also committed to spreading awareness and greater understanding of the issues surrounding poverty and homelessness among community residents in the D.C. area. At SOME, volunteers have the opportunity to engage in Social Justice work, Adult Education, Mental Health, K-8 Children Services, Elderly Services and Financial Management.

- *Transitional Housing Corporation* (THC) is a non-profit partnership that provides housing and comprehensive support services to homeless and at-risk families so that they can make transformational changes in their lives. *THC* has two transitional housing complexes serving 27 homeless families at any one time with an array of programs. During their two-year stay, families are provided with a program of services that include employment and career counseling, family dynamics, parenting skills, substance abuse counseling, and therapy for adults and children. At *THC*, volunteers work directly with the residents of the housing complexes in a variety of ways.

- *Second Chance Employment Services* (SCES) provides employment placement for domestic abuse survivors and other at-risk women. *SCES* partners with large DC corporations to place employees, as well as other businesses such as clothing stores, salons, GED programs and their own training initiatives to ensure their clients are fully prepared to find a meaningful career. Volunteers at *SCES* assist with one-on-one client work including resume development, marketing, PR, Capitol Hill advocacy, Spanish translations (conversational Spanish for interview follow-up and outreach), fundraising, database entry, and website creation.

- *Vietnamese American Community Service Center (VACSC)* was created to assist Vietnamese-Americans and other recent immigrants in suburban Washington, DC with assimilating and integrating into American society without sacrificing their cultural heritage and identity, and with an aim toward promoting friendship and understanding between diverse communities. Volunteers serve as mentors, tutors and advocates for the community.

Community Development and Environment

- *Washington Parks & People* is the capital area's network of community park partnerships. Parks & People is working to revitalize Washington by reconnecting two of its greatest but most forgotten assets: its vast network of public lands and waterways—comprising one of the highest percentages of park land of any city in the world—and its core of dedicated community leaders and organizations.

- *Capital Area Food Bank* is the largest, public nonprofit hunger and nutrition education resource in the Washington Metropolitan Area. Volunteers assist with packaging, sorting, and organizing various products that are sent to different assistance agencies around the area.

- *Sierra Club Recycling Initiative* is designed to educate students on the value of recycling, give them an understanding of the process, and empower them so that they can make a difference. Volunteers visit schools on a quarterly basis to lead sessions on environmental education. The curriculum and activities are based on established programs such as those produced by the U.S. Environmental Protection Agency.

Health, Aging and Disability Services

- *Emmaus Services for the Aging* provides services for seniors such as food shopping, medication delivery, supplemental food delivery, cleaning services, and friendly visiting for companionship. Emmaus concentrates on services that allow seniors to continue to lead fulfilling, independent lives.

- *St. Mary's Court* is a non-sectarian residential community of seniors 62 years of age or older, or individuals with accessibility needs. St. Mary's attempts to provide a community environment for seniors so that they do not suffer from isolation or detachment. Volunteers provide basic services and companionship.

- *IONA Senior Services* is a nonprofit community organization in northwest Washington, DC, dedicated to enabling older people to live with dignity and independence. Through its professional staff, corps of volunteers, and close collaboration with other organizations, IONA provides services and access to programs designed to meet the needs of seniors and their families.

- *We Are Family* is an outreach organization for the seniors of the North Capitol Street and Shaw neighborhoods. The staff and volunteers of We Are Family bring advocacy, services, and companionship into the homes of the elderly while helping to build friendships across the boundaries of race, class, religion, age, culture and sexual orientation.

Hunger, Homelessness and Poverty

- *Bread for the City* is a community resource center which includes a full-service health clinic, in addition to legal and social services, emergency food, and clothing. *Bread* has actively served families for twenty years in two community locations. The health clinic serves individuals and families who do not have health insurance and do not qualify for insurance according to city and federal assistance laws. Volunteers assist with distributing food, promoting personal fiscal responsibility, and identifying medical services.

- *DC Central Kitchen is o*pen 7 days a week, 365 days a year. *DC Central Kitchen* works to recover excess food from restaurants and food service businesses across the city and reprepares this food to be sent out to feed over 3,000 people each day. In addition, *First Helping*, the *Kitchen's* street outreach program, allows homeless individuals to receive proper meals, as well as information of the different resources that are available to them.

- *Dinner Program for Homeless Women (DPHW) is* a non-profit organization located in downtown DC that serves homeless women and their children by providing a hot nutritious dinner and support services in a stable and safe environment. DPHW provides emergency supplies onsite as well as access to showers, laundry, telephone, and mail. Volunteers work in the kitchen, provide programming and provide technology assistance for clients.

- *Foggy Bottom Food Pantry's* goal is to offer those of low income households enough groceries to last them for two weeks. This program distributes approximately 700 bags of food, or close to 9,000 lbs, each month and is run solely through the efforts of volunteers.

- *Food & Friends* prepares, packages and delivers meals and groceries to more than 1,000 people living with HIV/AIDS and other life-challenging illnesses throughout Washington, DC and 14 counties of Maryland and Virginia. Food & Friends chefs and registered dieticians design meals that meet the special needs of persons living with a broad range of life-challenging illnesses. Food & Friends also provides nutritional counselling and education. Volunteers assist with all aspects of Food & Friends mission.

The role of each service coordinator is to link the needs of the organization and community to the skills of student volunteers. The staff of the Neighbors Project works closely with a designated site supervisor at each organization to ensure that the student volunteers are learning as well as contributing. The staff, site supervisor, and service coordinator develop programs that engage volunteers to the benefit of the community.

As reflected in the following comments from site supervisors about the Neighbors Project, meaningful relationships are formed between the student leader and community partner. These relationships are influenced by the work of student leaders.

> They have helped build bridges, not only between generations, but across cultural, class, and racial divides as well, delivering crucial services and genuine caring with creativity and unflagging energy. I have seen how the experience has transformed the students themselves. By stepping out of the comfortable bounds of typical student life to encounter the realities of aging, mortality, poverty, and racism in D.C.'s inner-city, all [students] have become more thoughtful, caring and active citizens (Mark Andersen, Associate Director for Outreach, Emmaus Services for the Aging, Interview, 1998).

> The Neighbors Project has been instrumental to the development of our organization . . . Project volunteers helped our clients write 327 resumes and in turn secure

43 job placements. Students also placed 805 calls on our clients' behalf to connect them to housing, food, legal and other resources in their efforts to pursue self-sufficiency . . . When we have specific needs, among all our contacts at the universities in DC, the [GW] Service Coordinator is our first call to help generate volunteer support (Nathan Kamesar, Site Coordinator, National Student Partnerships, 2007).

LEADERSHIP OPPORTUNITIES

These comments and others like them, reflect the reciprocity present in the ways Neighbors Project volunteers interact with community partners. Students involved in the Neighbors Project benefit from the strong ties between the university and community. Each year fourteen students are chosen to serve as student leaders on the basis of their previous service, commitment and understanding of community development, and their potential to lead their fellow students. The process of selecting the team is competitive and entails a series of steps, involving the Neighbors Project staff and the community partners.

Diversity amongst the Neighbors Project service coordinators is valued. Students of a wide variety of cultural, racial, and religious backgrounds are chosen to lead service efforts. By working together as a tightly woven community, Neighbors Project service coordinators experience and explore issues surrounding diversity, both as a small group as well as within the community.

Students selected to lead the Neighbors Project begin their service with a two-week "Pre-Service Training" that builds camaraderie among students, introduces the community and agencies with which we work, and provides skill training. Community partners and campus staff play primary roles in the initial training of the student leaders, leading sessions focusing on the seven issue areas addressed by the Neighbors Project, the challenges of volunteer management, and strategies for social advocacy on a college campus. Neighbors Project service coordinators visit community partner organizations, read reflections on social issues and begin to build relationships with staff and clients at our partner sites.

COMMUNITY PARTNERSHIPS

The Neighbors Project's partnerships with community organizations are developed throughout the year. A site supervisors' training is held each summer during Pre-Service Training in order to familiarize community partners with changes in Neighbors' structure and expectations, as well as to discuss mutual goals and expectations, and build partnerships among community partners. Later in the year, the site supervisors play roles in selecting service coordinators, educating GW students about social issues and engaging in volunteer appreciation.

As the year progresses, the Neighbors Project professional and student staff visit the community partners while service coordinators and volunteers are in action, attend special events, send out regular email updates to site supervisors, and meet for a midyear evaluation of the performance of the service coordinator and GW volunteers at-large. The actions of Neighbors Project staff represent the university's commitment to the community. As a result of consistency and passion for the service taking place, successful and constantly deepening partnerships are fostered.

EMPOWERING GW STUDENTS

To reach out to as many students on campus as possible, the Neighbors Project forms partnerships with student organizations seeking to participate in service. The Neighbors Project serves as a catalyst for service for students and student organizations throughout the University. Through the Neighbors Project, this diverse cross-section of students then becomes engaged in service with the larger Washington, DC community. Most student volunteers participate on an ongoing basis, for a semester or the entire school year, while others participate on a one time or periodic basis. Students' ongoing service includes:

Delivering supplemental groceries to senior citizens residing in subsidized housing on Saturday mornings;

Staffing telephone and online hotlines for victims of rape and sexual assault;

Providing financial intervention services, assistance to low-income clients with managing bills and fiscal responsibility;

Tutoring middle and high school students twice weekly; enabling students to reach grade level proficiency in reading and math.

Developing curriculum and facilitating a weekly service-learning program at an elementary school focused on recycling and environmental sustainability.

ENTRY POINTS FOR SERVICE

Several special events, planned by student leaders under the guidance of site supervisors, take place during the course of the school year. Special events are usually linked with national or local initiatives and offer an opportunity to open the door to service for students who have not previously been involved. In addition, these one-time service projects provide major service in a short period of time. The following are special events that took place during the 2006-2007 school-year:

> *Make a Difference Day* is a national service sponsored by the USA Today newspaper and other organizations each fall in late October. Neighbors Project service coordinators organized *Kidsfest*, a Halloween-themed event for children from across Washington, DC to come to campus and experience educational activities with college students as well as trick-or-treating in the residence halls.

> *National Hunger and Homelessness Awareness Week* is focused on calling attention to the issues of hunger and homelessness throughout the country and world. Service coordinators organized an Oxfam Hunger Banquet to provide an educational simulation of hunger across the planet, a Food for Thought Poetry Slam including GW poets and poets from a local homeless shelter, a food drive to bring together donations for local food banks and, finally, a group of over 100 students to attend the Fannie Mae Help the Homeless Walkathon that focuses on raising funds for local organizations that serve homeless and low-income families.

National Youth Service Day is an annual event sponsored by Youth Service America to raise awareness about services provided by young people throughout the United States. For the 5th year, service coordinators organized a Senior Prom which brought low income senior citizens from across Washington, DC to campus to participate in a banquet and dance. This GW tradition is a service highlight for both the students and the senior citizens, and many lasting multigenerational friendships are formed as a result.

DC101 brought together several hundreds of students in one or more of a series of workshops and panel discussions designed to educate GW students about social issues through the eyes and work of community activists. As a result of learning about the realities of inequity, students increased their participation in outreach to senior citizens, affordable housing advocacy and HIV/AIDS education.

COMMUNITY IMPACT

The Neighbors Project accomplishes its mission by working with students, community members, and affiliated organizations. The Project is practical, results based, and need driven. The positive results of these collaborations are abundant. Neighbourhood parks are cleaned, community festivals are staffed with volunteers, medication is dispensed to patients at the local health clinic, and senior citizens receive visitors and helping hands to collect groceries and medication, clean their apartments, or deliver supplemental food. Children from first grade through high school are tutored in a one-on-one supportive atmosphere during and after school, and preschools drastically lower their child/adult ratio with the assistance of a large group of weekly volunteers. On an organizational level, the collaborative work of the Neighbors Project allows local organizations to meet their service missions. Many organizations, especially those that provide early childhood education, have highly transient staffs. The Neighbors Project promotes ongoing service of volunteers and student leaders to help provide a stable force in the neighborhood, thereby supplementing the efforts of our community partners.

CITIZENSHIP

The impact of the Neighbors Project on GW student leaders and volunteers are difficult to quantify. One 1999-2000 Neighbors Project student leader wrote:

> The biggest improvement that I have
> seen in myself this year has to be my sense

of accomplishment. I've really participated in something that I will never forget . . . . I have learned that one person can make a big difference! I've learned how to recruit, train, organize, and maintain a force of volunteers [and] how to keep people coming back. I've learned better communication skills [and] to be aggressive when the situation calls for it. I've learned how to be more flexible [and] how to take compliments, and how to take criticism. I've learned about how a non-profit works and how to be an administrator. I've learned how to lean on other people for help when I need it. I've learned how to plan humongous projects that actually work [and] how to get 18 crazy three-year-olds to listen to me, and how to dodge baby throw-up. I've learned from my Corps members [fellow Neighbors Project leaders] about their lives and about diversity . . . I've learned how to balance my life . . . I've learned about leadership and most importantly about friendship (Amanda Crowell, May, 2000).

Additional testimonials are shared by former Neighbors Project leaders:

There has been a wonderful change in me throughout this year and the change happened because of Neighbors. There is a confidence in me that developed this year—one that makes me feel strong and capable of anything. I'll never forget when I stood up in front at the first Senior Prom team member orientation. At the meeting I spoke about the mission of Senior Prom, and our plan for the coming months, and I just felt so excited and proud that the plan other service coordinators and I developed was being implemented by these eager students. And then, on the day of the event, to see it run so smoothly gave me a sense of accomplishment unlike anything I'd ever felt. This job has made me a leader and I know I will use these skills to help implement social change in the future (Jenna Fields, 2007).

Because I did not come from a poor family, I have grown to understand the less fortunate. When I first came to this school I was exposed, for the first time, to the homeless and the poor . . . As I matured mentally, I began understanding . . . I think today, most people in DC still think the way I did when I first came to DC. Today, my primary objective is to pull out of people's minds the ignorance of the poor by educating them and showing them that the less fortunate are not as society sees them.

Instead of service being merely a part of my weekly activities, it has become a great part of myself, my thinking and emotional state. Instead of feeling erratic changes of intensity about social issues, I have stabilized myself to a constant level of compassion (Jim Lee, June, 2000).

Students leave the Neighbors Project with an understanding of civic engagement and a lifelong commitment to serving others. As a result of their service, many students pursue careers as teachers in inner-city schools, social work, non-profit administration, psychology, law, and medicine to help communities and people in need.

FINDING SUPPORT TO CONTINUE

While the Neighbors Project has many strengths, it also faces several limitations. These limitations include reliance on grant-based funding, the transient schedules of college students, and the challenge of supporting a large number of community and institutional partnerships. The Neighbors Project was originally funded by the Corporation for National Service, which is the umbrella organization for AmeriCorps, otherwise known as the

U.S. domestic Peace Corps. This funding stopped in 2002 and income streams transitioned to private donors and foundations. Today, the Neighbors Project is generously supported by the Cafritz Foundation, which makes a large number of social investments in the Washington, D.C., as well as the Herb Block and Hattie Strong Foundations.

The grants supply funds for the salary of a Neighbors Project Coordinator, hourly wages for Neighbors Project service coordinators, funding for retreats, training, supplies, and recognition activities. GW supplies many in-kind resources including office and meeting space, phone and computer access, and technological resources. Various University departments including Athletics and Recreation, catering, and the student government donate tickets to events, food, and space for children to come to campus. While support, both in-kind and financial, is strong, the challenge of funding remains. Because the Neighbors Project is not institutionally financed, external funding must constantly be sought.

Like many university programs focusing on community service, the Neighbors Project faces the challenge of educating student participants about service-learning and the philosophy of the volunteer work. The GW campus highlights the exceptional work of students through its own version of the Academy Awards, a formal evening affair including a reception and ceremony. The Excellence in Student Life Awards program recognizes students involved in campus life through student government, year book, Greek life, and community service. Many students involved in community service programs do not want to be thanked for their service. The Neighbors Project encourages service coordinators to develop and implement creative ways to maintain a high level of energy and motivation among student volunteers through volunteer appreciation.

Many volunteer students find their education is more meaningful because of academic links that are created to their studies through the increasing use of service-learning by GW faculty. These classes, in disciplines like Human Services, Writing, Geography, Business Administration, and Psychology, require students to participate in service as a part of their learning experience. While the support that the Neighbors Project receives from individual faculty in these departments is strong, additional, more structural, linkages with academic departments are needed. Further University support for service-learning would enhance the experiences of other students.

The Neighbors Project is successful because of the commitment of its staff to write and maintain grants for funding. Reliance on grants requires dedicating a significant amount of time to researching, writing, editing, and communicating needs. The reliance on grant funding makes long-term strategic planning difficult because grantors often change priorities or grants are written in order to fill expectations of a grantor, thus requiring changes in the program based on regulations rather than identified needs. An increase in institutional funding for service initiatives would alleviate this problem and enhance community belief in university commitment.

The transient schedules of university students are an additional limitation of the Neighbors Project. Students come to spend their four years at GW from across the nation and the globe. Few students are from D.C. or its metropolitan area. Numerous students study abroad during their undergraduate years, and many leave the University during summer and the month-long winter break. The University year is two distinct periods: September through early December and January through April. During the time beyond the semesters most students take on internships and part-time jobs as a result of opportunities in Washington.

Midterms and finals are obstacles because they do not correlate with breaks in the public school system calendar. When breaks and scheduling conflicts are considered, there are essentially only about six months during which student volunteers are involved in service. Student volunteers are thus often seen as inconsistent members of the community, unable to make service a priority. This problem is addressed through open communication with community organizations and planning programs to follow student schedules and neighborhood needs, such as scheduling major events.

CONCLUSION

Although the Neighbors Project is fortunate to have a rich history and strong ties to the community, the Project faces several challenges and limitations which are similar to those faced by all universities seeking to make social change in their communities. The Neighbors Project is a program which links people who otherwise may not build relationships with each other. The individuals who lead the project in its many facets, and their passion for social justice, are what makes this program valuable and substantial. Student leaders, staff at community partner organizations, community members, and university faculty and staff, working in collaboration, all play an important role.

The Neighbors Project is reciprocal; the community, the students, and the university as an institution each profit in different ways. The community gains hands needed to provide essential services on an on-going and periodic basis. The students have a unique experiential learning opportunity, which develops their sense of civic responsibility and their understanding of complex social issues, which, in turn, influences their future career plans.

The program helps the university to achieve an important, but often neglected, mission: to serve as a member of the immediate community in the best interests of the larger community. The Neighbors Project, in collaboration with strong community partners in Washington, D.C., is making a significant contribution city-wide, while providing an opportunity for its students to learn and grow as citizens and leaders.

EDITOR'S COMMENT:

The large number of organizations makes it difficult for these organizations to be coordinated for change in their community. Immediate needs may be met but policies to overcome poverty are not considered. If coordination of some of the organizations could be achieved as in the Atlanta Project developed by Jimmy Carter, there might be rich possibilities for change (Mitchell, 2003). It is not just a small group that must be coordinated in a coalition, but a group with new and original ideas. Homogenous planners do not produce creative solutions.

The large number of groups supported by the Neighbors Project challenges GWU; involving and controlling many different students. Unlike public schools, universities have been the scene for many student demonstrations and protests, particularly since the civil rights movement of the l960s. Partnerships are much more widespread in universities than high schools. Faculty and administrators are more involved with business people and politicians than they are always with students. The interests of the universities are much more closely linked to the power structure. The more involved people are in making decisions for the economy and society, the more likely they are even to form partnerships (Mitchell, 2003.

Even radical organizations that criticize partnerships for schools form partnerships to develop studies and alternative policies, such as the Canadian Centre for Policy Alternatives. Making partnerships for ordinary people is more difficult.

The key issue in terms of development of people power is whether a large number of partners are more advantageous or if partners should be organized into blocks so as to achieve limited goals. Amanda Tattersall is looking at this issue from the standpoint of coalitions while Melinda Pollack and Kerry Kidwell-Slak are seeing grass-roots activities between George Washington. Fewer are better, but many are plentiful for the large number of organizations that provide credit and informal experience for the university students. However, neither the organizations nor the students change the university's policies. There is no indication that students actually change the policies of the many organizations that work with the university.

Empowering students to change the poverty conditions in the District of Columbia is a different order from alleviating the conditions of the poor in any city. A subsidy for the poor on welfare or a living wage for the poor who work for less than a minimum wage are issues that are raised in Chapter 11. Policy changes are the direction that a coalition attempts to tackle, particularly if unions are involved. Students are not expected to join such efforts, at least not as a part of credit courses at a private university.

The students require a coordinator not a broker who wields the ability to coordinate local groups and to link with national and international ones. Being a broker would involve a different kind of personal experience, one that requires multicultural and multilingual experience as we shall see in Chapter 7. Learning about the other half overcomes the isolation that GW students have experienced before coming to the university.

PART II

COMMON GROUND

Most partnerships are temporary alliances often lasting less than three years (Jenkins, 2002). In Europe, partnerships have lasted longer as organizations, such as masters and unions, have found ways to work together in skilled apprenticeship programs. In North America, partners show signs of working together over longer periods of time as they find more than superficial reasons to cooperate. However, North American partnerships have to remain dynamic and open to change in order to reflect the nature of their societies.

Michael Zanibbi shows how a partnership which he helped create to recycle construction material and preserve the environment has changed. Even from the start this partnership was open to the interests of its partners. Businesses wanted to avoid yet another attempt by schools to have them donate money. The schools and the community could improve the environment by reusing, rather than discarding building materials from new construction. Students who were not successful in an academic route would have an alternative.

A partnership that benefitted many different groups had a broad appeal. The teachers and students could learn from a program that cast a wide net and that would involve materials from movie studios as well as residential construction. The program changed as different administrators were hired and became a part of alternative education, including special students. The program has been made attractive to students and staff with changing interests.

Similarly, a credit union program widens to include the rebuilding of a theater, reading of literature and mentoring of students. None of these projects were narrowly conceived. The community, arts, and education were all beneficiaries of this partnership. The staff personnel found the programs interesting and career relevant, even though achievements in the arts are often thought about as distant from businesses or schools (Mitchell, 2000). Individual schools and partners celebrate their successes but the calendar of student art remains the most striking shared symbol of this partnership.

In a music partnership in which Roberta Lamb was an original partner, the symphony, university, and school systems have come together. Their unity, symbolized by the firing a cannon from a fort above the city during the *1812 Overture,* commands the attention of an entire community to music and the partnership of the university, schools and orchestra. Getting beyond the self-interest of the orchestra in building a client base or of the schools in following the curriculum challenge these partners to find a common ground. Their program develops a practical answer when student teachers with music training focus teachers and performers on a program for grade four students. The perspectives of different partners are still shown to differ as they discuss guides to music, such as the one by Benjamin Britton. The program contains individual approaches and different philosophies.

The last selection in Part II reveals how some players, other than music professors, can build bridges between schools and communities. These boundary spanners can link two very different socio-economic communities together. Specific programs, involving early childhood education, bring out the potential of creative leaders. Lynn Bradshaw worked as an administrator in one of the districts before she became a professor doing research. The connection between theory and practice is one that is pursued in concrete ways and suggests ways in which leaders can be trained in the future. Links between different communities, schools, and cultures can lead to new celebrations of success.

In chapters 1 and 3, we saw how individuals found partnership based upon their survival, career advancement, and understanding of the poor in their community. In chapter 2 conflicts between partnerships was revealed. Though out Part II, partnerships are discussed as corporate activities. However, most partnerships for schools or other organizations involve committed individuals. In the last chapter of this section, we see how marginal individuals in areas that are not central to schools or society are the leaders in creating change through partnerships. Business programs for failing students in Chapter 4, music programs for grade four students in Chapter 5, credit union activities in the arts in Chapter 6 are examples of the programs that result from boundary spanners, although Dr. Bradshaw, in Chapter 7, does not address, perhaps as much as the early childhood programs that she does discuss. These connections further suggest how change can be bought about by boundary spanners who build coalitions, not just partnerships.

Chapter 4

A Business Teacher Plans for the Environment

Michael Zanibbi, Former Director, Enviroworks

> Enviroworks certainly exhibits very high
> qualities of innovative ideas, organization
> wide impact, collaboration, sustainability, and
> outcomes that meet ongoing environmental
> challenges—Dawn Ralph, Executive Director
> of the Peter F. Drucker Canadian Foundation
> (Letter, October 27, 1997)

Enviroworks is a program of the Limestone District School Board (LDSB) in Kingston, Ontario, Canada, which has received national and international attention as a partnership model. By pooling the resources of the private sector, the public sector, the education system, and the community, an alliance has been created that benefits all partners. Students are being better prepared for the changing world of work, local businesses are reducing costs, and the community is addressing important environmental issues. The program started fourteen years ago with only 15 partners and has worked with over 300 organizations since its inception. The program and its partnership model have taken several forms and have continuously evolved over the course of its existence.

While this article focuses on the early years of the program from its beginning in 1996 until the time I left in 2000, I will reflect on how Enviroworks has changed into a new program.

THE IDEA

I knew something had to change when I was standing at a chalkboard in my first year of teaching watching my students looking glassy eyed and bored. Despite my best efforts to make my business courses interesting, the students were just not engaged. Students complained that they were getting tired of simulation exercises in which they 'pretended' to operate their own company. I didn't blame them; I was also bored with the traditional, 'hypothetical' approach to teaching business. I thought there has to be a better way to teach students about business. I also realized from my own experiences in business school that the best way to learn about business is to run one. The problem was to come up with an enterprise where students could take an active role in daily operations and successfully operate the business. Another big challenge was figuring out where the money was going to come from to start up and operate the venture. Lastly, as the whole idea was going to take a lot of time and work, I needed to find people with different areas of expertise to help me. I needed partners to help with the enhancement of the existing Ministry of Education curriculum, to lend their business knowledge, funding and materials.

The idea for Enviroworks came from my students who would come into class in the morning and talk about all the stuff people were throwing out on garbage day. They would see all this material on the side of the road on their way to school and they were amazed because some of the material looked good enough to use. They could not understand why someone would throw it out. After hearing the same stories week after week, something finally clicked. Here was a large supply of free product that we could collect relatively easily. The prospect of a retail store was attractive because it was an environment that many students were used to working in already through their part-time jobs. The difference between Enviroworks and their part-time jobs would be that students would have a hand in how the business was run and would make decisions that directly affected the operation of the enterprise. Our partnership was a right idea coming along at the right time. Several factors in the community were coming together that helped set the stage for the program. Enviroworks is an example of an entrepreneurial effort starting when problems are seen as opportunities.

THE CHALLENGE AND RESPONSE

During 1997, immediate problems were caused by the city of Kingston's growth. The area experienced its greatest construction boom ever led by the industrial, commercial, and institutional sectors. From 1996 to 1997, building permit values for construction more than doubled, which greatly increased the amount of construction and demolition waste. The Kingston community was concerned because of the increased pressure on local landfill sites; the cost of disposal soared, increasing by 30 per cent. This cost affected local businesses and Kingston residents. The environmental crisis was matched by the difficulties encountered by the education system. Schools in Ontario were feeling the effects of a new provincial government whose mandate included large cuts in grants to Ontario School Boards. At the same time, increasing pressure from the business community called for young people to be better prepared for the work place. The education system was challenged to become more innovative and entrepreneurial.

Any group can augment its effectiveness through the formation of powerful alliances (Cramphorn, 1999). The issues faced by the education system, the private sector, and the community were difficult to address individually. Under the direction of the LDSB, partnerships were created to pool resources and address all the issues simultaneously. The end result was the formation of Enviroworks, a used building materials store that is owned by the LDSB and operated by the students in the Board.

Enviroworks attracted extra funding for the School Board and provided a unique vehicle for training students. This program was modelled after many of the used building material stores that were starting all over North America in the early 1990's. What made Enviroworks unique was that it is owned by a School Board and operated by students. The program was based at Queen Elizabeth Collegiate and Vocational Institute (QECVI).

Although Enviroworks was based at QECVI, it is not run from there. It is housed in an 8000 square foot warehouse. During the period from 1996-2000, I was a business teacher at QECVI and ran the program along with Steph Running, a former student whom I hired to help manage the store. A primary goal of the program at this time was to divert construction and demolition waste from Kingston's landfills. The program started by obtaining materials, such as doors or sinks, from households and contractors who were disposing of them, and sold them back to customers who could reuse them.

Enviroworks was designed to provide students with a learning opportunity to operate a business. There were 15 to 20 students from several different schools in the program at any one time. Participants gained valuable experience in a number of areas including: marketing, sales and customer service, accounting, human resource management, computers, technological studies, and entrepreneurship. Young people developed the skills and attitudes established by the Conference Board of Canada's *Employability Skills Profile*: problem solving, responsibility, adaptability, team work skills, communication skills, and positive attitudes and behaviours (Corporate Council 1998).

While the vocational goals of the program were important, another critical goal related to empowerment for both the students and community partners. Students were empowered to take responsibility for their own learning and for their work. They were able to decide what they wanted to learn and how this learning would occur. They were also given a say in how the work of the store would be performed and by whom. I realized that students would be set up to fail if they were not ready to be empowered. They were trained how to make decisions and were given support and confidence. The most important aspect in their support was providing them with an environment where they could gain confidence in their decision making by experimenting, making mistakes, and learning from these mistakes. The luxury of making mistakes was not something students were used to in their regular classes or even in their part-time jobs. In terms of the community partners, they were empowered to have direct input into the curriculum the students learned and even how this curriculum was delivered.

PROGRAMS

The Enviroworks runs for two semesters. When I ran the program, students were at the store all day and received four credits a semester in different subject areas (Marketing, Accounting, Computers, Entrepreneurship, Management Studies, or Business Communications). These courses related directly to the operation of the business. When performing duties, such as making the budget, entering information into the computerized accounting system, or producing monthly reports for the School Board, students earned credits in accounting. When working on the marketing plan, conducting market research, or creating advertising (TV, radio, and newspaper), students earned credits in marketing.

There is no distinction between the business and classroom; *business is the classroom.* Students have an opportunity to gain excellent work experience to put on their resumes while completing their academic requirements. Young people are in a better position to sidestep the catch-twenty-two, "no job without experience, and no experience without a job." Students were encouraged to become "intrapreneurs" (entrepreneurs within an existing organization) and were allowed the freedom and resources to develop their ideas. A special budget was available to students who have ideas to make a business operate efficiently. Over the years students suggested ideas relating to operational planning, cash management, financing, advertising, public relations, and sources of supply.

Enviroworks is part of a large partnership model that makes up the Focus Program system in the Limestone District School Board. Focus Programs are packages of courses offered at Limestone District secondary schools. They concentrate on a particular field that will give a foundation in a career or area of study. These special programs enable students to come together to benefit from specialized equipment and training. They are to help high school students make well-informed career decisions to post-secondary education or the world of work (LDSB

2000). Currently, there are over fifty programs, ranging from business and construction to theatre and art. A student from any of the eleven schools in the LDSB can enrol in a focus program; LDSB absorbs transportation costs for these thirteen programs that include theatre, construction, creative arts, and marine technology. Enviroworks fits well into this innovative school environment because of its emphasis on 'at-risk students.'

VISIONS: PARTNERS FOR THE SCHOOL BOARD

Enviroworks is a new approach to developing community partnerships and a radical departure from traditional education. It illustrates a proactive approach to develop employment opportunities for today's youth. The world of work was and is undergoing a major transformation, shaped by the globalization of labour, technological change, growth of the service sector, and corporate downsizing and outsourcing. Young people have to be taught not just how to 'get' a job but also how to 'make' a job.

For the LDSB, this means teaching a new set of student skills: opportunity identification, idea evaluation, literacy skills, technical skills, and thinking skills. It also means a new set of student attitudes: creativity, initiative, responsibility, collaboration, and learning as a way of life and work. Enviroworks is a model that pools the resources of the education system, the private sector, the public sector, and the community. The government supplied the initial funding, the private sector provided the training, the education system made available human resources, and the community donated the materials. When the approval for Enviroworks to proceed with its program was given, a major stipulation was that it could not cost the LDSB any money. When the LDSB was approached about Enviroworks, a grant from Human Resources Development Canada for $103,000 was already in place. The School Board provided the salary for one teacher, myself, and this was conditional on attracting twenty students.

My role was to coordinate all business operations in addition to developing and teaching the curriculum. As I was already being paid as a business teacher at QECVI, there was no additional expense incurred. Enviroworks generated other funds to support the program either through revenue generation, grant support, or in-kind donation. Although they do not provide direct financial support, LDSB is supportive of the program. Negotiations with the City of Kingston were required to alter a city by-law, which stated schools can not be located in industrial zones. Enviroworks needed to operate out of a warehouse and most warehouses were zoned industrially. The board's organization resolved this problem and its staff established accounts and monitored purchasing activities for this project. Enviroworks used the bussing in place for Focus programs. At the school, the project teacher was supported by the principal of QECVI for student discipline, or to maintain academic performance.

REASONS FOR BUSINESS SUPPORT

An effective partnership is mutually beneficial to all parties involved (NBEC 1999). Private sector giants, such as DuPont and Alcan, are leery of entering into partnerships with the LDSB since, for them, partnerships means financial commitments. Most school principals and superintendents think that anyone who gives them money is a partner. For such partnerships, the benefit to business is good corporate citizenship. This benefit is available from donating money to any one of the thousands of organizations constantly soliciting big businesses. Companies do not want to be only a funding source for education. From a public relations standpoint, many companies try to spread their philanthropic activities around, supporting an organization for one to three years at most and, then, moving on to another organization.

School boards must learn there are other resources in the community. More and more businesses are seeking to donate their human resources and look forward to the opportunity to do so. Many members of the private sector believe that while their money is welcome in the classroom, their employees may not be. Enviroworks utilizes human resources by involving partners in a number of ways. Some, like Human Resources Development Canada, provide funding for the program's training component. Others like Cataraqui Cabinets and Queen's University donate materials. Still others, such as Vista Enterprises and the Greater Kingston Chamber of Commerce, advise the students and the LDSB.

When Enviroworks conducted market research and needed help in developing the survey, several marketing research firms, like Thornley Stoker Advertising, volunteered. Local companies such as CKWS Television and GTO 960 helped the students develop TV and radio advertising. Partnerships with the Enviroworks program are beneficial in three ways (1) by providing an opportunity for partners to have a say in the education process (2) by saving organizations money in disposal costs and (3) by providing employers with better-trained students.

The Greater Kingston Chamber of Commerce, which represents over 900 businesses in Kingston, as well as the Junior Chamber, was proactive in providing businesses to work with the students when needed. Business 'mentors' donated their time to students. They helped Enviroworks in the areas of marketing (advertising, promotion, pricing), accounting (checking financial statements and budgets), computers (web page development and use of computer hardware such as LCD projectors), and placed students on various Chamber committees. Their input led to a new environmental business and technology curriculum.

Business partners realize that young people are the future for economic and community development.

The benefits for company time and effort are in the development of a pool of skilled employees. Small business operators want generalists, people who have experience and skill in many different areas of business. In most small businesses, employees are required to do many different tasks. Enviroworks provided students with the opportunity to perform many tasks owners themselves would do: marketing, bookkeeping, sales, customer service, strategic planning, and networking. Potential employers are free to watch the students operate in a real business setting before hiring them or taking them for a work placement. In both cases, LDSB invests in the training of students before sending them to potential employers. The business community is impressed because education is taking responsibility for the preparation of their students in a realistic learning environment.

Organizations realize the cost savings a partnership can provide. Disposal costs are a great expense to many businesses and non-profit organizations. Our program works with local businesses to save them hundreds of thousands of dollars in disposal costs. Manufacturers are often stuck with products, such as doors, counter tops, and windows, which have minor defects or have been cut to sizes other than specified. These companies can not sell these products and either put them in storage or have them removed at a cost of $90 per ton.

Enviroworks does not charge for a pickup. The companies, who partner with the program, are seen by the community as environmentally responsible, and supportive of the education system. In both instances, there is publicity generated at no cost to the businesses. Large corporations, such as Alcan, Dupont, and Bombardier, and small companies, like Bathworks, Cataraqui Cabinets, and Lowen Windows, have all participated. Every year more businesses were utilizing the services Enviroworks provides.

COMMUNITY ASSISTANCE

The free pickup service is a great advantage to many non-profit organizations. Non-profits, especially those affected by government cutbacks, save significant amounts of money in demolition and disposal costs. Currently, Queen's University saves over $50,000 a year in disposal fees. Before our project, this university ran its own small reuse centre where the public could come two days a week to take away materials. They would pay someone to run the reuse centre and organize the materials. If materials did not sell, they stored them in needed space. By allowing us to take the material, the university disposes of a large volume rapidly. Fewer materials are also sent to the landfill, which upholds Queen's environmental reputation.

Some other examples of non-profit partnerships involved the former City of Kingston and its townships. The roads department provided Enviroworks with items to be picked up and phone numbers of residents needing a collection. Enviroworks contacted people with reusable building materials, collected discards and saved the roads department work while diverting materials from the dump. Before our project residents waited as much as two months to have their materials removed.

Enviroworks also partnered with city agencies such as the Kingston Area Recycling Corporation (KARC). KARC is in charge of the blue box program in Kingston. They recycle paper, glass, plastics, and even hazardous materials. Many Kingston residents call about disposing of materials that KARC does not take, including building materials and furniture. When calls such as this came in, KARC referred them to Enviroworks and we arranged to collect the material. Conversely, when we received calls about recyclable materials, we referred these people to KARC.

In an effort to offer greater cost savings to local businesses and community organizations, Enviroworks started a Demolition and Deconstruction operation, which worked with local renovators and homeowners to save them money and remove the materials in better condition. Our deconstruction team, students and a supervisor, went onto renovation job sites to dismantle and remove materials or to demolish smaller structures. This service was offered free to contractors. We only asked they give us the materials removed or demolished. This new service expanded our training program.

Expanded services are especially attractive to small businesses and non-profits that are financially strapped. The students developed web sites for several different organizations in both the private and public sectors. They provided consulting services and market research. Like the demolition and deconstruction services, assistance was offered free since students gain excellent experience in exchange for their work. In the early years, Enviroworks frequently worked with non-profit groups limited by finances and expertise. Many non-profit organizations needed assistance with the challenges they faced. Students in the program needed real problems to solve. Organizations, such as the Kingston General Hospital (KGH) and Hospice Kingston, organized fundraising events. Hospice Kingston operated Chilifest and KGH organized the Festival of Trees. In order to gauge the success of these events, survey research was conducted. However, staff could not tally the results and generate reports. Our students created the database needed to analyze the results. A report for both events summarized their results and made recommendations. Organizers of the two events told other non-profits that immediately contacted Enviroworks to do similar work for them.

Other examples of partnerships include one with the Voices, Opportunities, and Choices Employment Club, which seeks to develop employment opportunities for psychiatric patients being reintegrated into the community. We developed a business plan for a store operated by the patients. Partnerships were also developed with the St. Lawrence II, Kingston's tall ship. The St. Lawrence II offers sailing trips where people learn to operate the ship, teamwork, and discipline during an adventure. The organization that operated the ship wants to attract consumers from a younger age segment.

Enviroworks tried to come up with a strategy to promote both itself and business studies to younger students. The combined result was the Enviroworks Elementary School Business competition that involved students from surrounding schools who are in the target market for St. Lawrence II. The goal was to have the students create a radio commercial that would appeal to the ten to fourteen year old youth segment. Enviroworks coordinated this day long event with the Kingston Tourist Office, the Greater Kingston Chamber of Commerce, Vista Enterprises, and Country 96 FM.

Students heard from representatives from the Kingston Welcome Center concerning the importance of tourism in Kingston, Brigantine Incorporated about the St. Lawrence II and their market, and Country 96 FM on how to make a radio commercial. The winning group was invited to Country 96's studio to record their commercial, which was played free on the radio during Tourism Week. The advertisement increased the number of young people and adults who use the St. Lawrence II and younger students learned about Enviroworks.

CONTINUING EFFECTS

In the first three years of Enviroworks' development, we initiated partnerships. Over time, companies started approaching us about possible partnerships. A good example of this was a proposed partnership between Robinson's Solutions, the City of Kingston, and our project. Robinson's Solutions, a multinational firm of more than 1,000 employees in three countries who specialize in janitorial and property management services, asked us to consider a unique partnership. Robinson's was trying to develop a private/public partnership with the City of Kingston. It wanted to take over the collection of garbage and recyclables and believed it could save the city at least $1 million per year. The company promised better service, new equipment, and less garbage going to the dumps. Since building material makes up thirty percent of the waste stream, Enviroworks was asked to take these materials.

Another opportunity that was investigated included partnerships with companies in the movie industries. Kingston is one of the oldest cities in Canada and is the first capital of the country. Its well-maintained historical architecture makes it very attractive for movie companies shooting historical films. *Vendetta*, a movie starring Academy Award winner Christopher Walken, was filmed using parts of Kingston and the City Hall area. Elaborate sets were built to remake Kingston into New Orleans during the 1800s. The same production company was filming the CBS miniseries, *Feast of All Saints*. The production spends about $200,000 for construction of the sets. Usually after a movie is finished, the sets are torn down and brought to the dump. The producers were happy to let us take the materials.

Enviroworks measured its success by monitoring its objectives. I had several goals for the program and we were successful in meeting most of them:

- We diverted over 70 tons of construction and demolition waste from Kingston area landfills. This number was expected to jump to over 100 tons a year.
- Our program helped the LDSB bring in over $1 million dollars in additional funding from both the private and public sector. The store itself generated gross sales of over $40,000 per year.
- The number of business partners in the program grew from fifteen to over 300 in the space of four years.
- Local businesses saved hundreds of thousands of dollars in disposal fees.
- Kingston residents were encouraged to change their disposal habits. Over 3000 Kingston residents diverted materials from the landfill every year by using Enviroworks.
- With the help of its business partners and the community, a new environmental business and technology curriculum was developed.

It is incredible to see students who have had a history of attendance problems, and who have lacked motivation in the classroom, now volunteer after school. Trucks can be donated or their rent equivalent paid if a promotional arrangement is made, and the manager is a teacher or a volunteer. The labour force is students who are paid with academic credits rather than money.

Financing is not the most important factor in duplicating the Enviroworks model. There needs to be an entrepreneurial mind-set at the administrative level. A teacher/director needs to understand both the business and training aspects of the Enviroworks model. It is essential that market research be conducted in order to determine the supplier potential and market demand. Nine months of research was undertaken before the doors of Enviroworks opened. Analysis of the competition is another key factor in order to obtain help from government funds and business volunteers. At the time, there was only one other used building material store in Kingston and it did not offer a free pickup of materials. Our competitor paid for material whereas we did not. Our source of material was mostly residential while our competitor's was mostly commercial. Enviroworks was organized with these differences in mind to avoid competition with a private business. Private business support was needed for marketing, promotion, finance, and strategic planning, and they would not provide this

> help if we were openly competing with
> another private business.

The merging of business and school evaluations is revealed here by the former school Vice-Principal Roxanne Flynn as it is by many business spokespersons.

Programs like Enviroworks, as well as the partnerships that are formed, are dependent on the people who coordinate the program. There have been two other directors since I left and each of them brought their own vision (based on their own experiences) of what the program and its partnerships should look like. In addition to the environmental emphasis, which all directors promoted, they concentrated on the business and vocational aspects of the program.

Students were involved in marketing, accounting, strategic planning, and customer service. They were empowered to make decisions relating to every aspect of the business. It should be noted that, over time, the level and interests of the students changed and the program had to change with them. At the beginning of my tenure we had a mixture of academic and workplace students although most students ended up going to college or university. Towards the end of my tenure, students were predominantly workplace bound and this trend continued after I left. There was also an issue with dwindling numbers in business education classes at QECVI (and indeed in most of the LDSB). As a result, there was a shift in terms of the type of student entering the program. As student interests changed, there was a necessary shift in terms of the curriculum and the partnerships that were formed. For example, the second director had a construction background so more emphasis was placed on the technical aspects of the program.

There have been two other directors since I left Enviroworks and each of them brought their own vision (based on their own experiences) of what the program and its partnerships should look like. In addition to the environmental emphasis, which all directors promoted, I concentrated on the business and vocational aspects of the program. Students were involved in marketing, accounting, strategic planning, and customer service. They were empowered to make decisions relating to every aspect of the business. The interests of the students changed and the program had to change with them.

Although the business component was still important, students also learned about making products of the used material such as tables out of old doors and furniture out of used lumber. There was also a large refinishing component to the program. Business support continued even though the program was geared more to student needs than it was in the initial case.

Partnerships with suppliers such as Queen's University and the local hospitals were still a focus, but business partners such as the Greater Kingston Chamber of Commerce, who traditionally helped provide business training, were utilized less than partners such as the Kingston Construction Association, who helped provide contractors to assist with construction projects or securing material. A third director arrived who had an interest in special education and guidance in addition to business. He had a vision for the program that brought it in a new direction and he implemented several changes that are still in place today. Because of the growing difficulty of getting business oriented students, and construction oriented students for that matter since there were so many construction programs to compete with, Enviroworks became a referral focus program. A referral program meant that the majority of students in the program had to be referred by their schools guidance department or administrator and that the level of student was almost exclusively workplace and at-risk.

More time was now spent in the store looking after warehouse management and customer service than with the operation of the business. Students had very little interest in the marketing and accounting aspect of the operation but were much more interested in learning job skills that would get them a job right out of high school. There was a return to the emphasis on business partnerships that I promoted, however, rather than have these partners help with instructing students on business topics, they assisted students with getting jobs and employed several of the students. At this point, a growing environmental consciousness amongst contractors and the construction industry, as well as a better understanding of the worth of used construction materials, meant that these groups were keeping more of their material.

Enviroworks started taking in more furniture and working with construction partners less as suppliers and more as employers.

I derived a great deal of personal satisfaction from the fact that I developed something that had an impact not only on the students who were in the program, but on the whole community. I still run into former students and community partners who say our program is unlike anything they had ever seen before or since. I am also very proud of the fact that Enviroworks is now entering its 14th year. Its longevity is impressive for a focus program, but even more remarkable for a business. Many businesses never live to see their third year.

Enviroworks is definitely one of the highlights of my teaching career and has had a profound impact on many aspects of my life. However, what I remember most relates to my students. For example, I think about the opportunities that this program provided for students to get involved with the community and the chances they had to get involved in networking activities and events they never would have normally. For example, students attended business mixers and breakfast meetings and helped organize Chamber events such as the Home and Leisure Expo and the Chamber Golf Tournament. Students also worked with the Kingston Junior Chamber of Commerce (Jaycees), a leadership group for young professionals, and helped organize and participate in events such as: the St. Lawrence Fishing Festival, the Polar Plunge, the Over-the-Hill-Soap Box Derby, the

Green Expo, the Santa Claus Parade, Chilifest, the Festival of Trees, the Citizen of the Year Awards Dinner, and the Young Entrepreneur's Networking Dinner. I will never forget the surprised look on the faces of Chamber members when students would come up to them at mixers, introduce themselves, and start discussing business issues at the store. It was funny to watch business leaders in the community discuss serious management issues with 16 and 17 year olds.

I also remember my student Chuck, who was an active participant in all these high profile network events. Chuck was a huge attendance problem at the school but really flourished at Enviroworks. His networking for our project led him to join the Kingston Jaycees. As a result of his hard work and dedication, he was named the Kingston Jaycee Rookie of the Year—the youngest winner in the 55 year history of the Kingston Jaycees. He was also selected as the first winner of the Mayor's Youth Award for Volunteerism. I felt very proud of his success.

Lastly, I think about Phil, one of my students. Phil was from a disadvantaged family and had very few opportunities in his life. At the age of 17, he had still never travelled outside Kingston. At the school, he had been in trouble constantly and was bit of a loner. He spent two years at Enviroworks and, while it wasn't always easy for either of us, he became a very important part of the operation and developed some good friends. When I got a call from the United Nations saying that our partnership was one of the winners of the Global 500 Award, and that they were going to pay to fly me and one student to Japan first class and all expenses paid, I asked him if he wanted to go. For a student who had never been outside Kingston, it was a bit of a shock. I don't think he understood the magnitude of what was going on when he went on stage in front of 2000 people, accepted the Global 500 Award from the Director of the United Nations Environment Program, shook hands with the Prime Minister of Japan, and then met personally with the Emperor and Empress of Japan. The Empress commented on Phil's Ontario trillium pin which he gave her as a gift. Ten years later, when I went to Phil's wedding, he was still talking about that trip!

From a personal perspective, the program built up my confidence. It showed me that I could come up with an idea and bring it from concept to reality. It was also a great opportunity for me to test my own business skills using someone else's money! The success of the program, and the fact that people in the community thought it worthy of nominating for awards, also made me feel proud. It meant that people really valued the program and the work that the students and I were putting into it. In Kingston, Enviroworks was the winner of the Local Industry Focusing on the Environment (*L.I.F.E.) Environmental Award* from the Greater Kingston Chamber of Commerce, the first School Board program to win a major business award in Kingston. It was also the winner of the *Ontario Waste Minimization Award* as the outstanding non-profit organization in the province, an award bestowed by Recycling Council of Ontario. At the national level, the program received the *National Partners in Education Award* in the "Broad Community Collaboration" category. This award recognized our program as one of the best partnerships in Canada. It received the Honourable Mention Award in the Peter F. Drucker Canadian Non-Profit Award competition.

At the global level, Enviroworks received the internationally acclaimed *Nova Corporation Global Best Award* in the "Caring for the Community and the Environment" category among entries from 13 countries. Finally, it was awarded the *United Nations Global 500 Award*. Our partnership was one of 17 individuals and organizations recognized worldwide for outstanding contributions to the protection of the environment and success in mobilizing community resources to address these problems. I also received several personal awards including one of ten Prime Minister's Awards for Teaching Excellence, the TV Ontario Teachers' Award of Merit, and the Roy C. Hill Award.

While winning awards and gaining recognition was great, Enviroworks also taught me some very important lessons. It really showed me what was required to run a business and the demand and sacrifice that entrepreneurs have to make in order for their enterprises to be successful. It also forced me to prioritize. I realized that I could not do this for the rest of my life. I really began to understand the importance of family and friends when I hardly saw them!

This partnership was a highlight of my teaching career, but it was a stressful time in my life. The time commitment and strain of operating a business in addition to being a teacher took its toll. By the end of my tenure I was close to being burnt out and desperately needed a change. It was at that time that I decided to go back to school and take a break from Enviroworks. I knew that once I left, I was probably never going back. However, the success of the program provided me with many opportunities and had a significant impact on my life after I left.

Upon leaving the project in 2000, I was accepted to graduate school at Harvard University to complete my Masters in Education. The admissions department said that this program was a factor in my acceptance. After graduating from Harvard I took a new position at a new school in the LDSB. After a year I decided to complete my Doctorate at Queen's. Again, Enviroworks contributed to my acceptance. My experience with this partnership and other school-based enterprises influenced the research for my PhD thesis.

Although I did not study Enviroworks specifically, I examined how other school-based enterprises (SBE's) from across Ontario helped prepare young people for the New Economy workplace. I strongly believe that programs like Enviroworks provide a learning environment which incorporates many of the practices used to organize work and learning in the New Economy workplace. Students are expected to adapt to work practices that involve working in teams, decision-making and problem-solving, being comfortable with autonomy and empowerment, and learning how to learn at work.

In terms of the future of the program, I think it's time for this school-based enterprise to take advantage of the growing interest in green industries. It could be a model for green industry training for students all over Canada. Enviroworks has developed partnerships to help train students in areas related to recyclable material sales, deconstruction, and solid waste collection. It also seems to have a good fit with the green building segment, also known as green construction or sustainable building. Green construction is the practice of creating structures and using processes that are environmentally responsible and resource-efficient throughout a building's life-cycle: from sitting to design, construction, operation, maintenance, renovation, and deconstruction.

There are several businesses in Kingston with experience in all these areas that would benefit greatly from working with Enviroworks and helping prepare students to work in the many green industry jobs that are going to be created in the next decade. Partnerships could also be created in the areas of energy efficiency retrofits, green woodworking, and renewable energy. Renewable energy is a great opportunity as Kingston has dozens of wind turbines and St. Lawrence College has just started a Wind Turbine Technician Program to address the demand for trained and certified Wind Turbine Technicians.

Although Enviroworks was intended to be a model for entrepreneurial education, it has evolved in response to changes in its environment. It turned into a model for technical education and then a workplace preparation model for at-risk and special education students. Where it goes next depends on how it chooses to adapt. In all its different forms, it pooled the resources of the community, the education system, and private and public businesses. What started as a school board initiative has grown to become a collaboration of the community. Each of the partners shared in the program's accomplishments. I will always be proud to be a part of it.

EDITOR'S COMMENT

The reasons for directors changing the program's perspective include the changing relationship between business and the schools. Whether special education or the arts is the focus of the program is a result of educational policies. During dire financial times for the schools, business interests dominate over such decisions. When the program began, budget cut-backs were the order to the day. When inflation or economic growth is occurring, then progressive education tends to flourish in the schools (Mitchell, 1998).

In either set of circumstances, creative individuals find ways to bring opportunities together. It is striking in Kingston that environmental conservation was woven into a dominantly business program Indeed, the environmental conservation was the cornerstone of the program that allowed it to support profits for business and social responsibility for business people, as well as the entrepreneur who founded the program with his students. The program's planning is a seamless connection between education and business. The creator's career has also been linked constantly to the program's evolution, an issue that will be raised in the remaining chapters.

Chapter 5

Credit Union Designs Partners in Education (PIE)

Kari Pepperkorn, Corporate Citizenship
Specialist, First Calgary

It is rare to find a job that is able to
satisfy a desire for professional success and
personal fulfilment. Fortunately, I have
found both. Growing up in Calgary, Alberta,
I learned early on that being an active part
of the community was going to play an
important role in my life. With a broad range
of volunteer experiences under my belt, I
began to consider potential career paths that
would lead me to a place where business and
community interests connect. In 2004, I
emerged from Mount Royal College (now
University) with a degree in Public Relations
and a strong desire to pursue a job that would
blend these two worlds. After working with
Big Brothers and Big Sisters of Calgary and
Area in development and communications for
nearly two years, I soon found what I would
call 'my dream job' with First Calgary Savings.

In my role as Corporate Citizenship Specialist at First Calgary Savings, I have the pleasure of satisfying my desire to work with the community—a place where I live, work and play each and every day—along with my desire to operate in the world of business. While First Calgary Savings' community investments are diverse and unique, of particular note is its Partners in Education program. The Partners in Education program is a unique initiative that stands to build relationships between First Calgary Savings branches and local schools in the community. The goal of the program is to bring educators, students and First Calgary Savings staff together to enhance the learning environment of children and youth in the community—specifically students attending the partner school. For each branch that is launched, a partner school is found. This program, the first of its kind for First Calgary Savings at the time of inception, was created in response to Calgary schools voicing a need for non-traditional support. Beyond a financial necessity, the schools wanted to engage the community and bring local business into the classroom. Community involvement has led to other groups, such as theatres and authors reading for word feats or fests becoming a part of the program.

When I joined First Calgary Savings in 2007, the Partners in Education program was well established. My primary objective was to support this initiative, from building the core relationships with community partners to educational programming. I have taken an active role in all of the following community programs that are mentioned in relation to First Calgary Savings, two of the first being the Book Rapport Educational Programme of WordFest and the First Calgary Savings Mentorship Program with Theatre Junction.

Ultimately, the foundation of our community involvement is our Partners in Education program. It is based on the philosophy of 'neighbour-helping-neighbour.' Branches and partner schools are encouraged to develop deep, long-lasting relationships as they find innovative opportunities to work on unique programs and activities that meet their particular needs. First Calgary Savings is pleased to be able to offer a variety of programs aimed at enhancing the learning of children and youth from kindergarten to grade 12.

It is important to remember the greatest element of these partnerships is adaptability. The school administrators, teachers, students and First Calgary Savings' branch managers, employees and head office understand and champion the necessity of creating and supporting programs that sincerely and effectively enhance the learning experience of the students. Recognizing that school partnerships don't have to exclusively contribute to the core academic programming, this relationship attempts to include students whose life passion may fall within a realm outside of math, science, English and social studies. Adapting to the immediate and long-term needs of the students contributes to a healthy school and consequently a healthy partnership.

COMMUNITY ADVOCACY

Nearly seventy years ago, a small group of people cared enough about Calgary's economic prosperity and community strength to form a community-based credit union. And while much about our business has changed over the years, the simple, yet revolutionary concept of neighbor-helping-neighbor, endures. As First Calgary Savings strives to be a leader in corporate citizenship, the words 'community advocacy' are ones that cannot be overlooked or undervalued. From the moment I started at the company, this was a philosophy and action I quickly embraced. First Calgary Savings' corporate citizenship vision is to be a leader in fostering vibrant communities by championing partnerships that allow us to leverage our business assets toward inspiring and achieving positive social and environmental change in the communities we serve. We will become recognized as community advocates over time by being present, turning possibilities into realities, by taking a stand on critical community issues and by proving we care. It is for these reasons I have found success with First Calgary Savings as a company—their vision for the future aligns directly with my own.

Community advocacy is more than providing necessary funding. It is about building key relationships, developing effective partnerships, sitting at the right community tables and lending a voice to issues of importance. As community advocates, we remain committed to seeing learning as a lifelong journey and will continue to build upon our already strong commitment to education. As we look to the future, we will ensure our resources are used to help those facing educational barriers overcome them and will retain a strong focus on financial education, literacy and capability in line with our core business.

BEHIND THE SCENES

It is important to note Partners in Education relationships are not formed without significant consideration and research. Before a partnership is ever announced, months of groundwork have already been undertaken. Much of this back-end work is undertaken by the Corporate Citizenship team—I have worked with schools and branches to find alignment in programming and involvement. As with any plan to create a strong and sustainable educational partnership, the following elements must be considered:

Location of school/location of branch

School needs and wants

Branch needs and wants

School expectations of the partnership

Branch expectations of the partnership

Who primary program contacts will be

Number of staff/hours needed to fulfill agreed upon expectations

Opportunities currently available for branch to get involved

How open is the school to new opportunities/ideas
First Calgary could provide
Mutual understanding of the partnership

WHY PARTNERSHIPS SURVIVE

Finding a partner school that is the right fit for the branch is often the single largest step in the Partners in Education process. With mutual understanding of each party's goals and expectations, and with the proper research, finding a partner school should be an enjoyable and simple adventure. Historically, the most successful partnerships are those that share a common objective and that agree on a common direction in which to move. Most likely, both partners will have similar values and will have agreed upon a set course of action prior to embarking on a formal partnership. Of course, as partnerships grow, some of these initial objectives may change; however, the foundation of the relationship will still maintain a healthy, honest and mutually beneficial base.

The majority of our existing Partners in Education are situated in a shared geographical area. This means that both the branch and school are generally within walking distance or a quick drive from each other. While this certainly isn't the only way a partnership can exist, current participants find being in close proximity to each other facilitates an easier working environment.

Once you have identified a partner that may be suitable geographically, it is time to make contact.

Whether you are a branch or a school, first impressions are important. Whether you feel more comfortable sending an introductory email or making a cold call, make sure you have knowledge about the background of the organization and that you are contacting the correct person. Some helpful tips to consider prior to making first contact are:

Research—Searching the Internet for information, most businesses and even individual schools have Web sites. On these sites you should be able to get a glimpse into the personality of the organization that may help you when initializing a conversation with a company representative.

Call ahead—Before you set up a meeting, call ahead and find out who is responsible for partnership coordination at the school or branch. If you are going to send an email or letter, make sure you have the correct spelling of the partnership coordinator's name.

Ask the Corporate Citizenship team for help—the Corporate Citizenship team is here to encourage branch partnership initiatives. We actively support the branch with research and work with them to make contact with their desired school and even join the branch representatives at their first meeting.

FIRST MEETING

With the right research already performed, branches are well equipped for their first meeting. It is important to remember that the Corporate Citizenship team is available for support during any part of the process and is willing to join in on meetings if given the relevant information. During your meeting, it's important to touch-base on a few significant points of action. Keep in mind, however, that this meeting should mainly be focused on getting to know each other and discovering if your organizations will make a good match. The following is an outline that an agenda usually follows:

Introductions

Organizational briefing of both parties

Share partnership objectives (use the information cited in your preparatory work)

Identify key contacts and contact information (should be at least two people to insure succession planning)

Agree on a second meeting where you will confirm new projects and develop a concrete time-line for the entire year

You may also want to bring supplementary information about your organization that can be left behind after the meeting has concluded. Consider the following;

Your business card
The organization's Web site (particularly if it's the Partners in Education site)
An annual report
A company newsletter
Promotional items

RESULTS FROM ESTABLISHING PARTNERSHIPS

The best time to make contact with a new school or existing school is the last week in August.

The most effective person to deal with when establishing a new partner school is the principal.

The first month of each semester, especially September, is a particularly difficult time to meet with the schools. It's best to get planning accomplished in August or at the end of the school year.

If you are coordinating a first-year program, choose between two and four events. This number is manageable and allows you to become acquainted with your school without feeling overwhelmed with programs.

When planning events, coordinate details at least two to three months in advance. It is helpful to create a semester event calendar in August or during the first meeting with your partner school.

Talk to other partnership coordinators and the Corporate Citizenship team.

Before going too far down the road, it is important to understand how educational partnerships are formed.

BRANCH INVOLVEMENT

It is important to remember the foundation of the Partners in Education program lies with the branches and their selected involvement with their respective schools. There needs to be buy-in from not only the school, but the teachers and administrators at the school. Similarly, branch buy-in is only as good as those who are planning to deliver on the agreed upon action items. Ultimately, a successful educational partnership will enhance curriculum, provide meaningful volunteer opportunities and engage branch staff, school administrators, teachers and students alike.

After the first partnership meeting, both the school and the branch should have a good idea of what each is looking for and what each is able to offer. One of the many benefits of a program that operates with so much flexibility between partners is that projects can be created for each grade and age level. There are no guidelines or rules for program development—projects are limited only by a lack of imagination. While there are moderate financial benefits to being a partner in education, the majority of educational adventures are based on learning, human interaction and/or non-traditional use of resources.

CORPORATE CITIZENSHIP

The Corporate Citizenship team at First Calgary Savings acts as resource-based program support for Partners in Education. As branches are encouraged to build relationships directly with the schools with which they are associated, Corporate Citizenship seeks to act as that 'behind the scenes' guidepost. The role of Corporate Citizenship in the Partners in Education program is fluid in that the team can adapt to work with the branch, no matter the circumstance. In the formative months, Corporate Citizenship will be involved in introductory meetings and will provide program as well as organizational history, examples of other successful partners as well as background on current programming and non-profit partners.

In the early stages of partnership development, Corporate Citizenship will do the groundwork to find local schools within geographic proximity to the branch. This list will then be provided to the branch for review and discussion before a short list is created. At this time, branches have the opportunity to contact their top schools to arrange meetings, or Corporate Citizenship may be asked to fulfill this role. Although the Corporate Citizenship team will participate in any meetings of introduction, the branch is encouraged to take the lead in the relationship and solidify itself as the primary contact for the school. Branches within the First Calgary Savings network are empowered to work with their educational partner to find the best possible programs and initiatives to meet both parties' objectives.

REASONS FOR PARTNERSHIPS

First Calgary Savings has two primary motivations for the Partners in Education (PIE) program: business and community. Not surprisingly, these two things are not mutually exclusive, but rather, have deeply connected foundational roots. Let us take a look at what each of these motivations entail. The Partners in Education business benefits primarily revolve around creating awareness and generating positive and unique ways in which to position the organization's brand. The Partners in Education program provides a wide range of communication channels (Web site, email updates, branch/school contacts) in which to engage key stakeholders (students, parents, teachers, educational boards) and is considered a 'value add' for schools looking to engage with First Calgary Savings for their financial needs. It should be noted that doing business with First Calgary Savings is not a criteria on which a partnership is built. This program also allows the company to identify and celebrate employee volunteer efforts in the community.

To understand the communication channels the PIE program opens (from a business perspective), we must look at the core offerings from each:

Web Site:

- Provides an outlet to house all PIE information
- Allows community partners to provide special offers to PIE schools
- Gives schools the opportunity to share stories about how their PIE program is working
- Gives First Calgary Savings staff the opportunity to profile their branch partnership
- Gives community partners the opportunity to profile their education-based initiatives

Email Updates

- Provides a direct line of communication from the First Calgary Savings Corporate Citizenship team to branch PIE contacts, partner schools and community partners
- Allows First Calgary Savings to highlight successful partnerships
- Encourages active participation through an interactive interface

Branch/School Contacts

- Provides direct relationship contacts to each party
- Allows active two-way communication regarding not only the program, but First Calgary Savings financial business offerings as well (and if desired)

PROGRAMS

Being successful is not about working in a silo, but rather, bringing a variety of resources together to maximize impact. It is not enough to have a cover on a book: one must have the pages to be bound. For First Calgary Savings, the Partners in Education program is that cover and the community partners brought together to enrich the program are those pages. Six key community partnerships continue to add value and augment local curriculum.

Theatre Junction and Mentoring

Theatre Junction is said to be "a 'culturehouse' of contemporary live arts," (Vision, 2008), where unique art forms can grow from seeds of theatrical innovation to groundbreaking productions. Theatre Junction is about the convergence of the individual, the artist and the art form, whatever that may be. Founded in 1991, artistic director Mark Lawes had a vision, "to create a space to think collectively and activate the individual as a participant in a vibrant society, where the artist and the spectator bring theatre to life and make apparent its diversity, vitality and necessity" (ibid.). In 2006, Theatre Junction moved into one of Calgary's oldest buildings, The GRAND (History—Theatre Junction, 2008). Having been built before World War I, this vintage art space provides a stage that merges the old and the new.

The First Calgary Savings Mentorship Program with Theatre Junction began in 2001 as a multi-week program that would follow a play from first reading to going live on stage opening night. Youth from across the city were encouraged to apply for this unique experience that brought to life plays from paper to reality. As Theatre Junction has grown and changed, so too has the Mentorship Program. Each year, 16 students from across Calgary are accepted into the program, with an aim to learn about the theatre on every level. From movement to lighting and costume design to directing, students are taken on an intrinsic theatrical journey, and one that is expected to change lives.

Theatre Junction

Running from November through April each year, the Mentorship Program is also able to engage the Theatre Junction Resident Company of Artists (RCA) from across Canada and around the world, specializing in all different artistic disciplines. Each of these uniquely poignant artists contributes their skills and ideas to the creative process by working together on a full-time basis. The RCA's work is incorporated into the Mentorship Program curriculum and is shown at all levels of development, from rehearsal to full production. As part of the First Calgary Savings Mentorship Program, students have the opportunity to learn from this talented group of artists through an intensive workshop series, invitations to private rehearsals and backstage tours. Mentoring relationships are developed throughout the year and students are encouraged to ask questions of any of the RCA or Theatre Junction staff.

As a partner in education, First Calgary Savings is proud to work directly with Theatre Junction to ensure the Mentorship Program continues Vision 2008 (http:// www.theatrejunction.com/cms/200.html). Grounded in the foundation of arts and culture as well as life-long learning, the ideals of youth mentorship in the theatre are pivotal in the enrichment of Calgary's cultural fabric.

This program seeks to give youth an outlet to explore their passions, no matter what educational system they are enrolled. As a program promoted through the First Calgary Savings partner school network, it is also made available city-wide through in-branch community boards, Web site presence, viral marketing and in-school information sessions hosted by Theatre Junction. Theatre Junction arose as an ancient art form that embodies the literary arts as not only a cultural identifier, but also a means of survival. Throughout history, people have been communicating through symbols and sounds, ultimately yielding languages. Today, the literary arts are a widely diverse set of prose: from fiction or nonfiction to poetry or from plays to musical lyrics.

WordFest: Banff-Calgary International Writer's Festival began in 1996 with a mission, "to enhance quality of life by stimulating literacy through bringing readers of all ages together with writers of local, national and international stature in events that are accessible and populist in nature" (WordFest History, 2008). Today, that mission can be seen through every element of the annual programming WordFest History (http://www.wordfest.com/media_history.php). The festival, which runs every fall, attracts more than 12,000 people each year. To that end, it is the caliber of literary icon, both up-and-coming and established, who draw local citizens into the magic. Celebrated adult authors such as Margaret Atwood and the late Timothy Findley as well as children's authors Hazel Hutchins and Richard Scrimger, are just a few of the hundreds of note-worthy authors seen at WordFest since it's inception.

Since 2003, First Calgary Savings has been an active partner with WordFest in the creation of literary adventures for school-aged children through the Book Rapport Educational Program. Book Rapport, the youth component of the festival, seeks to enhance the language arts curriculum (from kindergarten to grade 12) by providing innovative literacy programming. Schools from across the city are invited to Book Rapport events and are encouraged to use online learning resources to supplement the interactive experience.

As a founding partner of Book Rapport, First Calgary Savings offers six partner schools class sets of tickets to a Book Rapport event of their choice. Partner schools are encouraged to take their classes out in the community to not only gain first-hand experience of listening to a live author, but also embrace the opportunity to see a local arts venue. Book Rapport works with teachers and their selected author to build an event that aligns with the curriculum and suits the school's needs.

Additionally, each year, two partner schools are chosen from the First Calgary Savings network, to receive an in-school session. During these events, schools are able to open their library or gymnasium and fill the space with as many youth as they wish. First Calgary Savings sponsors a writer to go into these schools for a captivating hour and a half session, with plenty of time for students to interact with the author. Formally opened in 1985, the EPCOR Centre for the Performing Arts is more than 400,000 square feet of creative space located in the heart of downtown Calgary. Since its inception, the EPCOR Centre has been home to more than 1,800 performances a year. Not only is the EPCOR CENTRE renowned for unique performances and special events, they are also known for their One Day Arts School, proudly supported by First Calgary Savings. With the joint belief that theatre and the performing arts encourage communities to think differently, by expanding imagination and incorporating creativity into daily lives, First Calgary Savings has taken a proactive stance for arts education.

One Day Arts School

One Day Arts School is a program that works hand-in-hand with curriculum to provide integrated arts learning to subject matter. Students receive a customized day of arts-based learning at the EPCOR CENTRE. Through a program coordinator, workshops are constructed to engage children and youth (from kindergarten to grade 12), in artistic and theatrical adventures that relate directly back to the classroom; these include:

> *Kindergarten science: Seasonal Changes.*
> One Day Arts School curriculum includes:
> the use of visual art, creative movement,
> storytelling and music to explore seasonal

cycles, the environment and changes in plants and animals.

Grade five language arts: Poetry. One Day Arts School curriculum includes: the examination of imagery, language, symbolism and metaphors through visual art, creative movement, drama and writing.

Exploring Ancient Greece. One Day Arts School curriculum includes: Greek drama, choral speaking and Greek mask making.

In 2008, more than 3,400 participants and 36 schools took part in One Day Arts School. The partnership between the EPCOR CENTRE and First Calgary Savings enables students, who may not have otherwise had the chance, to attend professionally facilitated arts programs. Beyond a financial commitment to the general operating fund of the program, First Calgary Savings also provides reimbursement for arts workshop expenses, special consideration to address transportation barriers for schools with limited resources (priority given to partner schools) as well as a discount for six partner schools to participate in One Day Arts School.

In 2007, First Calgary Savings, alongside the EPCOR CENTRE, was honored at the Mayor's Excellence Awards for Business and the Arts, for the best multi-sector partnership for the One Day Arts School program. This achievement marked a significant milestone not only for First Calgary Savings, but for the recognition of arts-based learning as an important component of kindergarten through grade 12 education.

Between Generations

Big Brothers and Big Sisters of Calgary and Area (BBBS) is a leader in mentoring. From traditional community-based matches, to one hour a week in-school sessions, the benefits of mentoring can be seen in all facets of a child's life. In 2004, BBBS and First Calgary Savings recognized a community need and saw the opportunity to partner and formalize a mentoring initiative focused on elementary school students and local seniors. Between Generations is the evolution of an earlier Grandparent Volunteer Program that was founded by the Calgary Board of Education and later partnered with First Calgary Savings and the Calgary Catholic School District. The school-based Between Generations program matches caring adults, 55 and over, with children in local elementary schools; mentors are matched with two children and meet with each child individually for one hour per week. When BBBS and First Calgary Savings began talking about partnership opportunities, both organizations identified the need for a new inter-generational mentoring program—one that incorporated Big Brothers and Big Sisters' national standards and reputation with the community spirit of First Calgary Savings.

The program was born to the name Between Generations, and as of 2008, boasted 102 mentoring matches in Calgary and area. By connecting elementary school children with caring seniors, the goal is to raise a generation of resilient young people who feel connected to adults as they journey towards adulthood. In 2007, BBBS and First Calgary Savings also won an Imagine Canada Business and Community Partnership Innovation Award for the collaboration for Between Generations. This recognition not only brought attention to the significant venture between BBBS and First Calgary Savings, but also the importance of being able to bring new and innovative programs into local school systems.

Between Generations came into being because of an identified community need. Combining First Calgary Savings' desire to promote education and lifelong learning, along with the desire to make a positive impact with member-owners (a significant portion of whom are seniors), this is a program that is not only offered to partner schools, but the community as a whole. BBBS continues to seek a mentor for every child in the city. This ambitious vision is one that First Calgary Savings supports entirely. A recent study on in-school mentoring shows that this support is justified; 90 per cent of students had an improved relationship with their peers; 75 per cent showed an increase in grades and attendance; and 80 per cent were more likely to graduate than their unmatched peers. These statistics are ones that staff of First Calgary Savings get behind, not just on the partners in education level, but through fundraising and other special events throughout the year.

Corporate Christmas Calendar

A historic part of the Partners in Education program has been the First Calgary Savings wall calendar, celebrating arts and learning in Calgary, while raising funds for partner schools. This initiative has provided local students the opportunity to have their artwork featured in a public forum through publication, while also giving them portfolio pieces to carry into their future artistic endeavours. For a suggested $2 donation, member-owners have been encouraged to support the Partners in Education program, through the purchase of a calendar. The Corporate Calendar program has also acted as a valuable fundraising tool, but more than that, as an opportunity to give back to staff and community partners of every shape and size. Each partner school has been engaged with the program by receiving a stock of calendars to be distributed to staff, students and volunteers of the school. Staff members and community partners have been given these artistic calendars year over year.

In 2008, First Calgary Savings joined forces with their partner credit union, Envision Financial, to create their first joint calendar. Together, First Calgary Savings and

Envision Financial embraced the following objectives as touchstones to the Corporate Calendar project:

> To produce a unique and professional corporate calendar

> To create a partnership opportunity for a First Calgary Savings partner branch and school and an Envision Financial partner school district

To raise a nominal amount of money for partner schools and partner school districts; for First Calgary Savings, funds are distributed equally among partner schools—for Envision Financial, funds are donated directly back to the partner school district involved. Finding this synergy for the calendar is important, as both First Calgary Savings and Envision Financial value the role emerging artists play both at home and across the Rockies. Whether through work, play, hobbies or academic pursuits, taking time to express and integrate creativity into daily living produces extraordinary results.

12 Days of Christmas

Each year, when the calendar is being distributed, an event formerly known as the 12 Days of Christmas brings the warmth and spirit of the holiday season to First Calgary's many partners. This celebration is centered at

Calgary's Heritage Park, which is home to one of Canada's oldest historic villages. Heritage Park's Once Upon a Christmas is a tradition that has stood the test of time. The event boasts more than a dozen activities which include: carolling, cookie decorating, a Christmas play, a children's market, visits with Santa, holiday gift shops and the opportunity to learn how three different classes of homes prepared for the holidays.

First Calgary Savings has partnered with Heritage Park since 1991 to bring this festival to life. As a principle supporter of this event, First Calgary Savings is able to maximize value for staff, other non-profit partners, member-owners, partner schools and Heritage Park. The program Once Upon a Christmas is widely advertised. Posters and coupons on community boards advertise the program throughout the branch network. All branches are given 50 per cent off coupons for member-owners and local citizens to pick up at their will, while all staff are given free admission vouchers to enjoy with their families. Further to that, all community partners and family-serving non-profit partners are given free admission vouchers to enjoy this event.

EVALUATION

Christmas and partnership celebrations are a part of community life for First Calgary. The ability to give back to communities where the business operates and where the employees live and work is of paramount importance. It is about integrity and being accountable in social, economic and environmental forums. For First Calgary Savings, integrity in the community stems from the credit union's founding principle of neighbour-helping-neighbour. To support this integral value, First Calgary Savings works with a number of third-party groups in order to provide us with guidance and support to ensure we're responsible to ever-changing needs in our communities and our business. In doing this, a high degree of credibility is achieved, committing to a high standard of excellence on which to be held accountable.

London Benchmarking Group (LBG) Canada

First Calgary Savings is one of 10 founding members of LBG Canada: a community of companies working toward a higher standard in the management, valuation and performance measurement of corporate community involvement. Internationally, First Calgary Savings joins the LBG network, spanning more than 100 companies. Clearly understanding the value of corporate citizenship to the community as a whole, and to our business, is a priority. We joined LBG Canada because we're committed to creating and achieving value for our community partners, for our business and ultimately for our member-owners. LBG Canada provides us with a basis for measuring both the business and community impact of our initiatives, within our PIE program and in all our corporate citizenship partnerships. LBG Canada helps us measure what matters.

LBG Canada's model uses standardized, international methodology to value inputs and to establish and exercise the benchmarking process. Since aggregate information is shared, we have the opportunity to see how we measure up against the Canadian group of companies on a year-by-year basis. This gives us valuable management insights. This evaluation and measurement has, for instance, led us to understand the effectiveness of our programs more thoroughly. We can see which ones provide greater value to the community and to the business, based on the investment and the results. This helps us with our short—and long-term planning and program management. Thanks to LBG Canada we continue to set clearer program goals and more effectively link activities to our business and community objectives.

Imagine Canada

Imagine Canada is a national registered charity that advocates for Canada's charities and non-profit organizations. Imagine Canada's Caring Company program is this country's leading corporate citizenship initiative. Its more than 100 members recognize that 'doing good' is not only good for business, it also builds brand identity, enhances employee recruitment and retention and improves a business's public reputation. As a proud member of Imagine Canada's Caring Company program, First Calgary Savings is committed to giving back a minimum one per cent of our pre-tax profit to the community, following ethical and environmental business practices and engaging employee volunteers in the community. Our Partners in Education program effortlessly blends the ideals of giving time, talent and treasure in the spirit of an Imagine Canada Caring Company each day.

Canadian Business for Social Responsibility

Founded in 1995, Canadian Business for Social Responsibility (CBSR) is a non-profit, member-led organization that mobilizes Canadian companies to make powerful business decisions that improve performance and contribute to a better world. CBSR strongly believes that corporate responsibility and business success go hand-in-hand. The organization supports the corporate social responsibility agendas of its member companies and leads the national debate in this area.

First Calgary Savings takes a proactive approach to our community programs by investing in areas where we can make a difference, a platform CBSR stands firmly behind. We seek partners within these focus areas who demonstrate leadership and social entrepreneurship, and who are known for their respectful, inclusive and creative approach. Beyond that, we focus our corporate assets on positively impacting our business and community. We are not afraid to say 'yes,' when it means taking a stand on issues that may require long-term thinking and involvement. We recognize that change takes time.

To that end, we work tirelessly each day to demonstrate leadership in community advocacy in four areas:

- Education and lifelong learning
- Arts and culture
- Protecting our planet
- Strengthening our voluntary sector

Our involvement with CBSR inspires us to continue to strive to be positive role models and encourage other companies to adopt best practices in corporate citizenship.

THE FUTURE

We are always looking to the future to ensure our corporate citizenship practices remain relevant for the issues of the day and to be aware of the social and environmental climate in which our business operates. Partners in Education is no exception when it comes to future planning. PIE is a program as rich in history as it is in diversity, having been a flagship endeavour for more than 15 years. It is this substantial record that has led us to closely examine the program and determine the best ways to move forward.

In 2008, First Calgary Savings undertook a program audit (conducted by a third-party communications contractor) for Partners in Education in order to benchmark the current needs of the community as well as to find out about new and emerging trends in the area of corporate partnerships as they relate to education. While the audit looked at programs from both First Calgary Savings and Envision Financial, for the purpose of this discussion, the primary information shared will be that from the PIE program. Going into the audit process, we wanted to take a closer look at our past experiences with business-education partnerships, our present activity with our partner schools and branches, and our plan for future action in order to serve the community to the best of our ability. Alongside our communications auditor, we worked through the following 10-steps:

(1) Establish audit objectives, goals and outcomes
(2) Gather, simplify and compare program objectives and structures
(3) Conduct literature review of corporate and internal program documents
(4) Interview stakeholders
(5) Review program resourcing, implementation and communication
(6) Research business-education partnership best practices
(7) Perform cost analysis
(8) Complete S.W.O.T. analysis

(9)   Complete overall program analysis

(10) Provide recommendations for next steps

The fact of the matter is, this program has been in place for nearly two decades. During this time, community needs have changed, school boards have identified areas for new curriculum development and social serving organizations in Calgary have developed so far as to fulfill their missions by working directly with students. These are things that have changed over time. While much of our PIE programming was still found to be relevant, some components were identified as having run their course. For First Calgary Savings, this is exactly the type of information we were seeking. In thinking about your own organization, a similar openness may provide a solid foundation in which to build future programming.

In the end, we would recommend any long-standing program undergo such a thorough case study. In many ways, it is the only way evolution and growth can build stronger programs. If it were not for this project, we would not be able to make the strategic decisions needed to serve the community in such a meaningful way.

OUR PARTNER PATHWAYS

We share a common social vision with our Pathways partner, Envision Financial, in the neighbouring province and large urban Vancouver area. Together, we look for opportunities to demonstrate our role as community advocates by lending our business voice at community tables and leveraging our business assets to impact a cause.

As we move through our journey with Envision, there are many projects that have the possibility for alignment with them. Together, we see the need to develop a strategic and sustainable model for educational partnerships based on our common philosophy of supporting education in the community. In order to do this, we have organized our corporate citizenship teams in the hope of bridging our educational programming over the next fife years. With that, it's important to note that while we would like our educational partnerships to come together operationally, we would still have local, grass-roots programs running. Of course, we are always open to having the same programs run on both sides of the Rockies if it makes sense for the community.

We expect there will be challenges along our business-education and Pathways journeys; however, these obstacles will only serve to strengthen our ability to serve the community. Both First Calgary Savings and Envision Financial are organizations adaptable to change. Success in the future might look different for our organizations, but the one thing that will always hold true is our mutual commitment to education. There is a curve of change, especially as it relates to program structure. While our community programming will be similar with regards to partnerships, it stands to reason that the evolution of PIE might find us having an increased presence in a greater number of schools, as opposed to the stronger presence in our partner schools.

CONCLUSION

As is the case with anything undergoing revitalization, Partners in Education as a program is likely to look a bit different in the future. At First Calgary Savings we do not see this as a threat, but rather, an opportunity. Our role is to be community advocates, helping to fill-in and enhance areas of the educational system that can use extra support. We have many long-standing partnerships that link directly back to schools—Book Rapport, One Day Arts School, the First Calgary Savings Mentorship Program with Theatre Junction, etc—and it is unlikely this type of involvement would ever change. We are, however, open to finding new and different ways to serve the community through educational partnerships. One of our greatest strengths is in our ability to leverage our community connections to benefit local school systems. As our branch network grows, we have an opportunity to grow with them. This could mean we open up our one-on-one branch contact to more than just single partner schools, but to many schools in the community, or it could mean we take things in an entirely different direction.

The Partners in Education program has always been seen as an innovative model from which to provide programming. From a communications perspective, our community partners see PIE as a valuable addition to their sphere of influence and we continue to provide them with an additional outlet to tell their stories. Our partner schools tell us they value and appreciate the programming we are able to bring into their schools throughout the year; a distinct sign pointing to the fact we are making the right investments for the communities we serve. Just as it has been in the past, Partners in Education will continue to be a cornerstone in the corporate citizenship portfolio for First Calgary Savings well into the future.

EDITOR'S COMMENT

From neighbours helping neighbours, First Calgary has moved to corporate citizenship as its goal. Originally there was involvement of members, even members making decisions. Now a large number of programs are brought to members or future members; even the branches have to be introduced to the school program. The dominance of administrators and the difficulty of involving people in decision-making for the program mean that the programs will likely be influenced by corporate thinking in the future.

Although Alberta cooperatives and credit unions were not influenced by socialists; they were influenced by Social Credit and its reading groups. In the small towns, the credit unionsl did and still do speak more to their members' needs. In Calgary, the oil capitol of Canada, there is an admiration for corporate practice. Although socialists, trade unions and other non-profit organizations have been shown to follow the iron law of oligarchy where by control is centralized with administrators, there is increasing evidence that large organizations can be focused on their constituents and democracy increased (Voss & Sherman, 2000).

There are continuing attempts by First Calgary to be more than a business by objectives. Perhaps Image Calgary is the most interesting project, but unlike Chicago, this program does not reach to the poor families or students, and to try and bring them together with the decision makers in society so that change would begin. The Chicago interpretation would challenge First Calgary Financial. More active involvement of parents and students, as suggested by Black in Chapter 9 would challenge First Calgary's corporate mould in the future.

As the biography of the author of this chapter suggests the program of the credit union is trying to connect with social needs in the community. The arts program is an alternative to a link whereby students are drawn into being future customers. The credit union wants to be something different from a bank, a new way for neighbours to help neighbours.

159

Chapter 6

Conducting A Symphonic Partnership

Roberta Lamb, Associate Professor of
Music, Queen's University

The gymnasium is already buzzing with
wiggling, whispering girls and boys. Will they,
can they, sit still long enough to get through
the program? How will they like the show?
Those of us who feel inclined chat a bit.
"Which school are you from? Wow, you've
travelled all that way! What pieces were you
and your teacher working on? Hey, I think
we're playing that this morning. Maybe you
guys can join in . . . This is a viola . . . Yes, I've
been playing a long time. What kind of music
do you like? Ah, I think I can play My Heart
will Go On . . . I'm not sure about Blue, how
does it go again? Oh, looks like I'd better
get ready. Nice talking to you, have fun."
Wiggling, fidgeting, poking, and giggling—
will they last? . . . 'Are those guys really going
to play sandpaper?' They laugh. Their faces
light up, more poking—'Hey, that's the song
we did in class!' They're quiet, they're right
there, captivated by the music. They know
what's coming next: the clarinet, the flute, the

> piccolo. It doesn't matter where these kids are from their reactions are the same: they enjoy the concerts because they can participate. They're not just hearing us play, they're playing with us. They become the stars, and they love it! That's what we're here for, isn't it? (James Coles, personal communication, June, 2000).

These children are brought together because a symphonic triangle thrives among Kingston Symphony Association, Limestone District School Board, Algonquin and Lakeshore Catholic District School Board, and Queen's University School of Music. The triangle is the Symphony Educational Partnership (SEP). The metaphor of the triangle reveals the partnership as a stable, balanced, and yet flexible geometric form. This partnership consists of three equal partners: the schools, the university, and the orchestra, all situated within the context of a Canadian city and the surrounding rural area.

The triangle attempts to remain equilateral, although at one time or another, any one of the three segments (schools-orchestra-university) may exert greater than the others. The triangle suggests the competing values that may be found among various combinations of partners as they work together. Although the focus is on the symphony triangle, attention is given to some social contexts that affect, apply pressure to, or activate the triangle.

The orchestra partnership builds support in and around the city of Kingston, Ontario in Canada. Descriptions of this city and Ontario Ministry of Education and Training policies and practices provide a frame for portraits of the partners. Both disagreement and consensus are involved in the development of this partnership. From reflections by the partners on its evolution, explicit principles emerge. The principles and their implementation enable this grass-roots partnership to garner community support for music in the schools.

LOCAL CONTEXT

Kingston is a small urban centre (about 150,000) in a rural region. Though it is a city equidistant from Toronto, Montreal, and Ottawa, rural communities look to Kingston as their cultural centre. The first European settlement of this city was the French Fort Frontenac, but it is the English descendants of the Loyalists who fled the American Revolution who dominate the city's history. The second largest ethnic population is an older Portuguese community. There exists a French community, an established Indian (Hindu) community, and small but growing Asian and Hispanic communities. Queen's University, the Royal Military College, St. Lawrence Community College, half a dozen hospitals, and as many prisons are located in Kingston.

In the 1900's, the region was hard-hit by government cutbacks because much of the economic base is public institutions (university, hospitals, prisons) and government. Such cutbacks reduce grants from arts councils. Provincial grants that municipalities used to have to give, in part, to the arts, have decreased to the point of nonexistence. Unlike, Montreal, Toronto or Ottawa, Kingston boasts no major fully professional orchestra, dance or opera company. The city is simply too small to support major performing arts organizations.

The Kingston Symphony Association (KSA) is unique in Canada. The association includes the professional orchestra, a volunteer choral society, a youth orchestra, a junior strings training ensemble, and adult string orchestra that is a avocation for its members. The KSA sponsors unusual annual performances, such as the Canada Day *Beat Beethoven* "run." The Kingston Symphony Orchestra (KSO) plays a Beethoven Symphony in the city park and nearly a thousand runners and walkers race to complete the 8 km or 4 km course before the last note is heard. KSO also plays the 1812 Overture as Old Fort Henry fires real cannons, and the Opera-in-Concert presents feature singers, such as Jean Stillwell.

During 1998-1999, the Kingston Symphony premiered seven new Canadian works for orchestra. The KSO is the only symphony in Ontario to win two Lieutenant Governor's Awards for the Arts (1996 and 1999), a competitive award for an arts organization showing exceptional community service and private sector support. KSO remuneration for services is not sufficient to be the musicians' sole source of income. Musicians must engage in additional paid employment as high school music teachers, contract academic staff at the university, or other careers completely outside of music (Katharine Carleton and James Coles, personal communication, June, 2000).

The second point of the triangle, Queen's University, is a research-intensive university with a School of Music and a Faculty of Education. The School of Music has links with community arts and education organizations and with professional musicians. Just as Kingston does not have the resources of larger cities, Queen's University does not have the resources of prestigious music schools. Seventy-five percent of School of Music students become music teachers, although students are not streamed. Though the School of Music tries to improve the quality of music teacher preparation and strengthen music in the region's schools, the responsibility for teacher certification belongs to the Faculty of Education. The medium-sized Faculty of Education has fewer full-time music education professors than does the School of Music. Cooperation between the School of Music and the Faculty of Education ebbs and flows, but was greatly strengthened by the implementation of a concurrent Bachelor of Music / Bachelor of Education five-year degree program. The implementation of this cooperative program increased enrolment at the School of Music by 30 percent, while simultaneously the B. Mus. / B. Ed. students boast the highest entering averages in the Faculty of Arts and Science at the university.

The two local school boards comprise the third partner. The Limestone Public School Board is centered in Kingston but includes Frontenac, Lennox, and Addington counties. The Algonquin and Lakeshore Catholic District School Board is the largest separate school board in Ontario, expanding over 200 km. Rural schools are included because both school boards stretch from Lake Ontario in the south to north of the Trans-Canada highway. In addition, one county within the area of both school districts has had the highest long-standing unemployment rate in Ontario.

Locally, the quality of arts (visual art, music, drama, and dance) teachers is left up to each school board, but it is limited by the provincial funding formula and related regulations. An historic custom influences arts education. Elementary teachers are generalists; secondary teachers are more likely to be specialists. Music education programs at universities were originally established for training high school specialists while normal schools included some music in their programs for elementary teachers. The first Ontario music education degree program for the preparation of high school band or orchestra directors did not begin until 1950 at the University of Toronto (Green & Vogan, 1991).

Very few arts specialist teachers remain in either school district. Elementary students in both school boards receive little music instruction within the schools. Classrooms present a wide range of teacher and student capabilities and experiences. This variety makes it difficult to achieve a cohesive music curriculum.

DEMANDS BY THE MINISTER OF EDUCATION

The way the Ontario Ministry of Education and Training defines adequate subject preparation for teaching music limits the quality of music teaching in the schools. Elementary teachers are not required to have any pre-service preparation in music, although they are required to teach music as part of what appears to be a fairly rigorous arts curriculum. During the past fifteen years there have been three major curriculum shifts, and a fourth revision is in progress (2010); it is difficult for anyone to know which curriculum actually is used in any particular class or school.

In 1998, the Ministry of Education and Training implemented a new elementary curriculum that requires much greater musical knowledge (as well as much greater knowledge in all subjects) from teachers than their education provided. This curriculum requires stringent reporting on specific outcomes, which creates new problems. For example, identifying the instruments of the orchestra is required in grades two through seven, changing to "identify tone colors in various performing ensembles" in grade seven, a task that is likely easier than the grade two requirement to identify families of instruments. Grade 4 students are required to "demonstrate correct embouchure" even though instrumental music instruction does not begin until grade nine. Prescribed "creative activities" include limited skills that are not particularly creative, such as reading standard music notation (*The Ontario Curriculum*, 1998).

In 1998, the government amalgamated school boards, which increased the number of students and the geographic area for each board. In addition to amalgamating school boards, the legislation micro-manages the decreased powers of the local school boards, prescribes standardized testing, specific standards for specific marks, a provincial report card, increases assigned teaching time, decreases teacher preparation time, and reduces professional development. As a response, teachers engaged in a province-wide political protest against the provincial government, closing the schools for several weeks. Teachers continue to scramble to keep up with the government-imposed changes although some try to teach what they think is important, in spite of the government.

The stages of the Symphony Education Partnership (SEP) are not easily defined since it arose from community need rather than grants council or governmental agency regulations. The initial stage ends when all the current partners become active participants. Future commitments are still being developed. Challenge, conflict, change, and consensus flow through each stage in retrospect, although the partners were not fully aware of these processes at the time.

PLANNING (1991-1995)

The music director, the symphony manager, the recently retired school board arts coordinator (a KSA Board Member and symphony violinist) and the author (a music education professor) formed the first Symphony Education Partnership (SEP) Committee. These four people are the committed leaders who determine to make this project succeed. The KSA music director is flexible and humble, willing to collaborate with school and university personnel, while encouraging the musicians. The violinist-retired teacher is an orchestral musician who worked in the schools in this region for many years, and is a great facilitator, knowing how to communicate educational policies and practices to other musicians and to bureaucrats. The music education professor is the catalyst involving potential teachers and planning for the project's future.

Initially two partners, the Kingston Symphony and the School of Music, wanted to work together beyond the common promotional activities, such as reduced price tickets for music students, volunteer experience and scholarships. Prior to 1991, these three activities typified the relationship between the KSA and the School of Music. The school boards took some time to join. The public school board's arts facilitator hesitated, due to previous frustrating experiences with the School of Music. These doubts dissipated as the program developed connections with the elementary curriculum and a school board representative joined the committee in 1993. The Faculty of Education music education professor declined an invitation to join. From these first steps, this partnership is envisioned as one of collaboration, as defined by Nierman:

> . . . both organizations take an active role in formulating the goals or objectives that are mutually beneficial. A "We" process mode develops. Leadership is shared by individuals from both organizations. Both groups contribute staff time, resources, and capabilities to accomplish the task. (1993, 26).

Of course, the SEP involves three distinct organizations rather than the two referred to in Nierman's model.

According to the KSA, educational concerts provided in past years were not consistently successful and, thus, were discontinued. The music education professor suggests a program to combine pre-service teacher education with symphony school concerts. University students would present sample lessons to the elementary students to prepare them for the symphony's education concerts. Elementary lessons would be drawn from the curriculum in order to ensure symphony concerts become an integral part of that curriculum, not merely a field trip. With proper planning a program provides a meaningful field experience within the music degree, improves the quality of music instruction in the schools, and the symphony encounters a more receptive young audience for its concerts.

Acting upon the music director's suggestion, the partners decide the Symphony Education Partnership should target elementary students in grade four. The partners agreed on an essential component: grade four students would perform with the symphony in some musically and pedagogically meaningful way. The Symphony Education Committee implemented the program for the 1993-1994 academic year with only the public school board participating. The committee felt some urgency to begin the program with a minimal plan in order to prove its viability, rather than wait until all protocols were in place. The separate school board joined the program in the second year. During 1993-1995, the music education professor shepherded the academic course requirements through various levels of university governance.

The music education professor provided participating grade four teachers with copies of lesson plans and an audiotape of orchestral selections that university students would use in their classrooms. The university students facilitated a curriculum follow-through in each grade four classroom after the symphony concert, with the guidance of the music education professor. During their previous university class session, the students practiced peer-teaching the lesson. The university students then taught the grade four classes. At the conclusion of the project, the music education professor sent evaluation forms to the participating grade four teachers.

EARLY CHALLENGES AND CONFLICTS

Comments were collected from teachers in 1995, 1999, and 2000. In these evaluation forms, teachers wrote about grade four students attending a symphony orchestra concert: "Most had never been to a symphony concert and they were surprised by the pleasure it gave them." Since the first year of the partnership all have agreed that the value of these concerts to elementary students is the central purpose to the partnership. For the orchestra, the primary reason for scheduling school concerts is to develop a future audience. Unfortunately, the Canadian Opera Company chorus singers, who performed in the second season, did not understand the pedagogical import of their presentation or the purpose of the partnership. These singers concentrated on their roles as highly trained opera singers. Professional performing artists often focus on the quality of the performance, rather than the educational process, and consequently do not appreciate playing for a young audience as part of their artistry.

This attitude is a by-product of professional training and subculture, which traditionally values the soloist or virtuoso much more highly than the orchestral musicians or the audience. The same attitude could be seen in many musicians who viewed the school concert as primarily a performance. Some of them saw the performance as entertainment, rather than education. This attitude is reflected in one musician's comments:

> I prefer to focus on the orchestra rather than providing accompaniment for something else [like dance or opera]. We should wear tux to bring atmosphere of the concert hall to the gymnasium (James Coles, personal communication, June, 2000).

Teachers provided the most varied, challenging comments to the partnership. Their responses often conflicted with the musicians, the SEP Committee and other teachers. This can be due to the many educational philosophies and practices of the profession. One teacher raved over programming and the preparation of the university music students:

> My students were most enthusiastic about opera. It was great for me, too. I was very impressed with my two first year students: comfortable, fun, informed but properly controlled learning environment.

Another teacher tersely disliked the concert program and criticized the university music students' skills: "No opera. Better classroom management." Teachers consistently make concrete suggestions for improving the overall educational value of the partnership. These suggestions were often things the committee had not considered, but worked to implement the next year. The classroom teacher—if aware of the details of program content at the outset—could increase the merit of this opportunity through integration of its content. Teachers provided insights into equity issues that raise awareness among some of the SEP Committee members:

> I like having a male and female QU [Queen's University] student together, as students often perceive music as a female subject.

These insights from teachers provide commentary on authenticity and cultural practices that are a backdrop to the immediate musical experience. Teachers are able to see issues that SEP Committee members may miss.

DEVELOPMENT (1996-2000)

The Symphony Education Partnership built on the previous year's concerts, curriculum and experiences. Each year featured different content, albeit based on similar procedures and structure. Flexibility comes from the SEP Committee's problem-solving approach to the partnership. The school board representatives took on the tasks of confirming which teachers in specific schools were willing to take a pair of university music students, thus centralizing the placement process. They took over the responsibility for distributing and tabulating The school board representatives and music education professor worked together to write a curriculum that grade four generalist teachers could use in preparing their classes for the concert, especially if they did not have university music students placed in their classroom. These curricular materials were provided to all grade four teachers, whether or not they elected to attend the professional development workshop given by the SEP Committee.

Changes to the university curriculum had an impact on the program. In order to ensure university students know more music, the Introduction to Music Education/ Partnership Program was moved from a first-year to a second-year course. Although the students are much more knowledgeable and better prepared to teach, fewer university students registered for the course, decreasing the number of grade four placements. The university course materials were placed on the Internet, allowing all classroom teachers access to the lessons the university students were teaching.

The school board SEP Committee members wanted to expand the project so that those grade four students in outlying areas would have the opportunity to participate in the concerts. Distance limits the scope of university student participation, since they only have one time slot scheduled for this purpose, and it was impossible to pre-plan who might have a car available for transportation. All grade four classes within the two participating school boards were given the opportunity to participate every second year. Simultaneously, all university students were placed in schools accessible to them within their course timetable.

By 1998-1999, teacher demand for music practice teachers exceeded availability, so the university music students were placed individually in grade four classrooms in order to provide instruction in more classrooms. Individual placements proved a failure. The failure was due to lack of immediate peer mentor's support and shared perceptions of classroom experience. Another factor contributing to this failure was the mistaken belief in the university music students' advanced musical knowledge. They are often viewed as experts in a curriculum-driven classroom taught by a generalist. These novice university music students had no experience with classroom management, modification of curriculum for children with special needs, or the realities of school culture. Following the principle of mutual benefit for each of the partners, paired placement was reinstated in order to promote a comprehensive music experience in the grade 4 classrooms.

In contrast to the problems of placements, there is a challenge, which the SEP Committee thoroughly enjoys, to find ways for the elementary students to perform with the symphony. The value of an authentic musical experience was identified by most teachers as the key to the program. One comments: "I *loved* doing the Orchestra Song—giving kids a chance to participate!"

The different capabilities and experience of partners presented competing priorities and a wealth of experience for the Symphony Education Partnership. The university professors and orchestra musicians are skilled and experienced professionals in music. The university students are focused on becoming professional musicians and music specialists. The schoolteachers are skilled educators. Thus, musicians' and teachers' understandings of music education through the partnership often conflicted:

> The *Young Person's Guide* [Britten] is an excellent thing to do [musician].

> I don't think it was necessary to do *Introduction to the Orchestra* [Britten] as a performance piece, if teachers already cover it in pre-symphony package [teacher].

The SEP Committee tried to include teachers in the planning and implementation of the curriculum; however, generalist teachers have limited musical knowledge. This makes it imperative for the SEP Committee to consider carefully their feedback in order to develop a curriculum that encourages teacher growth.

The curriculum package must be one that is self-explanatory because not all grade four teachers wanted to attend the voluntary professional development workshop. A teacher who may have needed the professional development workshop wrote:

> I wouldn't have started a recorder unit if I had known this was happening in February. As a result, I didn't teach my class the Orchestra Song in time for the Symphony. Yikes! It would have been great if a Queen's student could have been able to come up to our school—even for half a day.

Teachers who do attend the workshop and have come to understand the program, expressed concerns about those who do not in the evaluation forms:

> It should be ESSENTIAL that the curriculum package is addressed by all the classes attending. Only then do the students realize the full impact of the performance.

The school partners wanted every school to have equal access to the concerts and university music students. The schools sought equal access to the orchestra and the university, but the resources of these two partners are limited. A school principal may have wanted to place a university music student in a classroom that needed the most support in the arts, and some teachers wanted university music students to relieve them of music teaching responsibilities. Both of these situations constitute inappropriate placements. The more fitting situations were when teachers wanted to attend the professional workshops.

UNIVERSITY MUSIC STUDENTS

Unlike the teachers, the music students are in a dilemma as a result of the education they do have. Their music professors and professional musician mentors see them as just beginning to learn their skills. Some orchestra musicians identify those music students who take music education courses as less talented or musical than those who take music to become professional musicians. A musician-teacher-researcher comments:

> I was thinking about the project in terms of teacher as learner and teacher as expert. The success of the step dancing part of the project depended on the teachers' willingness to become learners . . . . This is especially true in areas like music and dance, where you can't prepare yourself with just research (S. Johnson, email, June 24, 2000).

Simultaneously, when these university music students arrive in the schools they are identified as talented elite. To generalist classroom teachers music students are such experts that the teachers forget that they are still students lacking classroom experience. When the music students are placed in classrooms with experienced and highly competent teachers and given support as beginning teachers, they begin a successful teaching career:

> I was able to take what I was learning in my lectures and implement these new and different teaching techniques into the classroom. The practical classroom experience I received from this program was a great asset for future educational endeavors. When attending the symphony presentation students said to me: 'Look, that's a cello!' or 'Did you see how fast the timpanist played?' or 'I really liked the Stravinsky piece' (D. Clarke, email, June 15, 2000).

Most music students are motivated and enthusiastic. They want to please everyone—professors, musicians, teachers, children—and end up tripping over all the contrasting and contradicting expectations. For them the Symphony Education Partnership is a balancing act among their music education, the curriculum they teach, and their transition from university to schools.

THE MYSTERY OF THE ORCHESTRA

The traditional symphony orchestra structure that includes the practice of only the music director making decisions is not conducive to cooperative and collaborative efforts. This traditional structure does not work with a small symphony orchestra composed of a combination of contract players, university music students and per-service players. Most of the KSO contract players teach as applied music instructors in the university or at high schools.

The part-time work and low wage requires that the orchestra management not make excessive or autocratic demands on the musicians in order to maintain a skilled, cooperative, functioning and musical ensemble. A small orchestra like the KSO runs on volunteers and the goodwill of its musicians. An autocratic music director can destroy such a group, but aspects of the 'maestro myth' live on and are cherished (Lebrecht, 1991).

The male, typical "maestro" can limit an orchestra's repertoire. Many musicians and traditional audiences favor the 'great music' composed by dead, white, European males. It is difficult to introduce cultural diversity and new pieces in a small orchestra. As the SEP developed, the Kingston Symphony took greater risks in programming new music for the schools, including one piece commissioned specifically for the educational concerts. However, the composer of this new work ignored time requirements and expectations for an easy-to-sing melody. The modern melody was nearly impossible for grade 4 students to sing and the commissioned piece was too long for their short attention span.

Since western classical music training begins as training towards a soloist career, the same problems composers encounter with young audiences can be found among orchestral musicians. This attitude can be exacerbated if the musicians believe that 'those who can do, and those who can't, teach.' It may be that some orchestral musicians are shy people who much prefer being part of an amazing wall of symphonic sound than to interact with others. Professional development for musicians as educators assists the transition from solo-musician to musician-teacher. It is also a change of orchestral culture to develop a musical organization that is as pedagogically effective as it is artistic. In 1999, the Kingston Symphony scheduled a series of workshops to develop musicians' improvisational skills and increase their interaction with students and audience (Weigold, n.d.), Babineau (2000) and Weigold (1999). The KSA sponsored the same workshop for classroom teachers and university music students. Some orchestra musicians participated in these workshops.

Now the musicians no longer see the SEP concerts primarily as children's entertainment, but recognize the educational value, so the "orchestra participates in local education out of its unique capacities and concerns" (Myers, 1996, p. 102). The orchestra representatives on the SEP Committee believe: "We used to hear condescending comments about the 'kiddy concerts' but that attitude has disappeared." The concertmaster writes:

> The preparation for the concerts is crucial and makes it much more meaningful. The choice of music is largely very good. The

involvement of the kids in the concerts has
been central to their success. We're doing a
really good job.

He now values the forging of musical quality and
pedagogical value into one.

Many musicians participate with a whole-hearted
sense of community that is reflected to the audience in the
subscription concerts. One university music student puts it:

> The Kingston Symphony is definitely a
> strong part of the community in Kingston.
> Whenever I go to the symphony now, I
> recognize former instructors, students and
> faculty members. I have been to several
> community events where the symphony has
> played. I never get this sense of connection in
> Toronto. I feel there is a larger attachment to
> the community here. (Peter Kole, interview,
> June 14, 2000).

Community support for music grows in direct
proportion to SEP's progress although publicity is
essential.

RENEWED CONSENSUS

By the end of February 1999, SEP had completed
seven years of programming and was ready to examine

the terms of the alliance. The SEP Committee held a series of planning and reflection meetings. The Faculty of Education music education professor was again invited to participate, but withdrew after a few meetings, citing research priorities as the reason. The planning and reflection process continued. During this time, the SEP Committee identified six principles underpinning the SEP practices and program, and made commitments to continue developing the partnership.

SIX SEP PRINCIPLES

The principles that the SEP selected were defined after a lengthy process, highlighted the differences among the partners and tested their commitment to collaboration. The partners acknowledged the musical and marketing interests of the symphony may not always coincide with the pedagogical concerns of the schools, and the interests of the university are different from those of either the schools or the symphony.

The review discussions did not proceed in a linear fashion, but rambled from success to failure, favorite projects to pet peeves, and to impossible dreams. Achieving consensus in this review process enabled the SEP Committee to articulate priorities and direction.

These principles-by-consensus are:

(1) The SEP is a partnership of mutual benefit to which each partner contributes substantially in different but equally valuable ways;

(2) The Kingston Symphony performs a concert designed to meet objectives chosen from the Ontario Ministry of Education and Training grade four music curriculum by the Symphony Education Committee;

(3) The grade four students must participate musically in the concert;

(4) University music students teach preparatory and follow-up lessons, based on the provincial music curriculum, to grade four students in a supervised classroom placement that introduces them to teaching;

(5) Grade four teachers enhance their professional development through a prepared music curricula and a music workshop focused on the symphony experience and related curriculum;

(6) The Kingston Symphony reaches an extended audience of elementary students and teachers.

Each of the six principles now appears self-evident. There is not one principle that any member of the SEP Committee would leave out or diminish. Keeping the principles in the forefront of SEP planning is necessary, because it is easy for individuals to slip into representing the self-interests of their group more highly than the principles of the partnership. When the SEP Committee experiences difficulty—plans that have run amok, concerts that do not quite work, lessons that fall flat—it is because one or more of the principles is neglected.

The first principle of mutual benefit functions for the Symphony Education Partnership as a test; it is the one that resolves difficult issues. How is a new or different policy mutually beneficial? How does each partner contribute to this revision? When these questions are answered, the problem can be solved. This principle of mutual benefit is the result of having a clear vision of each partner's role in making the partnership work, nurturing flexibility, and grounding the partnership in community (Boston, 1996).

The second principle, choosing the repertoire and designing the supporting curriculum, is a major focus of the SEP Committee. Involving all the partners exemplifies the principles of high-quality teaching and learning that Myers identified. These include professional development for teachers, the many challenges and strategies of curriculum, teaching, and musician training, and performances. Myers argues this will happen:

> . . . when teachers—those closest to the children—are involved with each facet, from selecting age-appropriate concert repertoire to sharing successful teaching strategies with their professional colleagues. (1996, 105).

This is the case in the Kingston Symphony Education Partnership.

The third principle of participation at the level of grade four ensures meaningful engagement with the music through experiential learning. It emphasizes the value of musical learning. This principle distinguishes the orchestra concert from other assemblies or field trips. The authentic participation of the grade 4 students convinces some of the more resistant musicians and teachers of the program's value.

The fourth principle extends professional development to the musicians and university music students. This principle is one way the partnership supports existing programs and sustains relationships among those participating (Myers, 1996, 103), while the fifth principle addresses the more obvious professional development of classroom teachers (Myers, 1996, 105, 107), and the sixth principle shows that "the role of education is valued within the orchestra" (Myers, 1996, p. 101).

A UNIQUE PROGRAM

As review and reflection continue, including examining reports of other orchestra partnerships, it becomes apparent that the Kingston SEP differs from other programs. The following characteristics appear to be unique to the Kingston Symphony Education Partnership: the structure; elementary student performance; pre-service teacher education; focus on music; the manner of funding;

and, grassroots solution based on partner-identified principles. Other partnerships share some of these elements, but the idiosyncratic mix and the particular definition of these principles is part of the strength of this local partnership.

The three-party structure of schools, symphony, and university is unusual. Other arts education partnerships present a package to the schools, who purchase it as-is (Myers, 1996, 102). The SEP Committee developed their program to meet the needs of their constituencies. The schools, university, and the orchestra contributed to constructing the curriculum (Boston, 1996). Creating a unique package marshaled a cohesive community behind the program.

This partnership also differs from other similar symphony concert experiences or orchestra partnerships because elementary students prepare to perform with the symphony. This performance may be in different mediums: singing, dancing, or composing. The grade four students know from the beginning of the six-week study unit that they will be performing with the symphony. This performance is a major goal and motivator. Singing a song with symphonic accompaniment signals that the partners function in relationship to the community. The program combines important music with significant pedagogy (Boston, 1996).

The university music students who practice teaching are the link between performance and school education (Myers, 2000). The introductory music education courses are a part of the program for practice teaching. These courses are open to any students with adequate music preparation whether or not they identify themselves as music education majors. Some students are pursuing the Bachelor of Music degree; others humanities-based Bachelor of Arts Honors with a music concentration; others a music minor. While most of the students in the course plan on becoming teachers, a few see themselves as performers, composers, or music history majors.

These introductory music education courses function as the university students' first exposure to teaching in a classroom setting. The courses are required for anyone who pursues further courses in music education. The placement is part of a structured, regular course within an academic degree. This is an example of how partnerships can "foster sustained relationships and programs" (Myers, 1996, p. 103).

Music and education are consistently combined. Though this program does not include the other arts, it provides connections with other arts. An early and most successful programs (1997) involved dance in an intrinsic relation to music. Each program includes connections to other areas of the curriculum, e.g., dance, art, drama, science, geography, history. Although music is taught in a social context, the focus is always music. The concern is specifically music performed by the instruments within a symphony orchestra. This direction creates the opportunity for an intense and deep artistic and educational experience with music (Boston, 1996).

This unique music program is created from existing resources by SEP; an occasion when "resources and funding constitute a shared enterprise" (Myers, 1996, p. 108). Neither grants nor a wealthy benefactor are involved. One reason it is possible is the strong leadership from the orchestra manager (Boston, 1996). The performing and rehearsing expenses constitute a portion of the Kingston Symphony's education budget. The schools provide the buses to concerts, release time for teachers who play in the symphony, reproduction of curriculum materials, and facilities for meetings and professional development workshops. The university contributes the student practice teachers, curriculum development, and facilitators for the professional development workshop.

SEP is built from existing resources, a direct solution to the problem of relating the interests, needs and skills of the individuals present within the orchestra, the schools, and the university music department. The partners come together as a result of common concerns: music education; the precarious position of the arts in schools and universities; the partners understanding of and experiencing of the arts as a critical and a creative response to social structures that marginalize the arts.

Budget reductions to arts agencies/organizations, the schools, and universities require partners to find innovative ways to engage in the artistic/creative, educational/pedagogical, and professional projects vital to people who believe that the arts express their values and social knowledge. This grassroots solution exemplifies the direct relationship that others find between the strength of the partnership and the degree to which it is grounded in the community (Boston, 1996).

RECENT DEVELOPMENTS 2001-2010

When Roberta Lamb took a sabbatical in 2000, another Queen's music education professor, Karen Frediickson, joined the SEP team in order to keep the university contributions to the partnership in place. Her vision took the SEP far beyond the original plan to provide more cohesive and usable curriculum for the project. She was so successful that the entire SEP agreed she should stay on as the university representative. This music education professor's major innovation in 2001 was to introduce movement to continue the tradition that grade four students participate in the concert. This creative endeavor, choreographed movement to one of the orchestral selections, became fundamental to the SEP curriculum. Classroom teachers responded enthusiastically to the "dance" because the Ontario Ministry of Education and Training mandates 20 minutes of daily physical activity (DPA), so they capably connect music education with physical education in order to meet these requirements.

A second innovation to the 2001 curriculum added original lyrics to be sung with one orchestral piece. The KSA appreciates this innovation in particular, because they can focus the repertoire on actual orchestral works, rather than finding a song with orchestral accompaniment. The music education professor writes original lyrics that focus attention on the musical concept chosen for the curriculum and reinforce familiarity with the specific orchestral work, as well as reinforce concepts included in the curriculum. This scheme proved more successful than attempting to find songs with orchestral accompaniment; therefore, lyrics have been created each year for one of the concert pieces.

By 2002, SEP began requiring schools sending classes to the concerts to have a curriculum package and accompanying CD of concert repertoire, especially if university students are not placed at that school. Now the curriculum package is handed out only at the professional development workshop. In addition to introducing the curriculum to the classroom teachers, the dance is taught at the November professional development workshop. With these motivations for teachers to attend, workshop participation greatly increased. Consequently, the preparation of grade four pupils and classroom teachers improved steadily. A second "dance only" January workshop was added in 2004. The classroom teachers, who have a second opportunity to learn the dance and ask questions about the curriculum and logistics, appreciate this second workshop.

In spring 2006, the SEP committee adopted a rotation of five western musical concepts for the curriculum base: rhythm, timbre, form, texture and melody. The chosen concept is then integrated with another subject area of the elementary curriculum, which is selected at the first curriculum meeting of the season. SEP believes that focusing on the musical features of the music (Swanwick, 1988) rather than on the extra-musical aspects is the best way to introduce children (and classroom teachers) to unfamiliar music. The following elementary curriculum integrations have been explored to date: timbre with the science of sound; texture with drama; texture with dance; melody with algebra (patterning in both); musical form with poetry; and, rhythm with poetry.

The SEP continued the practice of commissioning works for the project through 2007. This is a challenging approach to concert programming, but is a means for children to experience the creative process and a way for the orchestral repertoire to expand to meet musical goals of music education. Unfortunately, grants to fund commissions for this purpose withered with the 2008 economic recession. Simultaneously, SEP produced a DVD of the collected dances (2001-2008) for classroom use. This DVD did not hinder workshop attendance because teachers receive personal help at the workshop. Instead, the DVD inspired creative use of the collected curricula. As a result of the collected dances and curricula, classroom teachers are able to include more music education within their teaching plans.

COMPARISONS AND CONCLUSIONS

Many orchestras maintain some type of partnership. Orchestras Canada provides models from major symphony orchestras around the world to its members (Orchestras Canada, 2000). Some of these partnerships are more technological, such as the MENC-New York Philharmonic partnership (MENC, 1996) that provides curriculum materials to accompany a PBS broadcast, available through the *Music Educators Journal* and/ or a website (Myers & Young, 1996). In addition to the Kingston Symphony's, Orchestras Canada reports the following Canadian orchestras with partnerships: Toronto, Scarborough, Saskatoon, Timmins, and Edmonton (Babineau, 1998).

Orchestras have participated in educational programs in Canada throughout their history, but contemporary practitioners appear to be ignorant of this history. During the 1920s and 1930s, symphony orchestras framed educational concerts within the rubric of music appreciation. The Women's Committee of the Toronto Symphony administered Music Memory Test contests as part of the concerts for secondary students. Winners of these contests were announced at the next concert (Green & Vogan, 1991, pp. 254-255). Connecting the repertoire to the required secondary curriculum was a feature of the 1942-1957 annual school concert series.

Although the Women's Committee saw the program's purpose as audience development (Millar, 1949), the participation of secondary students in post-war era Toronto Symphony Orchestra education concerts developed into planning the concerts and promotional and fund-raising activities for the orchestra (Rowe, 1989). Similar activities might be possible today, such as school-to-work, required volunteering or special community night concerts (Allen, 1997).

A high point for all partners was a feature report in the city's only daily paper (Brousseau, 1999). Teachers, school board personnel, musicians, the music director, music professors, and students were interviewed. The reporter visited one of the schools and observed a lesson taught by the university students. Several photos of both elementary and university students accompanied the story. Over the years smaller stories, always with photos, have appeared in the paper, in the partners' newsletters and on school board or university websites. More recently a local television station featured the SEP in its evening community news segment. This recognition is always welcome and increases community support.

The Symphony Education Partnership is now firmly established as a component of each partner's agenda. Not one of the partners would consider pulling out. Each year there are more people who want to participate than can be accommodated. Each year something new, even slightly different, is added to the way the partnership works. Each year the direct benefit for the orchestra, the schools, and the university increases. The commitment is unquestioned and growing.

The Kingston Symphony Education Partnership is a grass-roots model with mutual benefits to the groups involved, where no organization is short-changed, which respects all those directly involved. Each group is valued, listened to, and shares ownership of the project. The commitment to collaboration through the principle of mutual benefit is the essential factor ensuring the partnership's continuity and longevity as a music community and as a part of the large community.

This partnership went through several years of planning and programming prior to the appearance of handbooks for planning arts partnerships (Remer, 1996) and research on music education partnerships (Allen, 1997; Boston, 1996; Cutietta, 1997; Hamilton 1999; Lippert, 1999; Logan, 1997; Myers, 2000; Myers 1996; Rodgers, 1999; Tambling, 1999). SEP did not have the advantage of access to this body of thought, but it might not have become so unique if these researchers were consulted initially.

Although Remer's work is invaluable for bringing together the procedures used by different arts organizations and arts administrator as an organizational or advocacy tool, Remer did not deal with the same kind of partnership structure or specific subject discipline as the SEP. For the SEP, Myers' extensive research on orchestral partnerships in the United States is more pertinent (2000, 1996, and as reported in Boston, 1996). The National Endowment of the Arts tried to identify principles for effective programs. Their principles are based on the study of model programs (Myers, 1996). These models are not grass-roots partnership. When others move in our direction, we will be able to learn and partner with them.

At present the triangle partnership is unique. The enthusiasm of all of the partners allows it to thrive. The SEP holds the interests of the grade four pupils, the pre-service preparation of Queen's University music education students and the professional development of classroom teachers, as well as symphony orchestra members at heart. Each year more people want to participate in the program than can be accommodate. Each year something new, slightly different, is added to the program. It is truly a win-win situation and a genuine partnership.

POSTSCRIPT

When Dr. Karen Erickson joined the SEP team, she taught the Queen's music education classes during that year, preparing Queen's university students for grade four teaching, and contributed to the 2001 curriculum by creating some movements for the *Jamaican Rhumba* by Arthur Benjamin to continue the tradition that grade four students should participate musically in the concert. This creative endeavour was the beginning of many such dances that have been produced for the SEP in subsequent years.

The children especially enjoyed the conductor's narration and could hardly wait to the dance (anonymous comment from 2002 teacher evaluation). The new dance for each curriculum is taught at the teacher workshop in late autumn, and the committee has found that is motivation for teachers to attend the workshop. We changed our practice and began requiring schools that were sending classes to the concerts to have a curriculum package and accompanying CD of concert repertoire. This has been a significant factor in increasing workshop attendance and the preparation of grade four pupils and classroom teachers has improved steadily. We also provide a 'dance only' workshop in January and it has been very well attended since 2004. The new dance for each curriculum is taught at the teacher workshop in late autumn, and the committee has found that this is motivation for teachers to attend the workshop and have become more involved steadily with the whole project.

The 2008 curriculum produced, our first DVD of the collected dances for classroom use. The Ontario Ministry has currently mandated 20 minutes per day of physical activity and many teachers already use the dances in this way, connecting music education with another important aspect of the school experience. We hope that this will not hinder workshop attendance but will inspire creative use of the existing curricula.

The 2001 curriculum also included lyrics to be sung with *The Jamaican Rhumba*. This seemed to be more successful than attempting to find songs that had orchestral accompaniment; therefore lyrics have been created each subsequent year for another of the concert pieces. The lyrics focus attention on the musical concept chosen for the curriculum and serve to reinforce familiarity with the musical selection as well as reinforce concepts included in the curriculum. This has been particularly helpful for the KSA, as we can focus the repertoire on actual orchestral works, rather than simply providing accompaniment.

FURTHER CHANGES

In the spring of 2006, the SEP committee decided to observe a rotation of five western musical concepts for the curriculum base. The concepts of rhythm, timbre, form, texture and melody are then integrated with another subject area of the elementary curriculum and selected at the first curriculum meeting. We believe this is the best way to introduce people to unfamiliar music, by focusing on the musical features of the music (Swanwick, 1988) rather than on the extra-musical aspects such as history and cultural context, which characterize the music education programs of most orchestral organizations in North America.

The following program has been explored since 2002.

2003—Texture/Drama and dance
2004—Melody/Algebra (patterning)
2005—Texture/Drama and dance
2006—Form/Poetry
2007—Rhythm/Poetry
2008—The science of sound (Timbre)

The committee has also continued the practice of commissioning works for the project, with the most recent one for 2007. This is a challenging approach to concert programming, but is a means for young people to experience the creative process and a way for the orchestral repertoire to expand to meet musical goals of music education. It is the commitment and enthusiasm of all of the partners that makes this project thrive. We have the interests of the grade four pupils, the pre-service training of Queen's University music education students and classroom teachers, as well as symphony orchestra members at heart. It is truly a win-win situation at present.

EDITOR'S COMMENT

This is a challenging approach to concert programming; it is an opportunity for young people to experience the creative process and a way for the orchestra to expand its repertoire to expand to meet musical goals of the school and community. The program has the commitment and enthusiasm of all of the partners. It has the interests of the grade four pupils; it successfully provides pre-service training of Queen's University music education students and classroom teachers; the symphony orchestra members receive recognition and build a future audience. Each of the partners benefits, but there is a fatal flaw.

Although this music partnership contains all the constituents of a successful partnership, its very existence is threatened. The university does not see the benefit to itself in supporting the partnership projects and the other partners are not able to increase their funding for it. The triangle partnership has not built up support from businesses, unlike the credit union in Calgary or the vocational program in the same city. The music partnership has not mobilized political supporters since music is not seen as essential to the city's renewal. Other cities have obtained support from lawyers and politicians (Mitchell, 2000; Mitchell, Burger & Klinck, 2004). The program has a central role for the city but the city has not been convinced to support it financially.

The equal partners in the SEP partnership is a model for any reciprocal partnership as it is discussed in the literature. In many other partnerships one partner is dominant in either the practice of partnership or in the planning for the partnership. The ideal of partnerships is realized in the teaching of grade-four music. All the participants, including the concertmaster accept this equality and involve the students so that the students are active and creative in their music classes.

Although the music partnership contains the elements of an ideal partnership, its very existence is threatened. The university does not see the benefit in supporting SEP and the other partners are not able to increase their funding for it. The program has not built in support from businesses. Nor has SEP mobilized political supporters in a coalition. It has depended upon community support, but that support has been one of admiration rather than specific commitments.

There are further allies who could be linked to SEP partnerships, the other arts. The beauty of the Renaissance was linking music to the visual arts and drama. Today music is a part of the experience one encounters in art museums of Italy. Opera and ballet grow out of this interaction. Increasingly in schools the arts are seen as a basis for increasing academic performance. The arts are unified in these programs as they are in special arts schools. Music is a part of the rediscovery of the importance of arts and it can be more so in the future (Mitchell 2000).

The retirement of the key music education partner, Roberta Lamb, is perhaps the most important challenge to this program. Like Michael Zanibbi she has been the key innovator for this project, but Enviroworks was redefined by his successors, a process that will be more difficult for the music program. The credit union has already passed through several hands. The more unique and integrated a partnership then the more difficult its continuation will be.

Chapter 7
Boundary Spanners

Lynn Bradshaw, Professor, East Carolina University

> DEPC literally opened the eyes of our community to the need for quality childcare and family services. Thank you for improving the quality of life for children and families in Nash and Edgecombe Counties—Sylvia Harris, Director, the Rocky Mount Region, Inc.

The Down East Partnership for Children (DEPC) is an interagency partnership designed to model and support the delivery of integrated health, education, and social services to children and their families in two counties in northeastern North Carolina. When the DEPC was formed, the two-county community was preparing for the merger of the four school districts. Discussions were complicated by the fact that one of the city districts was split by county lines with accompanying racial and socioeconomic divisions, and there was interest in several strategies, including the option of merging all four districts into a single two-county district. Efforts to ensure that all voices were heard in the discussions of educational opportunities in the area expanded to include childcare and other health and human services. The mission of DEPC continues to be "to build a strong foundation for children and families by advocating and supporting both high quality early care and education and a coordinated system of community resources" (DEPC, 2009, p. 9).

The school districts in the two counties have been important stakeholders in the development of the DEPC and its programs. Some of the projects undertaken jointly by the DEPC and one or both school districts have been more successful than others. At times, changes in school district leadership and differences in policy and procedures have been challenging. This case allows us to explore the boundary spanning roles of principals and other school leaders; then theories are drawn upon and new directions suggested.

COLLABORATION THEORY

Literature and research from the fields of business and education are helpful in understanding partnerships and the various roles needed to develop and sustain them. Some theories of collaboration distinguish between collaboration and cooperation, but a more inclusive definition can be helpful: "Collaboration occurs when a group of autonomous stakeholders of a problem domain engage in an interactive process, using shared rules, norms, and structures, to act or decide on issues related to that domain" (Wood & Gray, 1991, p. 146).

The Stages of Collaboration

The collaborative process is developmental (for example, see Gray, 1985; Hord, 1986; Melaville & Blank, 1993), and the early stages of a collaborative effort are particularly important to the eventual success of the initiative. Reed and Cedja (1987) described organizational preconditions that support successful collaboration. Partners must recognize both what they need and what they can contribute to the collaborative effort. When the goals of partnering organizations are aligned and there is support for collaboration and strategic planning during the early stages of a project, participants are more likely to be able to build a strong foundation for long-term collaborative activity. There is no single recipe for organizational collaboration. The process is unique, depending on the needs and resources of the individual stakeholders in a particular problem domain. However, there seems to be a predictable sequence of activities even though the "steps" differ in number and name (for example, see Gray, 1985; Hord, 1986; Reed & Cedja, 1987; Wood & Gray, 1991; Melaville & Blank, 1993; Rigsbee, Reynolds, & Wang, 1995). Gray (1985) identified three stages of collaborative activity: problem-setting, direction-setting, and structuring. These three stages encompass additional steps identified by other authors and capture the prevailing forward motion of collaborative activity as new partnerships develop.

During the "problem-setting" stage, it is important for stakeholders to recognize the complexity of the problem and the interdependence of the organizations that are undertaking the joint effort. The degree to which all stakeholders are identified and involved will "influence the nature of the agreements reached as well as the ease of coming to an agreement" (Gray, 1995, p. 74). Effective problem setting requires asking the right questions, and the unique perspectives of multiple stakeholders (Knapp, 1995) enrich problem setting and other stages of collaborative work. During "direction setting," stakeholders work together to gather information and develop a strategic plan. As the plan takes shape, power must be distributed to allow all stakeholders to influence decisions about the collaborative effort. When the plan is implemented, structures and processes must be established to accomplish shared goals. The context for such "structuring" is complex, and the results will be influenced by the diverse institutional interests of the partners and the needs of the new collaborative (Crowson & Boyd, 1996).

Although the stages of collaboration are incremental, progress often looks more like a spiral than a straight line. When new members join the collaborative effort, old members leave, or changes occur in needs or resources, the partners must cycle back through earlier stages and make revisions before they can move ahead. Partners must balance their focus on long-term goals with flexibility in order to find the most effective way to "knit their local needs, resources, and preferences into a purposeful plan" (Melaville & Blank, 1993, p. 19). Ultimately, the successful implementation of collaborative agreements depends upon stakeholders' collective ability to manage continuous change. In fact, Mawhinney (1996) suggested that collaborative efforts are not really systemic reforms, but rather a series of incremental adjustments as projects unfold. In order to sustain a collaborative effort, an "enablement framework" must assure funding and communication linkages, and as the collaborative evolves, environmental scanning and adaptation must continue (Reed & Cedja, 1987).

Creating Partnerships

When schools and districts want to partner with parents and the community, but their leaders do not possess the knowledge, skills, and attitudes required for successful collaboration, they will find themselves stuck in the phenomenon of "rhetoric rut" (Epstein, 2001, p. 407), talking about their need for partnerships and expressing their support for collaborative work, but not being able to demonstrate results. The work of Epstein and her colleagues (1997, 2001, 2009) at the Center for School, Family, and Community Partnerships continues to provide valuable resources to help school leaders move beyond "token" or "superficial" practices in parent involvement and partnerships and toward more meaningful ways of reaching out to and partnering with parents and communities in order to meet the needs of families and students (http://www.csos.jhu. edu/p2000/center.htm).

Six levels of partnership help clarify how a specific effort will involve families and communities: parenting, communicating, volunteering, learning at home, decision making, and collaborating with the community. For each level of partnership, sample practices, challenges, redefinitions, results for students, and results for parents are identified. The "redefinitions" highlight concepts that may need clarification as partnerships develop and can support important discussions using a common language to help a partnership achieve its goals. The expected results for students and parents at each level of involvement can be helpful in setting goals and evaluating results. Actual results will depend on the types of involvement and the quality of the implementation.

When the school, family, and community contexts in which students learn and grow overlap, students are more likely to receive consistent, positive messages about the importance of school, getting help, and staying in school. These overlapping spheres of influence recognize that families, schools, and communities all contribute to student growth and learning. Students are at the center of partnerships because students are "the main actors in their education, development, and success in school" (p. 404). 'Family-like schools,' 'school-like families,' and 'family-friendly' services combine to create caring communities that support students and their families. Healthy partnerships establish a "base of respect and trust on which to build" (p. 406) and provide opportunities for differences and conflicts to be explored and resolved.

In addition to theories, frameworks, and research, Epstein's handbooks for action (1997, 2009) provide resources for organizing an effective action team for the partnership (ATP) and tools for developing the team and working together to plan and evaluate the work.

Boundary Spanning

The business and social science literature describes a phenomenon called *boundary spanning* that takes place at the edges of organizations that have decided to work collaboratively to solve a problem. Organizational boundaries define organizations and departments within organizations, and they regulate the flow of information from one to another. When problems extend beyond the boundary of a single organization or department, solutions require activity across organizational boundaries. Boundary spanners work in the area where these boundaries cross and overlap. They represent their own organizations, facilitate information sharing back and forth across the organizational boundaries, and help match needs and resources (Reed & Cedja, 1987). Boundary spanning contacts develop formally and informally, depending on the type of project, and individuals are more likely to serve as boundary spanners because of their work-related competence or credibility than because of their position on an organizational chart (Tushman & Scanlan, 1981).

Throughout the life of a collaborative effort, "boundary-spanners" communicate frequently within and across organizational boundaries and engage in a variety of activities that may support the new organization, protect their own organizations, or link organizations together. Sarason and Lorentz (1998) observed that the roles of these boundary spanners or "coordinators" were characterized by scanning, fluidity, and imaginativeness. Cordeiro and Kolek (1996) described the individuals who are able to cross the boundaries of organizations and agencies as multi-lingual and multi-cultural "compradors," and they challenged school leaders "to identify compradors within the organization and give them permission and a reason to travel" (p. 13).

Those who interact at and across organizational boundaries encounter unique opportunities to create and influence solutions to shared problems. These personal linkages can be "the most likely source of cooperation" (Eisenberg, 1995, p. 104), but because they are also difficult to control, boundary spanning activities have the potential to create conflict for the organization. The progress of a collaborative partnership is influenced by the activities and skills of the boundary spanning representatives of the partnering organizations, including the partnership itself. When boundary spanners understand the visions of their own organizations and the new partnership and have strong communication linkages within their own organizations, they are more likely to be able to anticipate and work through potential conflicts.

DOWNEAST PARTNERSHIP FOR CHILDREN (DEPC)

The early efforts to improve conditions for children in Nash and Edgecombe Counties and the preconditions established for this collaborative effort formed a strong foundation for its continuing success. Citizens were concerned about the quality of life of many residents of Nash and Edgecombe counties. Just as the governor sought to improve the condition of children in order to improve the state's economic outlook, business and community leaders in Nash and Edgecombe counties recognized the need to improve education and quality of life for children and their families in order to attract new business and industry to the area.

Indicators of child well-being monitored annually for all 100 counties in the state by the North Carolina Child Advocacy Institute highlighted serious issues related to the health, education, safety, and security of children in the two-county area. For example, Edgecombe County ranked among the "worst" counties in the State in terms of infant mortality, child abuse and neglect, juvenile arrests and violent arrests. While statistics for Nash County were more positive, Nash still ranked in the bottom half of all 100 counties in the state on six of the 13 indicators. Although the median family income was the same in both counties, more children in Edgecombe County were living in poverty and receiving aid for families with dependent children. In the area of safety, Nash had no violent arrests, but Edgecombe's juvenile arrest rate was almost the highest in the state.

In spite of the differences, leaders in the two counties recognized advantages of working together to address similar needs. They shared the city of Rocky Mount, where railroad tracks in the middle of Main Street established the boundary between the two counties. The former Rocky Mount City Schools served students from both counties, and economic development efforts focused on environmental scanning and school improvement for the region as a whole. Two earlier initiatives to improve economic and social conditions in the area, Project Uplift and Visions 2000, had identified serious needs for higher quality childcare. Once the magnitude of the needs was broadly understood, two funding opportunities motivated early discussion and planning: state funding for Child Care Resource and Referral (CCR&R) programs and state funding for "pioneers" in the governor's new Smart Start initiative.

The various stakeholders shared a strong desire to improve the quality of life for children and their families. They believed that both a quality education and quality, accessible, community services were keys to achieving their goals, and they articulated the link between the condition of their communities' children and families and their communities' economic future. Ultimately, they shared a vision of easy access to services through 'one-stop-shops' spread out over the region, less shuffling back and forth among agencies, healthier children coming into schools, and better support systems for children in schools.

Needs assessments conducted by multiple, and sometimes overlapping, community groups resulted in a growing recognition that Nash County had some of the same needs as Edgecombe County and could accomplish more through a collective or regional effort. Edgecombe County's more serious needs became an "advantage" when the funding process was based on need, and it was unlikely that Nash County could have received initial Smart Start funding by itself.

Education, health, and human service agencies recognized that the Smart Start funding would enable them to expand current programs and implement strategies that currently lacked funding. Agencies operating separately in the two counties, such as Social Services, the Health Department, and the school districts, had their own representatives in the early discussions. Parents and community leaders, including business and industry representatives, were also involved. Early boundary spanning activities consisted primarily of gathering, analyzing, and sharing information. Once the decision was made to pursue Smart Start funding, attention focused on planning and developing the Smart Start proposal. At this point, the planning was sufficiently general so as not to threaten the boundaries of any stakeholder's organization, programs, or administrative procedures. The ease with which the partnering organizations agreed on the goals of the DEPC simplified the work of the early boundary spanners, allowing them to support the new partnership without obligating their own organizations to change the way they did business.

Although the first two-county Smart Start proposal, submitted in 1993, was not funded, the comprehensive needs assessments and the commitment of so many stakeholder groups in the planning efforts positioned the group to respond proactively. They moved ahead with a two-county Child Care Resource and Referral (CCR&R) proposal and with the incorporation of the Down East Partnership for Children in December 1993 without the Smart Start funding or any other known source of continuing support. A one-time contribution of $50,000 from the business community enabled the DEPC to hire two employees, and one of the school districts provided office space in Rocky Mount that had been vacated as a result of the recent school district merger.

The failure of the first Smart Start proposal had raised new questions about the decision to pursue a two-county Smart Start partnership, particularly from the stakeholders in Edgecombe County, but the decision was made to move ahead with another joint application. The Executive Director noted, "It is much easier to coordinate if everybody from across the county line works together" (Vinh, 1994). In the spring of 1994, the NC Client and Community Development Center facilitated a strategic planning session for all stakeholders. The process helped clarify and reaffirm the focus of the DEPC and prepared the group of staff, Board members, and stakeholders to finalize a second Smart Start proposal and develop additional applications for funding from other groups. The DEPC received a Smart Start planning grant and assurance that the Smart Start proposal would be funded in the next grant cycle. In addition, the request for CCR&R funding was also successful.

During problem setting, stakeholders in a collaborative effort deepen their understanding of the problem domain (Gray, 1985). The immediate "problem" for the DEPC was to improve access to child care and the other services needed by children and their families. The problem was articulated in the Smart Start proposal as follows:

> Through our needs assessment we learned that much work is needed to create a comprehensive early childhood system, and then to develop an integrated funding mechanism to allow all children equal access. We learned that the quality of our childcare is low, but that childcare providers are excited about the opportunity to undergo self-assessment and changes needed to meet high quality, national standards. We learned that the expectations of parents are very different from the expectations of schools

regarding what children need to succeed. Our vision addresses the need to increase opportunities for dialogue and sharing between parents, child care providers, and kindergarten teachers. Finally we learned that there are many barriers to services, but the most difficult to overcome may be the attitudes that many people have toward using those services, even those that will lead to a better life for their children. By including prospective program participants in the design of services we expect to begin to overcome these negative attitudes (Smart Start Proposal, 1994).

As the Partnership evolved, stakeholders reaffirmed that the "problem" in Nash and Edgecombe counties included, and also extended beyond child care issues. Not only did they want children to be healthy and ready to learn when they entered school, but they also wanted children and their families to have the support they needed as long as their children were in school. In addition, they wanted children to complete school successfully. As a result, the DEPC has not limited its services to preschool children, but is committed to serving the needs of children of all ages and their families.

Once the stakeholders understood and defined the problem, they had to decide how the problem would be addressed. To insure that all children and families in Nash and Edgecombe counties would receive the education, health, and social services necessary to be economically successful, the DEPC adopted four goals and organized their activities accordingly:

(1) The CCR&R (Child Care Resources and Reform) supported *universal access to high quality early childhood education* by providing information to parents about the costs, availability, and quality of childcare in centers and family homes. Scholarships were granted to help parents with the costs of child care. In addition, training, technical assistance, and grants helped child care providers improve their programs and achieve accreditation.

(2) The Family Resource Program supported *improved parenting and parent involvement in education* through a growing network of family resource centers in the two-county area. Through the centers, the staff worked to improve links between those who need health and human services and the agencies and individuals who provide them.

3) The Family Resource Data Base helped *eliminate barriers to Services* by providing information and referrals for parents who were concerned about their child's growth and development. Standing work groups continued to address the needs for

service integration and transportation, and, with a growing number of Hispanic families in the area, services were expanded to include the Hispanic community as well.

(4) The DEPC supported Home School Coordinators and parent education in both school districts in order to *improve the transition to public school.* The DEPC also initiated and supported the development of a strategic plan for early childhood education in the two-county area. Specific programs were implemented to address the quality of care for school-age children and to empower parents to be more involved in the education of children of all ages.

Parents, representatives of community agencies and organizations, and the DEPC Board and staff have continued to be involved in the development of strategies for achieving the DEPC goals. State auditors commended the DEPC's strong commitment to involve clients and community representatives in addition to the "recognized" agency directors and business leaders (Coopers & Lybrand, 1996, p. 56). In addition, the Executive Director articulated a need for continuous strategic planning in a successful request for Babcock Foundation funding to support the organizational development of the DEPC through planning, evaluation, and staff development efforts. For a partnership to be sustained, it must have organizational structures and procedures, a group of "believers," effective communication linkages, and sufficient funding (Reed & Cedja, 1987). DEPC structures and policies have been established as needed. The early decision to incorporate allowed the DEPC to strengthen its position. Policies were established to support the CCR&R program. As the size of the DEPC staff grew and stabilized at about thirty people, personnel policies and procedures were established. As the annual budget grew, contracts management software was developed that was then used by other partnerships throughout the State.

Structures and processes that supported positive change were even more significant. For example, the DEPC has continued to make grants to community groups "with strings attached" to ensure that the groups receiving funding would obtain the training and support needed for their programs to be successful. Grass roots leaders were identified, and after these "Community Fellows" completed a year-long leadership training program, they were able to apply for grants to support projects they believed would make a difference in their own communities. A standing Evaluation Committee was created in the spring of 1995 to develop an evaluation process that would help the Partnership maintain its focus and ensure progress toward Partnership goals. Program evaluation activities have focused on both the Partnership as a whole and the individual program activities. Training and support for the development of measurable, client-focused outcomes has resulted in more useful evaluation data. A peer review process for DEPC programs and grantees was initiated to enable groups receiving DEPC funding to develop sound organizational policies and procedures so that they would be able to carry out their programs successfully.

Information is an important commodity in a collaborative setting. In the first DEPC offices, space was "tight" and shared communication was natural. When the school district reclaimed space used by the DEPC, the partnership purchased the former YWCA building in downtown Rocky Mount for office space and a model family resource center. In the new building, private offices were a welcomed luxury, but internal communication required more effort. Technology, including e-mail, Internet, and web pages, has been used to improve internal and external communication. For example, see the DEPC website (www.depc.org). Newsletters and mailings share information with the community, and the quarterly evaluation reports generate regular communication about program outcomes.

Continuing funding is essential for a collaborative project, but the decision to take action without Smart Start funding set an important precedent for the DEPC. Although the annual budget increased from $1,673,503 in fiscal year 1995 to more than $6,500,000 in 2009, DEPC has never relied upon a single funding source. Additional funds have been obtained through varied state and federal grants, grants from private foundations, and other contributors. Auditors noted that the multiple funding streams allowed DEPC to offer services that go beyond Smart Start and "implement programs that will have a long-term impact on the community" (Coopers & Lybrand, 1996, p. 25). For example, the Child Care Scholarship program has been conducted on-site in collaboration with Social Services, but the Partnership was able to use multiple funding streams to establish graduated eligibility criteria that allowed parents to wean off the subsidy as their income increased over time. The DEPC scholarship program continues to support families who have reached an income level that exceeds the Department of Social Services eligibility level.

Although DEPC programs were grouped loosely in three areas (Child Care Resource and Referral, Family Resource, and Information and Exchange), many initiatives were interrelated, and members of the staff "regrouped" to work on projects as needed. Many staff members were able to articulate the relationship between their specific job descriptions and DEPC goals. The broad recognition that specific activities supported multiple goals was consistent with the vision of integrated services, but it has complicated efforts to structure the administrative groupings. It is essential to monitor administrative structures to be sure that they support both the day-to-day operations and the long-term goals of the Partnership. In structuring a collaborative effort, there is a danger that the new collaborative could take on some of the bureaucratic characteristics of the unresponsive organizations it was designed to replace.

Important events in the early history of the DEPC highlight evidence of the developmental nature of the collaboration process. The fact that not all events were sequential demonstrated the need, from time to time, to cycle back through earlier stages before moving ahead (Melaville & Blank, 1993). For example, in 1999, severe flooding in the two-county area caused the DEPC to return to the problem-setting stage. Following the urgency of disaster relief efforts, the partnership reaffirmed its commitment to the original goals and chose not to take the ongoing lead in long-term recovery efforts.

The DEPC celebrated its fifteenth anniversary of the incorporation of the partnership in 2008. During the first fifteen years, positive results multiplied. Through the Child Care R&R efforts, resource and referral services for parents and technical assistance and training for child care providers are in place. The quality of childcare has improved as more facilities have become accredited. Of total childcare placements in 2008, 74% in Edgecombe and 55% in Nash were in the highest quality childcare settings compared to only 7% for both counties in 1993. Through the efforts of DEPC stakeholder groups, the network of family resource centers in schools and communities has grown. Millions of dollars from grants and other outside sources have benefited residents of the two-county area, and the partnership and its funded programs have served growing numbers of children and families annually, with approximately 30,000 people walking through the doors of the DEPC every year (DEPC, 2009, p. 9).

ROLES AND RELATIONSHIPS WITHIN SCHOOL DISTRICTS

The two merged school districts were important stakeholder groups as the DEPC began operation. The location of the first office space in the Nash-Rocky Mount Teacher Resource Center was beneficial in several ways. The in-kind contribution obviously reduced operating costs for the new partnership. In addition, the Executive Director observed that by providing this "incubation space," the school district "parented" the partnership and conferred a sense of legitimacy in the community.

Superintendents of both school districts have filled designated positions on the DEPC Board of Directors since the partnership was established. The early planning and incorporation efforts followed the successful culmination of more than twenty years of attempts to improve education in the two-county area by merging separate city and county school districts in each county. As a result, in the early days of the DEPC, both school superintendents were newly appointed leaders of new, merged districts. Community interest in education and expectations for improvement were at an all-time high. Politically, it was important for the school districts to be active partners in community projects including the DEPC. The superintendents' designated boundary spanners kept both superintendents informed of specific program activities, and the relationships between the DEPC and both school districts during the early years were generally positive.

While the Executive Director of DEPC has remained in place, there have been numerous superintendent changes for both districts in addition to frequent changes in principals and other school leaders. These changes make it difficult to maintain momentum in collaborative efforts with the schools. The DEPC offers opportunities and support for innovative school programs, but the boundaries of the DEPC and partnering organizations were more likely to overlap when new programs were implemented, making boundary spanning activities more uncertain and sometimes threatening. When schools were not interested in partnership opportunities, the DEPC moved on with those who were.

For principals accustomed to making decisions for their schools and controlling policies and procedures, the growing presence of the DEPC in the community and its interests and initiatives that crossed over school and district boundaries, concern and discomfort increased. Unfortunately, it is not common practice in education for superintendents or principals to have accepted the challenge of Cordeiro and Kelek (1996) to identify boundary spanners in districts and schools and give them "permission and a reason to travel" (p. 13). Without supportive Board policies in place and a superintendent who clarifies expectation and consistently models collaboration and empowerment, principals are less likely to feel permitted to travel or recognize reasons to do so.

Relationship-Defining Incidents

The relationships between the two school districts and the DEPC have continued to evolve in unique ways. Just as shared successes strengthened the partnership, negative incidents challenged the relationship with the DEPC, and some have been difficult to overcome. In the beginning, representatives of both districts participated in early needs assessments and planning. Over time, however, school district involvement in DEPC initiatives became more reactive, and district representatives were less likely to seek joint efforts. A number of incidents that influenced the relationship between the DEPC and the two school districts are discussed below.

Needs assessment and planning. Representatives of both districts participated in the pre-DEPC needs assessment efforts of Project Uplift, Visions 2000, and Common Ground. Edgecombe County had a longer history of collaboration around the efforts to understand the problems of children and their families, and the needs in Edgecombe County were recognized to be more serious than the needs in Nash County.

Quality of education in the two-county area was an important concern of the community and the DEPC stakeholder groups. The school districts were needed at the discussion table, and they wanted to be there. Funding agencies, including Smart Start, expected to see evidence that the school districts were significantly involved in the proposed collaborative programs. The school districts recognized the need to participate, to monitor the discussion, and to be aware of, and possibly prevent, any "threats" to their own organizations and programs. The new partnership, an "unknown" group, was delving into education, health, and social issues; empowering parents and other community groups; providing information; and encouraging parents and community representatives to ask questions. At times, school district boundaries seemed to be threatened. School leaders' interest and involvement in the work of the DEPC tended to vary over time, depending on the current focus of the partnership, the specific project under discussion, and other demands facing the school districts at any given time.

Incubation space. The first office space for the DEPC, provided by the Nash-Rocky Mount Schools in their Teacher Resource Center, was a major boost as the DEPC was formed. In addition to the financial benefit, the district's visible support helped legitimize the new partnership. The school district's decision to reclaim that space in 1996 could have dealt a serious blow to the credibility of the young partnership. However, the DEPC was able to purchase its own facility, the vacant YWCA building in downtown Rocky Mount, thereby increasing its visibility and the number of services that could be provided by the partnership.

Funding for special projects. Along with other groups in the two-county area, both school districts have had opportunities to submit grants to support special programs in the schools that are aligned with DEPC goals. For example, in the early years of the DEPC, the partnership supported training and follow-up support for schools in both districts that wanted to establish peer mediation programs. Although remnants of those programs remain, changes in district priorities and the availability of district financial support limited the ability of individual schools to sustain the programs, even with support of the DEPC that included, but were not limited to K-12 education. Other school projects funded by the DEPC included parent education, pre-school programs, developmentally appropriate playgrounds, and school transition programs. As the DEPC matured, the Board became more interested in grants that were part of long term strategic plans aligned with the shared goals of the DEPC.

Conditions were placed on DEPC grants to the school districts. As the expectation became more explicit that DEPC funding should support programs aligned with a strategic plan rather than isolated, single-shot initiatives, some proposals submitted by schools and districts were returned for revision. While one district has been able to weave its initiatives into a strategic effort that includes Title I and Even Start funding streams, the other district has continued to struggle to articulate long-term goals and develop "acceptable" proposals. School district personnel is the second district expressed concern that they didn't

227

know "what the DEPC wanted" and questioned the value of continued attempts to figure it out. To them, the proposed projects were not essential, and there were plenty of other responsibilities that demanded their attention.

Aborted pre-kindergarten programs. DEPC grants supported pre-kindergarten programs in schools in both districts. While the DEPC was interested in creating new programs in areas where child care spaces were needed, classroom space was not always available in underserved areas, and principals were not always willing or able to collaborate with the DEPC. When two pre-K programs in one district were "closed" by the principals because they were "too much trouble," the relationship between the district and the DEPC suffered.

Reverted funds. DEPC staff took pride in the responsible management of their financial resources. They were sensitive to funding deadlines and meticulous about using all available resources to benefit the communities. When the same district that closed the pre-K programs failed to spend all their allocated funds within the fiscal year and caused the DEPC to revert $35,000 to the state, the collaborative relationship suffered another serious blow. Although $35,000 was not a large amount of money compared to the school district budget, it was a more significant portion of the DEPC budget. The DEPC staff and Board took the loss seriously and resented the damage done to their own credibility as a result of the school district's mistake.

Successful family resource centers. Both school districts and the DEPC have been proud of the growing network of family resource centers. The centers have benefited from the support of various agencies. The local Communities in Schools organization is an active partner in two family resource centers. One is located in an urban elementary school, and the other is housed in a surplus school building that was once the center of a small rural community. Additional services are provided by business representatives, the Community Colleges, the Health Departments, and the Departments of Social Services. When family resource centers are located on school grounds, the role of the principal and the teachers and their commitment to the community have been key factors influencing success.

One district's early childhood center and the threat of competition for day care providers. A new Early Childhood Center, built by one of the districts, alarmed the child care community. In both counties, child care providers feared that they would lose clients as school districts began to serve younger children. District representatives pointed out that their programs were supported by categorical funding and designed to serve children with specific needs. Although these were not the children who were being served in private child care facilities, as the new facility opened and grew, the providers continued to look to the DEPC for support and 'protection.'

Leadership changes. Building positive collaborative relationships is more difficult if the school district representatives or boundary spanners keep changing. Continuing turnover in superintendents, principals, and other district contacts has required all stakeholders to "spiral back through" the stages of collaboration (Melaville & Blank, 1993) on several occasions. At times, these changes delayed forward progress.

Components for Successful Collaboration

Three themes emerged in the search for components of successful collaboration between the DEPC and the partnering school districts. A clear understanding of and commitment to the shared vision of the partnership, the ability to resolve or accept differences in administrative procedures, and effective boundary spanning activity within and across organizational boundaries contributed to successful implementation of collaborative projects and activities.

Value of shared vision. Representatives of each school district reported that the district and the DEPC shared a vision for their partnership, but the visions they articulated differed in specificity—a vague 'doing what's best for children' versus a more specific match 'making access to all services available to everybody.' The second interpretation was more closely aligned with the vision and goals of the DEPC and affirmed more specific and systemic initiatives. It is interesting to note that the emphasis on access to services was articulated by the representative of the district with the longest history of involvement in needs assessment and planning efforts. The longer history of working collaboratively to understand the problem domain could be an important factor in the stronger alignment of vision and strategies. (See Bradshaw, 2002).

Visioning continues throughout the life of a collaborative effort. As the participants and the context for the partnership change, stakeholders must continue to clarify and refine the vision. When new partners enter into a collaborative effort that is already underway, it is difficult to ensure that all partners achieve the same level of understanding of the conditions that led to the formation of the partnership, but the challenge must be addressed.

The ability to resolve or accept differences in administrative procedures. Differences in administrative procedures, the ways organizations do business, are sources of potential conflict in partnership efforts. School district representatives tended to be inconvenienced or even offended by a variety of meetings, reports, and other requirements associated with DEPC grants and other joint activities. At the same time, DEPC staff were frustrated when school district contacts missed meetings and reporting deadlines. Ultimately, however, each school district responded differently. In one district, the problems with administrative procedures were potential deterrents to future collaborative projects. In the other district, however, the inconveniences were described as a "small price to pay for the benefits to children and their families."

Differences in administrative procedures are predictable sources of tension in collaborative efforts, and additional discussion could lead to a better understanding of the needs and concerns of both school districts and the DEPC. In turn, efforts to simplify procedures or craft collaborative solutions could benefit relationships with other stakeholders as well.

The importance of effective boundary spanning activity. Both school districts and the DEPC engaged in boundary spanning activity at many levels. As noted earlier, when the district vision was aligned with the DEPC vision and goals, efforts were more likely to be successful. The high level of alignment in one school district was achieved as a result of effective boundary spanning activity within and across the school district's organizational boundaries.

Effective boundary spanning requires consistency, communication, and coordination. However, in the district where shared vision was most evident, one key boundary spanner had been in place prior to the formation of the DEPC. As a teacher, principal, and Director of Federal Programs, she had participated in the early needs assessment efforts. She understood the problem domain and worked to build awareness and support within the district for developmentally appropriate practice in early childhood education, parent education, and meaningful parent involvement. In her eventual role as Director of Federal Programs, she was able to access and leverage varied funding sources to put different 'pieces' in place, including a Title One pre-school program, Reading Recovery programs, and a major Even Start initiative. The systemic results demonstrated how personal linkages provide opportunities for unique and creative solutions (Eisenberg, 1995). At the same time, her ability to share information and build and maintain support within the school district assured success of the programs.

PRINCIPALS AND SCHOOL LEADERS

There are many reasons to be concerned about the condition of children. Some progress steadily through our public schools to higher education or the world of work, but poor academic performance and other problems plague a significant portion of the student body. Policy makers and the general public are seeking ways to hold schools accountable for the education of all children, and various reports call attention to problems with their physical, mental, and social health (Annie E. Casey Foundation, 1999). Dryfoos observed that the threats to the well-being of today's children are unprotected sex, drugs, violence, and depression. These "new morbidities" are drastically different from the "old morbidities" of chronic diseases, nutritional deficiencies, acne, and head lice (1994, p. 2). There are both moral and economic reasons for addressing these health and social issues (Galvin, 1998). When serious health and social needs are unmet, children are more likely to be unsuccessful in school, drop out, and be unprepared for the world of work. The strength of the economy depends upon the quality of the workforce, and business leaders are concerned about the quality of the labor pool.

Because children spend large, predictable amounts of time in school settings during certain years of their lives, those who wish to address children's health and social needs in a systemic way often seek to involve schools and school personnel in the solution. When children's needs are entwined with the dynamics of their families, solutions must extend beyond the scope of the traditional roles of teachers and other education professionals. The education partnerships of the past were often "charitable" arrangements that involved new resources for the schools. As partnerships have become more client-focused, there has been a movement toward "bringing service systems into schools to respond to the needs of today's children and their families" (Dryfoos, 1994, p. 6). These newer partnerships, including community and full service schools, seek a broad understanding of the problems encountered by students and their families and the coordination of resources to meet those needs. Linkages may be established among programs and agencies to improve the delivery of education, health, and social services. (For example, see Cibulka & Kritek, 1996; Dryfoos, 1994; Hooper-Briar & Lawson, 1996; Rigsby, Reynolds, & Wang, 1995.) In order to successfully develop and sustain these complex partnerships, all stakeholders and service providers, especially principals and other school leaders must understand the dynamics of collaboration (see Bradshaw, 1999), and the representatives of the partnering organizations must be effective in their unique roles.

While the term *boundary spanning* might be a new one, most principals have had quite a bit of boundary spanning experience. It is not uncommon for principals to work with faculty at other schools, district office personnel, parents, community groups, school of education faculty, or state agency representatives to resolve problems or create innovative programs to address student needs. They understand the need to listen, conduct needs assessments, identify resources, build consensus, and develop plans. However, the trend toward more systemic solutions, including full service schools, takes boundary spanning to a more challenging level and requires the principal to be able to navigate boundaries between education, health, and social service bureaucracies and between education and other professional disciplines.

The principal is in charge of the school, but that control is not always clear when the school site serves as a hub for services that extend beyond teaching and learning. In community and full service schools, the principal will be called upon to obtain and share information and to encourage an ongoing dialogue concerning the ways clients are and should be served. Dryfoos (1994) listed these components of the principal's role with integrated services: "(acting) as an interpreter between the school staff and the outside staff, (controlling) the traffic flow, (facilitating) the use of services, and (being) in charge of whatever happens under the school roof" (p. 152). The principal must have positive attitudes toward collaboration and strong boundary spanning skills in order to carry out the complex role effectively.

Recognizing how collaboration can address the complex needs of children. Successful boundary spanners want to improve conditions for their clients. Sloan's model of collaboration in school based health centers shows how the principal's boundary spanning activities were directed toward building an empathic professional culture within the school that responded to a societal imperative to resolve the complex needs of children (1996). Principals should have a vision of where the partnership is going, and they should be committed to collaboration as the process for achieving the goals. As boundary spanners, principals must also be flexible, with room in their vision that allows them to respond to and use important new information and developments.

Develop and refine the ability to obtain and distribute information strategically. Successful boundary spanners understand the "outside layers of their own organizations" (Cordeiro and Kolek, 1996) and the practices of all partnering agencies so that strategies can be developed for obtaining, documenting, and sharing necessary information as well as distributing the information across internal boundaries. Sloan (1996) found that principals who were successful boundary spanners found many ways to facilitate dialogue among the different professionals in a school based partnership and to make them feel a part of the school. They included all professionals in faculty meetings, helped them address confidentiality issues by understanding other professionals' needs to know, facilitated discussions of referral issues, and provided team building workshops. Successful boundary spanners know or are willing to learn the language and culture of other professions. Cordeiro and Kolek (1996) noted that educational leaders must be multicultural, "facile with the shared language that is created as different organizations with different cultures come together (p. 13)."

Develop the ability to see problems in new ways. Successful boundary spanners are able to diagnose problems and prescribe appropriate strategies (Mannes, 1996). Boundary spanning principals monitor the organizational environment, gathering and analyzing data to identify and better understand the needs of students and their families. They see connections and commonalities (Sarason & Lorentz, 1998), and bring together or are willing to join groups of stakeholders to discuss a problem domain. For them, a problem is "a series of intersecting events and resources, all providing opportunities for intervention and instruction"(Cordeiro & Kolek, 1996, p. 7).

View problems in new ways. Successful boundary spanners imagine innovative strategies. They have can-do attitudes (Galvin, 1998), are willing to take risks, and recognize resources. They know what individuals, agencies, and programs can contribute to the partnership (Sarason & Lorentz, 1998), and they understand and have the support of their own organizations so that they can serve as a broker when developing and implementing collaborative strategies. However, successful boundary spanners do not impose solutions. They are more like founders than leaders who have to be in charge (Seitsinger, 1996).

Develop the ability to craft collaborative solutions. Successful boundary spanners have a unique sense of timing. They work purposefully, "making and nurturing connections, constantly scanning the environment for opportunities that match identified needs, waiting for the time to be right politically, and planting seeds in several 'fields" (Cordeiro & Kolek, 1996, p. 10).

Successful boundary spanners are not threatened by questions about how the schools have traditionally done their work. Dryfoos (1994) understood how complex partnerships can open the school to questions about discipline policies and practices from those with "new" professional perspectives: "When a clinic opens in a school, the school is exposed to close observation by personnel who are sensitive to the effects of repressive environments on the health and well-being of youth" (p. 155). A principal who is a successful boundary spanner will use such questions to facilitate conversation among those involved and to adjust those policies and practices, if necessary, to better serve the clients of the school.

Develop and support the boundary spanning skills of others. Although the principal's own boundary spanning activity is critical to the success of complex partnerships, the principal cannot accomplish the partnership's goals alone. Principals must also encourage other staff members to communicate across organizational and professional boundaries and support them in their boundary spanning roles. Principals must recognize that leadership in collaborative ventures is no longer limited to line positions on an organizational chart. They must know when to direct, when to delegate, and when to move out of the way. Cordeiro and Kolek (1996) observed that leadership in collaborative settings "emerges depending on the situation and needs of each participant. When people from different organizations and agencies collaborate with educators, leadership becomes a part of each participant's role" (p. 5).

Connections between frontline staff might be more important than top-down strategies when implementing change (McLaughlin, 1990). Frontline personnel must be encouraged and allowed to work through barriers and push the limits of their own professional perspectives to effectively serve children and families in need (Mannes, 1996, p. xi). Eisenberg (1995) observed that "personal linkages, while risky and difficult to control, are at times the most likely source of cooperation" (p. 104). When comprehensive programs that integrate services for children are established in the school setting, school personnel may be particularly uncomfortable. Boundary spanning principals must recognize those feelings and help personnel work through them. Principals should also "offer a sense of purpose and safety" (Seitsinger, 1996), and they must be able to resolve conflict among diverse professionals in the collaborative setting. They must become "adept at managing novel interdependencies among adults as their organizations become more complex" (Finch, 1977, p. 298) and in developing a team.

Managing the Challenges of Boundary Spanning Roles

Boundary spanning roles can be stressful, but the lack of clarity in the way the roles are defined is also a source of flexibility to create and maintain innovative strategies. The following strategies may reduce stress.

Maintain strong internal linkages. Work with the Superintendent and other school leaders in the district to maintain an ongoing discussion of collaboration in the community. Keep everyone informed as you search for better strategies to address the needs of your students and their families. Know and understand the positions of the Superintendent, the Board of Education, and other important district stakeholders, and work with other school leaders to clarify expectations and develop policy to support collaborative efforts. When collaborative efforts to resolve a problem pull you toward a "new" strategy, share the developments with your internal stakeholders, and involve them in brainstorming alternatives. Help them understand the complexity of the problem and the need for innovative action.

Build strong external linkages. Regularly engage in environmental scanning. Learn all you can about the needs of your students, their families, and the professionals who serve them. Listen for opportunities to link services in more effective ways. Identify potential resources. Engage stakeholders in a continuing dialogue about the problems, and include additional stakeholders who can share new perspectives as you learn more about what needs to be done. Work with others to build a shared vision of how students' education and development could be more successful.

Accept, and even celebrate, the uncertainty of your boundary spanning role. Successful boundary spanners must be able to tolerate role ambiguity and role conflict. They operate "on the edge" of organizations, where roles are often undefined and continually changing. The uncertainty can be stressful, and it is difficult to bring even temporary closure to the work in a problem domain. However, this uncertainty provides opportunities to recognize and act on new ideas that can resolve problems in innovative and lasting ways.

Recognize differences in organizational structures for what they are. Boundary spanners frequently encounter problems when schools and partnering organizations have different systems for keeping financial records, assigning and evaluating personnel, referring clients, and maintaining program data. These are structural "conflicts" that need to be resolved, and boundary spanners may be the best source of innovative solutions. However, structural conflicts are not sufficient reasons for discontinuing collaborative efforts.

CONCLUSIONS

Individuals working at the edges of organizations and in their overlapping spaces are essential to the success of organizational partnerships. The Downeast Partnership for Children (DEPC) is a layered partnership, an umbrella for a wide range of collaborative efforts serving children and their families across a two-county area in eastern North Carolina. The DEPC is unique in the number of parallel stakeholders it brings together across the two counties: school districts, health departments, social services, juvenile justice systems, community colleges, libraries, and a variety of community organizations. Stakeholders also included state agencies and a number of private foundations. While we focused primarily on the roles and relationships of superintendents and other school leaders with the partnership, the story would be similar from the perspective of other stakeholders.

Organizational boundaries must be spanned and crossed in order to develop and sustain effective partnerships. Often, individuals with the potential to fill those roles are neither aware of nor prepared to seize those roles. More importantly, they may not have the permission of their own organizations or understand the reasons to do so. School leaders are the agents of this change; both positive examples and examples 'less than best' have been shared to illustrate effects of various activities on the development of the partnership. Recommendations were made to support those who realize that they have boundary spanning opportunities and seek to develop their ability to take advantage of them in order to support partnerships.

EDITOR'S COMMENT

Dr. Bradshaw tells us more about the links between partnerships than any of our previous writers. The ability of the marginal leader to cross boundaries is a key to such developments. All of the previous contributors have crossed theses boundaries whether as an individual in the North, a broker of coalitions who coordinates local and national programs, a coordinator of student programs at GW, a high school teacher who found opportunities for nonacademic students, or university visionary who created a music program. Just different boundaries are crossed.

Unlike the other contributors, Dr. Bradshaw's personal experiences are not revealed. She has moved from school administration to a university position and was very much a part of the partnership that she analyzes so objectively. Partnerships are always a part of subjective experience and actual types of organizations. The other contributors described the context in which their stories emerge. Usually, as we have seen, the business model is dominant. The model is probably dominant for Dr. Bradshaw, but it is not direct and she has not worked with business leaders.

PART III

MAKING CONNECTIONS

How do partnerships spread? The initial answer of both Wade Rathke, who founded a large community group, and Rosalyn Black, who worked for the Australian Foundation, is that individuals had experience in one country and they brought the innovation with them to the new country or when they returned to their place of origin. However, the innovation changes rapidly and surprisingly moves in a similar direction even when separated from its place of origin. Advocacy groups try and help poor people obtain better homes, jobs and credit. Corporations attempt to become a part of the communities that they service and contribute to the arts, public education, and annual ceremonies.

The people who are describing the programs that spread are creative boundary spanners themselves who connect communities and countries. Ann Jones describes how she brought partnership models with her into a rural community, but she found others already meeting at kitchen tables as a place where the largest projects could emerge. Indeed five different states and provinces came to focus upon environmental education that provides an opportunity where outsiders can join with local residents in a common cause. A summer program becomes a ceremony that unifies those who 'come-from-away' with those who have lived there for generations.

In a changing urban world, many issues and events have to be sought by organizers. Judy Duncan and her colleagues find slum landlords, a living wage, and environmental challenges are opportunities for publicity and legislation. ACORN is able to form alliances with environmental groups and even the chamber of commerce for social ends in Canada, if not the United States. In any country, the issue is how partnerships are able to empower students or other young people.

. The complexity of partnerships makes it difficult to achieve only a few results in a complicated and changing scene. Creating partnerships involves politics and cultural differences; these differences are substantial among schools when educators are confronted with innovations as they are between countries that are borrowing from and competing with each other. Spreading partnerships involves empowering students, often the weakest group and others with less power than the planners. Specific strategies for change balance considerations of power and vision for the have-nots.

The have-nots are revealed more clearly in international relationships. Canadians have long admired and resented Americans. Poverty in underdeveloped countries is more of a challenge to those who, like the founder of ACORN, Wade Rathke, tries to empower the people through partnerships and coalitions. No difference is more enduring than that between rural and urban centers. In either developed or underdeveloped countries, linking these sources of stratification is a continuing challenge. Political organizations of partnerships, coalitions, take up this challenge.

Chapter 8
The Tie That Binds Local and International Organizing

Wade Rathke. Founder, Association of Community
Organizations for Reform Now (ACORN)

As an organizer, one of the most important lessons I have learned over the years is how to learn to follow the members. Sometimes this means running to catch up with where they want to go. Other times, it means following them to where they have been including distant countries as I have learned in recent years working with ACORN International. This new organization is also known as Community Organizations International.

Having founded ACORN as a membership organization of low and moderate income families in 1970 in Little Rock, Arkansas, it all seemed simpler forty years ago and just a matter of black and white, though that was more than complicated enough in the South at the tail end of the civil rights movement (Fischer, 2010). Over the years though, as the organization spread its work, first into neighboring states near Arkansas like Texas, Missouri, and Louisiana, and then over decades as it grew to have offices in more than 100 cities and forty states and organize in thousands of neighborhoods in hundreds of towns with nearly a half-million members, the organization's membership was a microcosm of the world's population struggling to survive and forge their way forward. Chicago, New York, Seattle, Los Angeles, Houston, Miami, New Orleans, Phoenix, Philadelphia, and other cities where ACORN had grown were burgeoning and brawling communities with scores of languages and millions of stories all leading to these crossroads.

It goes without saying that Canada and the United States are nations of immigrants in the "new world." Many observers trumpet Toronto and Vancouver as two of the most "international" or cosmopolitan cities in the world in terms of their great diversity due to the welcoming immigrant practices that prevailed in Canada within the last generation. The historic reputation of the United States and the Statue of Liberty acting as a beacon signaling in immigrants has been tarnished in recent years as conservatives have targeted immigrants in the wake of 9/11 with constant invective, high walls along the southern border, and a resistance to even the legislative reforms that would unite families. Globalism had made the world even more economically interdependent and technology seemed to be shrinking the world's borders almost by the day.

I should not have been surprised as ACORN's membership in the United States grew that many of our members with one foot on this ground and sometimes their hearts and homes still in another would increasingly make the case that we should work in other countries. In fact I was not surprised, so it was easy for years for me to simply smile and figure out a way to say no with some grace. It was not as if there were not a million things to do and undone in the United States, so it was not that hard to shrug most of the members and leaders off until some fine day in the future. But the more I listened to the members and followed the leaders in the directions they wanted to go, the harder it was to ignore and sluff off everything happening in the rest of their world, especially because the narrow compartments of borders and boundaries did not exist for many of them at all. The world kept slipping around the walls.

BRINGING PEOPLE INTO THE FOLD

There were several strands that finally came together no matter how many years I had worked to keep them separate. Eventually, as an organizer, "no" was the easy answer, but "yes" became the right answer.

Alto Manhattan

One of the fastest growing parts of our membership in New York City in Brooklyn and Washington Heights (Manhattan) was among Dominicans. I can remember mentally scratching my head when I had to field a request from ACORN's Vice-President Maria Polanco in New York about whether or not the President Maude Hurd could be in the city to meet with a candidate for the President, and then to my surprise realizing this was a candidate for the Presidency of *Republicana de Dominica!*

We deftly took an institutional position that ACORN in the United States did not endorse candidates for election in other countries, but as simple as that sounds, it was anything but. Dominicans, like the residents of other countries it turns out, can often vote in elections in both the United States and in the Dominican Republic, recognizing their dual citizenship. ACORN because of its large Dominican membership on the East Coast was seen as a powerhouse and a coveted endorsement. Years later I saw an article for one of the candidates that included a picture with Maude Hurd, which on the island might have been worth a thousand votes. This was a wake-up call for me! Later Maria and others took the leadership in organizing the ACORN Dominican Council which not only won the creation and use of *matricula* cards as a form of identification after a meeting with the Consulate and organized an annual party and fundraiser for Dominican projects in the motherland, but also lobbied successfully on two different trips of ACORN leaders and staff to Santo Domingo, Santiago, and Samana which later led to ACORN International organizing in Santiago and finding people block by block who had been members in *alto Manhattan* and knew ACORN.

Rebuilding Civil Society in Peru

The Alberto Fujimora repression of the *Sendero Luminiso* (Shining Path) in Peru had led to widespread political discontent and a fair number of student and other exiles to the United States. Interestingly there were sizable pockets of Peruvians in ACORN's membership and on our staff in Los Angeles as well as in northern New Jersey. Importantly, Norca, the wife of one of our senior organizers, Craig Robbins, was also well known to all of us. The election of Alejandro Toledo coursed through the Peruvian community in the USA like a spring breeze of new hope. As it became harder to say no, I found myself travelling with Jeff Ordower, a seasoned ACORN organizer, who had visited Lima recently on his vacation, to spend several days meeting with a wide variety of people and groups from the slums to the Capitol and Congresso to try and find an answer to the question of whether or not ACORN could be helpful in the efforts to rebuild civil society in Peru. It was a heady and amazing experience within six months of Toldeo's election. The meetings would sometimes begin early in the morning in a dingy coffee shop in the barrios and end past 11 at night being ushered into the office of the First Lady's chief of staff or meeting with the executive committee of Lima's Legal Society or drinking pisco sours in old clubs with former officials and lobbyists right on the central plaza.

We were looking for partners with whom we could make a contribution, which was not easy. We had very simple requirements. It had to be a *real* partnership where ACORN was not simply *giving* but also *getting*. There had to be a deep recognition that we were essentially poor people partnering with poor people, members dealing with members, and not based on an assumption of superior first world resources, which we honestly did not have. As fascinating and exhilarating as the meetings had been throughout the week, nothing was really clicking. We had one last meeting in the early afternoon before our planes left in different directions back to the USA with the executive board of the *comodores*. We located their headquarters in a non-descript neighborhood and found ourselves sitting in their small office that seemed to look like scores of ACORN offices with posters on the wall, folding and plastic chairs, and makeshift tables and desks. The all women leadership of middle aged women who hardly came to my shoulder sat around the table and passed us Ritz crackers and paper cups of Inca Cola. I told them in halting Spanish with Jeff's help that where I came from my mother would up braid me forever for my bad manners were I to touch a drop until they were all seated and served and took the first sip. They broke into peals of laughter and we were great friends from that moment on. It's the little things sometimes. They were running 1500 kitchens feeding about 150,000 people a day for next to nothing other than some surplus foodstuffs from the government. They wanted to expand into health as well and wanted our help. I agreed to loan them an organizer somehow and to host their president for training with our Peruvian leaders in Los Angeles.

Subsequently, we also added another partnership with the FENTAP, the union of water workers, and fought together to prevent privatization of water services in many cities in Peru. The partnerships ebbed and flowed, and before long the people we met in the comodores wanted something that was not there: their own organization. We began a project in San Juan Laragancho which became the founding group of ACORN Peru and the first project of what would become ACORN International.

Bridges Across the Southern Border

ACORN's Latino membership was growing rapidly along the borders from San Diego to Tuscon to El Paso to Brownsville. ACORN in the USA had been heavily involved in housing financing and predatory lending issues for years sitting across the table with some of the largest banking institutions in the world. Leaders from SEIU Local 100 in the Texas Rio Grande Valley lived below the border and commuted up to work in the schools and county jobs that allowed them to live even better south of the border. The director of ACORN's San Diego office and much of the staff were living in Tijuana and its suburbs and driving up to work to organize in the low and moderate income neighborhoods of this growing city. ACORN's immigrant members everywhere were always talking about the high price of *remisis* or remittances between their work and their distant families, and nowhere was this more common than along the border between the US and Mexico. The additional irony lay in the fact that when we were sitting across the table from Citibank or HSBC or Bank of America, we were also sitting across the table from the executives owning the largest banks in Mexico. In a global, computerized economy, why weren't these simple money transactions almost trivial matters? On one hand we had members not exactly demanding that we organize south of the border, but increasingly confused about why we weren't doing so, and on the other hand, it seemed that we had were at the table where we needed to be to impact on key issues and leverage the relationships into both support and change. We were able to partner with projects on both sides of the border, which eventually led to ACORN Mexico's first organizing operation opening in Tijuana. Moving forward to create the organization was easier than solving the intractable remittance issue, which continues to be a central concern.

Community-Labor and Great Canadian Organizers

In Vancouver a unique combination of union-owned businesses directed part of their profits to create the Columbia Foundation, and a farsighted entrepreneur, David Levy, with a sense of social responsibility and his debts to unions, as well as a board composed of union leaders from the head of the Canadian Labor Congress at the time, Ken Georgetti, and others, asked John Kay, its acting director, to help design a new project that could create a new kind of organizer in Canada with the ability to organize community-labor projects overlapping the workplace and neighborhood. I was fortunate to be drafted to design and head up the training program for this great and exciting experiment, which also immersed me in the labor and organizing politics and experiences within this great country for a year. The will and commitment to such a community-labor program did not survive, but meetings with activists and unions all over the country produced a steady sleeve tug of requests to work with them to build "an ACORN" in Canada. Seattle ACORN was an interesting operation in these same early years of the 21st Century. After a time of troubles the operation had learned to walk the tightrope of the "executive city" where fewer and fewer of our low and moderate income families could afford to live in Seattle itself, but were everywhere in the suburbs of Burien, White Settlement, and even commuting from Tacoma. ACORN's campaigns addressed like living wages and district elections and deepened its base. Judy Duncan, the lead organizer of the Seattle operation, was an interesting and talented organizer from Winnipeg in Canada. We kept trying to extend her Visa to work with us longer by six months here and six months there, but finally, despite our best efforts, it was clear she was going to have to return to her home country. I asked and she was game to see if we could build an ACORN Canada and as she mustered out of Seattle, we found ourselves not long afterward driving for hours through Jane and Finch, Scarborough, and a host of other working, "new Canadians," and diverse communities in greater Toronto. Now a short five years later there are 30,000 members in ACORN Canada in offices in Vancouver/

New Westminster, Ottawa, Toronto, and Hamilton and a score of campaigns, victories, and accomplishments for the organization and its great leadership and staff that Judy Duncan has painstakingly pulled together throughout the period. Sometimes in organizing, it is as devastatingly simple as following the river where the water wants to flow.

Organizers' Forum International Dialogues

Another strain running through many of our initiatives has been a small, almost ad hoc project, we put together more than a decade ago called The Organizers' Forum (www.organizersforum.org). Although this would almost seem like a footnote, the annual international dialogues of the Organizers' Forums put between one and two dozen community and union organizers together from the US and Canada to meet our counterparts in a non-stop diet of meetings for solid weeks in various countries. We have now been to Brazil, India, South Africa, Indonesia, Turkey, Russia, Australia, and Thailand all of which underscored the remarkably common quest for equity and justice by the disenfranchised no matter what their circumstances in the world, and the tremendous commonality of the challenges we faced organizationally and individually in doing the work. The Organizers' Forum for me as chair and for many of my *companeros* and *companeras* has been a profound and life-changing experience in understanding the world differently.

THE HUMAN CONNECTION FOR ORGANIZING·

I could go on. There is a story for each country that is both different and the same. In recent years the obvious takes over. More and more from the beginning when there seemed no way to say "yes," increasingly now the harder problem is saying "no." It seems trite to say that the world of our people is inextricably connected whether through the board rooms or the migration routes or internet, fast planes, or Skype. It seems myopic to have believed otherwise for the first 30 years of ACORN's work, but it was a self-curing coma. Unable to do more, it may have been just as well that we tried to mind our own shores. Sometimes the connections were both dramatic and almost fateful in an eerie and almost magical way.

At one of the first meetings between ACORN leaders in the United States and ACORN Canada leaders on a beautiful July day in a small meeting room in a dorm of the University of Toronto, as leaders from both organizations were introducing themselves their stories started to intertwine. A member of the ACORN Canada board from Pakistan mentioned having migrated from there to Dubai to the US before finally ending up in Toronto. One of the members of the ACORN US delegation was Johnny Clark, the treasurer of the organization at the time and a recently retired postal worker in Dallas. He started asking his brother member penetrating questions about where he worked and within five minutes it became clear that he worked with his brother at a convenience store in Dallas and Johnny had delivered mail to him on his route. They laughed and went on, but I was awestruck at the way people have now trumped all boundaries that we might want to imagine in ways that are virtually inconceivable.

Though the very short history of ACORN International as an emerging membership organization among lower income families has strong roots in the United States, looking forward, the organization faces much different challenges and opportunities. After leaving ACORN in the USA after 38 years in June 2008, I have been fortunate as chief organizer to give more time and attention to the unique contribution that the organization can make in the countries where we work. The relentless partisan and conservative attacks on ACORN in the USA during the 2008 election campaign which saw a former community organizer, Barack Obama become President of the USA, and the subsequent media stings and distortions in ACORN offices in New York, Baltimore, Los Angeles, San Diego, and Philadelphia that led to an illegal, but lethal, Congressional defunding, and a desertion of support from all but its members, which has crippled the organization to the degree that where it once was a powerhouse, the organization is now fragmenting in a Darwinian way in a struggle to survive with doubts that even the King's soldiers could ever reassemble Humpty-Dumpty. The impact of these threats was severe enough that for any current projects in the United States, we are now identifying ourselves as Community Organizations International, while we remain ACORN International for our global work and in the countries where we have affiliates. The ripple effects of the anti-ACORN activities in the USA have been profound and forced extensive self-examination and assessments of our program.

THE STRUCTURE OF ACORN INTERNATIONAL

Part of our strength going forward is rooted in the federated nature of ACORN International and the separate strengths of the formative parts of the organization in the seven countries where we work as we enter the second decade of the 21st Century. Part of the emerging lesson of the demise of ACORN /USA is that a stool needs many legs to stand. Though that had seemed to be the case in the US, the walls and moats built around various parts of the organization were allowed to erode and crumble as the assaults raged and the structures were scaled, allowing the barbarians to enter. Countries are different than corporations with their own laws and requirements allowing ACORN International to assist in assuring that each of the affiliates is registered and structured appropriately in their home country, while creating the formal and informal relationships vital to success that welds the parts into a whole when useful while maintaining the flexibility of individual national action as the normal rule of the work.

We are also quick to acknowledge that the increasing strength and robustness of ACORN Canada has given our international work support, capacity, and range that would not be possible without the diversity and leadership of our ACORN Canada members and staff, which has been sustaining. Canadians as opposed to Americans are not under any illusion about the need to bind them to the rest of the world in something other than arrogance and might. As ACORN International builds a new organizing model for a new constituency in a new century, the role of ACORN Canada has been foundational. The top leadership of ACORN International is a Canadian in the best tradition of our work, Kay Bisnath, a woman of Indian origin who migrated to Canada from the Caribbean islands, bridging virtually the world of ACORN International in her own life story. Judy Duncan, as head organizer of ACORN Canada, has been a leader in making sure that the international operations were integrated with the national operations in Canada, including assigning regular hours from her special projects staff on a weekly basis to support the international work. Our webmaster and web design is centered in Toronto.

We have a vibrant intern program in Toronto that takes responsibility for the regular upkeep of our website, translation of articles, and even an intern-based fundraising program at places like Tequila Bookworm where volunteer salsa teachers help cement more ties to ACORN International as well. The leadership of the first international campaign and actions in the spring of 2009 came from ACORN Canada as well, so it was not surprising that, as a result, the first victory also came from concessions made by Scotiabank based on the demands and actions by Toronto ACORN.

Dues and Fundraising

All are important because the strains of attempting to build a sustainable organization on membership dues that adds soles, rupees, pesos, and shillings to support the organization that can reach past its beginnings and achieve some organizational scale within the areas where we organize is very difficult. Clearly, dues alone are insufficient to allow us to invest in expansion within existing countries or meeting the demands placed on us in new countries. At the same time we are resistant to the donor-based culture that both shrinks the autonomy of the organization and its program as well as inserting a culture based on external favor and resources that is crippling to the long-term future of the organizing project. Most of our energy is focused on finding, at the grassroots level and through new available internet and social networking tools, ways in which we can bridge the resource needs of our international organizing by linking people to people and tightening these ties. Most of these projects are still in the formative stage including the standard solicitations but more interestingly street canvassing which is used in India and other large cities and partnering with a women's coop in Honduras (soon to be our eighth country) to sell coffee where we both would benefit. We are convinced that we have the will and now must find the way.

Partnering:

'Partnering' has been more than a word for ACORN International. It has been more a way of life. Earlier I mentioned the importance to ACORN Peru of the partnership with the FENTAP union around water, but just as essential has been the emerging partnership with the great British Columbia Government Employees Union (BCGEU) and its leadership. They have been great supporters of the growth of ACORN Canada of course, but they are also true internationalists in the best sense of the concept and have been the constant support for our organizing of informal workers in Mumbai, Bangalore, and Delhi, as well as regular, leading participants in the Organizers' Forum. The same has been true of small funders (Frontera Fund, Paradox Fund, Vista Hermosa, the Chrysalis Fund, and the Tides Foundation) who have embraced the mission of ACORN International and steadfastly—and patiently—invested in the fragile opportunity of building something where the odds were so great for failure but the rewards so powerful and permanent in success. On the local level, we have found partners that see the potential of a membership organization of the poor, rather than "just another NGO," as so many have said. Their contributions have often meant life and death to the local organizations whether the *Comedores Populares de Peru* and FENTAP in the first projects in Peru or COPA-K, the aptly named Community Organization Practitioners of Kenya, which has been our friend, landlord, advisor, and jack-of-all-trades in Nairobi, or most recently COMUCAP, the women's coop in Honduras, which is so helpful in opening up that country for a new ACORN International project in 2010.

Our partnership with COPA-K is a good example of how critical such deep relationships can be in enabling organizing to develop. Originally, we had planned to begin organizing in early 2008 having traveled to Nairobi several times earlier in the year to meet with a variety of groups, NGO's, and unions. Suddenly everything was postponed and cast in doubt with the closeness of the election for President in the fall of 2007. In a surprise to many in Africa that had touted Kenya as the most stable democracy on the continent, the accusations of election fraud claiming the re-election of the existing leadership despite overwhelming popular sentiment and belief that he had lost, erupted into deadly tribal violence that was especially pronounced in some of poorest areas in the city and countryside. Clearly ACORN International had to adjust its plans, and as fundamentally, being able to work in Nairobi at all was going to depend much more on the strength of our partnerships, if we were going to go forward at all. COPA-K became more than a partner. They became both gatekeeper and guide advocating constantly for us to move forward once calm was restored, and convincing us to visit again in early 2009. Lawrence Apiyo, the director of COPA-K, personally walked with me through a half-dozen slums introducing me to people they had worked with closely and making the case pro-and-con on where we might begin the organizing. Perhaps more critically, we knew we needed to hire a least two organizers to begin, one from each dominant tribe, so that we would be able to organize successfully and not be drawn into the vestiges of the recent violence.

With COPA-K's intercession, I was able to interview a good number of experienced activists with community experience to find the right two people with the skills, motivation, and interests necessary to begin our work. The success of the launch in Korogochu of ACORN Kenya in 2010 was due to hard work by an organizing committee of more than 30 people from the communities and the two excellent organizers, Sammy Ndirangu and David Musungu, but without being able to forge the kind of partnership with COPA-K with frequent work and discussions over close to a decade, it would never have happened.

On the other hand, grassroots organizing of low-and-moderate income families, and flatly speaking, the poor in the mega-slums, faces huge barriers in finding support outside of the immediate constituency being organized. The work of ACORN Canada has been virtually the exception proving the rule. ACORN Canada has been able to build bridges of support to diverse middle income constituencies for its work, has regularly launched appeals in such communities for its work, and has created political coalitions that advance campaigns and the membership agenda. The isolation of the poor in the other countries is virtually absolute with expectations of servility rather than potential partnership. The only emerging hope of a different level of support may be now emerging in our work in Mumbai, India through our ACORN Foundation (India) and ACORN India. There our work in the Dharavi slum with ragpickers in the wake of the hit movie, *Slumdog Millionaire,* has become a cause for some in Bollywood, for the Blue Frog jazz club, and even startlingly for the U.S. Consulate and some larger corporations like Bharrat Petroleum and their corporate social responsibility program. A cause and 'doing good,' though is not a partnership of course.

Where that is evolving slowly, and interestingly, is on a joint project between an initial list of 23 schools, including the American School and the French School, where a partnership between the schools and ACORN International has the students and schools collecting all wet and dry trash so that the waste pickers organized through our Dharavi Project can pick up and sort the trash to increase their livelihoods. This has been slow going, but we are optimistic that a real partnership might evolve here replacing a demeaning notion of our membership as a social work project. Additional efforts being organized by sponsors to do a half dozen concerts for the ACORN Foundation in Dharavi, celebrations at the Nature Center to support us, and other work, may also lead to some support that breaks through the class and caste barriers of India, but, frankly, in many instances, it is too early to tell. It takes a huge village to organize across the time zones of the globe!

Focus on Mega-Slums

The other early lesson of our work has been the need to focus. Yes, right, it's a *big* world! Where we have found ourselves moving more and more of our concentration in many countries is towards the mega-slums. Our work in San Juan Laranguancho, the 1.5 million person squatters' community at the outskirts of Lima was a natural place to work with ACORN Peru without realizing at first that this was one of the largest slums in the world. La Matanza on the outskirts of Buenos Aires also had more than a million residents while NEZA on the fringe of Mexico City, with almost 3 million inhabitants, might be the largest. Korogochu, where we began our work in Nairobi was not even the largest in that African city, but with 350,000 people was the oldest and the place where it seemed we could make the most difference. Dharavi in the center of Mumbai in the wake of *Slumdog Millionaire* had its own sudden cachet, but with almost a million people was certainly one of the larger mega-slums not only in India, but all of Asia. Delhi's program of slum removal to the outskirts of the city in the mask of public policy and in preparation for the Commonwealth Games provided other challenges. With the worldwide trend of migration to the cities, ACORN International was surprised at the number of traditional government supported NGOs whose focus remained in rural areas, while so little attention was being given to the screaming infrastructure and survival needs in these mega-slums. These were poor, working families often employed in informal labor and living in highly informal conditions that seemed to jump at the opportunity to build their own organizations with the help of ACORN International and support them enthusiastically and aggressively.

Organizing Informal Workers

An early meeting of our waste-pickers association in East Delhi led to a meeting with the board after the more than 200 person Sunday afternoon session with the members in the middle of their living and sorting areas had finished, and produced an interesting but not surprising conclusion. When asked where they wanted to focus and their central priorities, they boiled them down to two: first, they did not want their work "privatized" by city subcontractors, and, secondly, they wanted to find a way to have a teacher or school for their children after the working day was done.

TIES THAT BIND TO A POWERFUL FUTURE

In our short history, ACORN International has repeatedly found that there are similar demands and themes, whether the pressing demands of basic livelihood for *cartoneros* in Buenos Aires or rickshaw pullers in India or the living wages in Ottawa and New Westminster in Canada, or forcing landlords in Toronto to make repairs or trying to get title to housing units in Lima and sort out who owns the vast squatting units in Kibera and Korogochu where there are landlords and tenants somehow co-existing on vast acreage that the City of Nairobi does not even record on municipal maps.

The answer is not simply that ACORN International works in countries that are often at various stages of emergence from repression and authoritarian governance that stifled the peoples' voice as was the case for many years in Peru, Dominican Republic, and Argentina, as well as arguably the long stranglehold of the PRI in Mexico, the huge multi-party democratic contradiction of post-colonial Indian that made it ungovernable, the dysfunction now in Kenya in the wake of the 2008 post-election violence, and even the military coup in Honduras that has released the demands for organization in San Pedro Sula and Tegucigalpa, which have led to the invitation for ACORN International to organize there, although this is undoubtedly part of the problem. The deeper dilemma is that these are divided countries submerged in challenges that have turned dead hearts and tin ears to the problems of the poor within their cities. The global concern is stability, not democracy, and international donor agencies like the IMF and World Bank classify these countries as "middle class" and able to solve their own problems with their own resources. People and the poor are therefore on their own.

It may be far afield, but it all sounds like home. Certainly these are themes that echoed for ACORN for 40 years, and are now a standard for ACORN International and its country partners and affiliates have now raised to make it their own mission to bring participatory, democratic, empowering, membership based organization to low and moderate income families around the world. Since we have lost the ability to say, "no," the fight is now to organize the millions of people necessary to make sure that the powers that be, country to country, and around the world also learn how to finally say, "yes!"

EDITOR'S COMMENT

Unlike previous writers, Wade Rathke makes partnerships political and personal. He is also demonstrating social democracy as a goal that everyone in the world can pursue. At times, he reveals his tactics by reaching across borders. It may be the accident of a staff member having to return to Canada, but the decisions are also based on funding that he is able to obtain. His community action approach is also compatible with the approaches of government, business and community arts groups, as our next contributor demonstrates.

Although there are common problems in different countries, there are unique problems to different countries which is a problem that Mr. Rathke does not reconcile. For example, he notes the classic Indian paradoxes of "registered" slums that receive some sanitation and water support even though they abut teeming slums with nothing other than the lack of registration. Why do not other countries contain similar contradictions? Other writers juxtapose contradictions which in each case are revealing in their distinctive interpretation. The authors who are primarily professionals are not as revealing about the conflicts and challenges of partnerships and coalitions as are advocates.

Chapter 9
Linking Community, Business and Schools

Rosalyn Black, Senior Manager, Research and Evaluation,
The Foundation for Young Australians

International commentary on the priorities of nation building recognizes the central role of schooling in building economic prosperity, civic engagement and social capital. Many national vision statements present a charter for progress based on the twin goals of community cohesion and quality education. There is now an established view that these goals cannot be wholly met through top-down public policy. Instead, cross-sectoral partnerships have for some years brought together the skills and resources of the public and private sectors and to redefine their roles, responsibilities and relationships in regards to numerous policy domains including schooling. While these new sectoral collaborations proliferate, the creation and maintenance of effective and fruitful partnerships remains a challenge for many schools.

The Foundation for Young Australians (FYA), which includes the Education Foundation division, is an independent not-for-profit organization with a mission to empower young Australians to be successful learners and creative, active and valued citizens. A partnership approach is at the heart of FYA's strategy. FYA plays a powerful role in leading and informing partnerships between schools, business and the community, both at the system level and on the ground. Through its research and initiatives, FYA analyses the forces enabling or inhibiting partnerships, models and brokering effective partnerships, helping schools build the skills for partnership, creating a platform for young people's involvement within their schools and communities and working with government, peak bodies and other influential agencies to create the systemic conditions under which partnerships can flourish. This examination of some of the work of FYA provides insights into the ways in which an independent organization can lead educational reform and improve life opportunities for young people by building the capacity of schools and their communities. FYA works collaboratively with the government, school, business, community, not-for-profit and philanthropic sectors across Australia. It also leads and brokers collaborations across these sectors; its roots are in the history of FYA and its Education Foundation division.

PARTNERSHIPS' HISTORY

Originating from the Small Change Foundation, Education Foundation was formed to meet a need within the Australian educational landscape. Its founder, Ellen Koshland, grew up in the United States in a culture with a strong history of community participation and philanthropy in relation to public education. By contrast,

Australians have historically tended to see government system schools as the responsibility of government. While private donations for public education—directly or through an intermediary organization—is a longstanding and accepted practice in the United States, the Australian taxation system still provides no incentive for direct contributions to government schools.

Building on a model well established in the United States through organizations such as the San Francisco Education Fund but relatively unknown in Australia at the time, Ellen launched Education Foundation on the basis of six central ideas: that small funds could make a big difference to teachers and students; that schools represented a rich laboratory for innovation; that individuals, companies and trusts could support needed innovations in schools without replicating government funding; that schools needed greater public recognition for what they did well; that powerful learning could take place beyond the classroom through rich tasks and authentic contexts; and that whole school change could be leveraged through outside support.

In its earlier role as a grant-making agency, Education Foundation channeled funds from individual and corporate donors and philanthropic trusts to hundreds of innovative projects in metropolitan, regional and rural Australian schools. Small grants and simple processes meant that teachers could apply for funding without navigating school and other bureaucratic processes. One year funding cycles meant that projects delivered tangible outcomes within a timeframe that schools understood. The flexibility of the grants provided a license for teacher creativity in a way that found real resonance in schools and boosted morale even where the actual funding was minimal.

At the same time, because this grant-making process did not require the involvement of school leadership, it worked against the likelihood of whole school reform. Education Foundation seeded significant innovations that were incorporated as mainstream practice in individual schools, but by the late 1990s it began to want to effect wider improvements. As the enrolment drift towards private schools accelerated, its trustees perceived that a more strategic intervention was required to prevent public education becoming a peripheral system. They identified a wider role for Education Foundation in analyzing issues affecting public education, raising the profile of the sector's achievements, encouraging new policy and practice and prompting business and community support for government system schools.

This awareness coincided with the emergence of a number of synergistic forces for change in Australian education. New cross-sectoral approaches began to emerge, supported by policy, which combined the energies and resources of the public, private and philanthropic sectors in efforts to bring about improvements in a range of social domains, typically at the community level. As part of this, there was a fresh recognition of the importance of public education in meeting a range of social goals. Leading voices in the philanthropic sector began to argue for more strategic grant-making to bring about lasting change in relation to school practice and young people's outcomes. At the same time, recognition and development of new practice of corporate social responsibility began to generate more strategic interventions in school education from companies.

These alignments during the 1990s were part of a well-documented international movement from 'big government' to various interpretations of a state that achieves its core social policy aims by fostering communities of mutual interest within sectors other than government and at the local level. While this Third Way agenda has attracted justifiable criticism, its legacy continues to be felt in the integration of economic and social goals that permeates the policies of Australian federal and state governments and in the willingness of business and other sectors to assume genuine roles and responsibilities in relation to the improvement of young people's educational outcomes and wellbeing.

In this environment, there continues to be a clear role for an organization like FYA and its Education Foundation division that serves as a focus for cooperative action designed to achieve this improvement. FYA conducts powerful, partnership-based programs with the potential to achieve sustained education reform, engage new community support for education and inform policy. These include: ruMAD? (are you Making A Difference?), which is discussed later in this chapter; the Classroom to

Community program that helps schools form learning partnerships with their own immediate communities; and the Worlds of Work program that engages city-based workplaces to increase young people's awareness and ability to access opportunities in life and work outside their local environment.

It also conducts commissions, and is contracted to undertake research into new directions for Australian schooling including education partnerships and networks. Its work in this area to date includes studies of the capacity of schools in high poverty contexts to initiate and sustain partnerships (Black, 2007), reports for government that analyze the barriers and enablers to effective school-community partnership and partnership-based models of schooling (Black, 2008b, 2009; Black et al., 2010), and books, chapters and papers that consider what a more collaborative approach to education provision could look like for Australia, what is required to bring such collaboration about and the role of young people within this (Black, 2008a; Black, forthcoming; Black & Walsh, 2009; Walsh & Black, 2009). The phenomenon of school-community partnership is not a new one in Australia: especially in low socioeconomic contexts, Australian schools have a history of working in partnership both within and beyond their immediate local communities. At the same time, recent policy initiatives such as the Australian Government's **School Business Community Partnership Brokers** program means that partnership is even more strongly on the agenda for more schools and that business and communities are more directly supported in seeking and developing partnerships with schools.

Australian schools develop partnerships with business and the community for multiple reasons. These relationships take multiple forms. When they work, they have powerful outcomes for young people including greater engagement in school, better learning and post-school pathways and enhanced resilience and social functioning. They also have powerful outcomes for the community because they bring people together to create fresh solutions to local problems, combine knowledge and resources across the community and boost purpose and confidence amongst previously marginalized groups. Schools benefit from greater dynamism and reform, a new role as a lifelong learning hub for the entire community, a more open school culture and increased human and capital resources (Black, 2009; Black & Walsh, 2009; Johns et al., 2000; Kilpatrick et al., 2002).

Ensuring the effectiveness of partnerships can be a hard task, however. One of the obstacles to success is the variation of assumptions about what is actually meant by partnership. With the proliferation of partnership practice has come an accompanying terminological proliferation where terms like partnership, linkage, alliance, collaboration, network and joined up approach are used interchangeably to describe what is actually a multitude of very different arrangements. One extensive study (Jordan et al., 2001) has identified 13 distinct areas of school-community connection, less than a third of which might be defined as partnership. At the level of policy and research, this looseness of definition makes it almost impossible to analyze what is actually taking place or to ascertain its effectiveness and impact. At the level of local practice, it can make it difficult for schools and their partners to find the common language and common ground that is necessary for the development of the shared goals on which success depends. It also contributes to contradictory expectations about the partnership and the roles of each partner within it.

Partnerships may be linkages between a small number of similar organizations in order to achieve a limited range of outcomes. They may be multifaceted arrangements with multiple goals involving a large number of organizations with diverse purposes and structures. They may be directly negotiated by partners or brokered by a third party. Partner organizations may be involved in other partnerships, contributing to a complex web of extended relationships. While this diversity of practice is both desirable and unavoidable, there is a consensus that an effective partnership is an intentional relationship guided by a vision linked to the organizational aims of each partner and translated into achievable common goals that cannot be accomplished by the individual partners alone. This relationship should be an equal one that is driven and led by the partner organizations and that fosters trust between them. It should recognize differences in organizational and sectoral culture while enabling the cross-fertilization of ideas and building the capacity of each partner. It should provide the necessary time and resources to achieve its goals (Edwards et al., 2002; Jordan et al., 2001).

FYA's own research suggests that few school-community or school-business partnerships meet these criteria (Black, 2009). This raises a number of key questions that are pertinent both for government and for other agencies fostering education partnerships. These include the question of whether positive change can in fact be achieved through forms of cooperative endeavor that do not meet the definitions of effective partnership. They include the question of how government and other agencies can nurture schools' capacity to develop the processes for effective partnership, especially in the case of schools serving high poverty communities with complex needs. They also include the question of how young people can be brought into the partnership picture, not only as its beneficiaries but also as its active drivers and leaders.

PARTNERSHIPS FOR CHANGE

FYA's experience over many years suggests that innovative schools are good at building short term relationships but that many lack the necessary capacity to set longer horizons. This may be a natural outcome of a sector that typically operates within short time-frames of terms, semesters or single years. It may reflect a need for observable outcomes in a field where teachers rarely see the tangible products of their efforts. In sectors whose practitioners are time-poor and permanently suffering from overload, short bursts of new practice bring fresh energy, but continuity may require more than many schools have to give. It may also reflect a cynicism about the short horizons of many government reforms. The uncertainty that new programs will survive beyond a three year electoral cycle does not support a culture of long term thinking.

This climate of flux means that even strong partnerships are vulnerable. Some of this vulnerability is also a function of the way in which many schools conduct partnerships as icing on the educational cake, that is, as initiatives that operate outside the school's central frameworks. In these instances, the partnership remains invisible within the school's organizational vision, future planning, budget, staffing arrangements or timetables. This means, in turn, that it operates outside the measurement and reporting regimes required by educational systems.

One risk of this situation is that these partnerships are operating under the systemic radar, unrecognized and unsupported. In an era of growing educational measurement, initiatives that are not seen to contribute to schools' central accountabilities are highly vulnerable: they are the first to be discontinued as pressures mount on schools to meet centrally set targets (Angus, 2006). Another and related risk is that the partnership will not be subject to proper monitoring or measurement. This further exacerbates an existing trend whereby surprisingly few school-community partnerships are subject to any evaluation, either by the school or its partners. This reduces the capacity of the school system overall to benefit and learn from proven models of practice. More fundamentally, it means that the impact of partnerships cannot be known (Black, 2009).

In too many instances, school-community partnerships are engineered by a single heroic teacher or small group of teachers. This has multiple negative effects. Trying to innovate in the face of the dominant school culture is a recipe for failure and teachers who push for new approaches without bringing other staff with them face isolation, exhaustion and the demoralizing knowledge that their work will not have a broader impact in the school. It also makes the partnership highly vulnerable. What happens if its lone advocate changes roles, moves schools or becomes too exhausted to maintain it? Effective partnerships and partnership thinking are highly dependent on school leadership. They flourish when school leaders have an outward looking vision which welcomes new opportunities and when they see themselves as "learning leaders" for the whole community (Kilpatrick et al., 2002, p. 105). This mode of leadership integrates the learning from new relationships into teacher practice and into the school culture and it fosters an internal culture of cooperation that has been shown to have a powerful impact on student outcomes (Black, 2007).

Teachers in these schools work together to plan teaching and curriculum have a role in school decision-making and share intellectual and social resources. This provides an internal strength on which the school can build collaborative relationships with the external community. Unfortunately, this collaborative culture is still alien to many schools. Without it, new partnerships will evaporate with time and leave little behind.

This raises the question of what the legacy of partnership should be. On the one hand, it has been suggested that the process of partnership may be just as valuable as its outcomes (Raysmith, 2001). In that case, the sustainability of individual partnerships may be less important than the social capital they generate. On the other hand, cultural change requires the accretion of initiatives and experiences over a long time-frame and with the support of policy. The Australian educational landscape is littered with discontinued or underutilized programs and partnerships that leave little legacy except in the experience of individual students or small cohorts. As research conducted by FYA shows, it is also a landscape strongly characterized by structural and increasing inequities (Keating, 2009). In such a climate, educational activity such as partnership formation must be able to improve outcomes for a wider number of young people.

Over the past decade, numerous initiatives and agreements have pumped corporate, philanthropic and public funds into school-community partnership programs around Australia. This has had clear and observable benefits. It has helped to create a climate within which partnership has become an accepted approach. It has seeded practice in a wide range of schools and settings. In many instances, it has led to direct and tangible improvements in the quality of young people's learning and wider life experience. In many instances, however, partnerships have been funded or fostered as pilot projects without clear mechanisms for continuity. The pilot project model is a favorite vehicle for agencies wanting to make a mark on the landscape or to seed change without committing ongoing resources. On the one hand, schools need these external resources and triggers for change. On the other hand, the multiplicity and uncoordinated nature of these resources and triggers can easily overwhelm schools, especially those that serve high poverty and high need populations.

Short-term relationships may also present risks for the school. Where external funding or support is too limited to ensure the maintenance of a partnership-based initiative, this can leave the school attempting to meet those costs from its own limited resources, conducting the partnership at a lower level than intended or facing the almost certain knowledge that it will not continue once the funding runs out (Carrington, 2003). There is an apparent trend for schools in low socioeconomic areas of the state to be more involved in partnerships than schools in more affluent areas (Black, 2009). While this looks at first glance to be a positive trend, some of these schools are juggling large numbers of partnerships and relationships with no assurance of quality or sustainability. This may create innovation fatigue in teachers, drain school capacity and have a limited impact on student outcomes.

There are hopeful signs, however, in the changes that are taking place within the corporate sector and its relationship to schools. The establishment of corporate social responsibility as a fixture of corporate activity has seen a burgeoning of new relationships that require direct linkages and dialogue with the community and that represent a major shift from the traditional practice of arms-length or 'chequebook' sponsorship. Like their counterparts elsewhere (Hood & Rubin, 2004), Australian and Australian-based companies are showing signs of moving away from individual school assistance and the adopt-a-school initiatives of the 1990s and towards support for change at the regional or systemic levels, where they believe they can have the greatest impact in the medium to long term.

This is most evident in the rapidly growing trend of employee volunteering (Volunteering Australia, 2006). This recognizes that employees are also community members who provide a natural point of connection between the company and the community. Building corporate community involvement through their employees builds capacity for the company. Benefits include improved organizational effectiveness, a positive workplace culture with higher employee morale and cooperation, a reputation as a good corporate citizen and improved community relationships, greater standing and credibility on specific community issues, attractiveness to potential employees, retention of valued employees and a more productive workforce (Suggett et al., 2000). Corporate employees, especially younger employees, now expect that their company will provide opportunities and support for volunteering in the community. As a result, more than 60 per cent of Australian companies provide up to three paid days per year for staff volunteer activity and nearly a third of companies have a dedicated member of staff responsible for coordinating and supporting this activity (Centre for Corporate Public Affairs, 2007).

Schools First is a national awards program that has committed $15 million in awards funding over three years to recognize and encourage excellence in Australian school-community partnerships. The National Australia Bank (NAB), Australian Council for Educational Research (ACER) and FYA are working together on this national initiative. This partnership between one of Australia's largest financial institutions, a not-for-profit research organization with an international reputation, and a not-for-profit organization specializing in programs for young people, shows what can be achieved through shared commitment. All three organizations are committed to the goal of fostering sustainable, effective school-community partnerships as a means of improving outcomes for young people. The program draws on the expertise, goodwill and resources of each organization.

This partnership has its origins in 2008 when senior staff from ACER and FYA met to identify ways in which their respective organizations could collectively make a difference to young Australians' educational outcomes and increase their sense of connectedness to their local communities. Meanwhile, NAB realized that it, too, could contribute positively to the lives of young people by playing a more significant role in the education sector, using its considerable resources to support a high profile project that could improve student outcomes and school capacity. As a result, NAB agreed to fund ACER and FYA's proposal for a national school-community partnership program and to become a partner in the initiative. The Schools First Board includes all three partner organizations. It meets regularly to monitor the progress of the Schools First project and provide ongoing support and advice (NAB, 2010). In 2009, the program's first year of operation, 1,552 applications were received from a wide range of schools in every state and territory: this represents an application by one in six Australian schools. More than 35 per cent of these applications were from schools in areas that are among the most disadvantaged in Australia. The total award funding provided in 2009 was AUS$4.95 million. This provided 68 Impact Awards for outstanding school-community partnerships and a further 20 Seed Funding Awards for developing partnerships with potential.

The winning projects are characterized by regular monitoring and review processes. They show clear evidence of collaborative decision-making and planning from their outset and their activities are educationally valid and student-focused. The best applications also demonstrate how the partnership will be sustained into the future. The inaugural winner of the National Impact Award is Canberra College, which has partnered with the Child, Youth and Women's Health Program from the Australian Capital Territory Department of Health to create the CC Cares unit. This is a separate senior campus established alongside the main school to support the needs of pregnant or parenting students as well as young students not experiencing success in mainstream school settings. Of the young parents who attend, 95 per cent bring their children with them to the school. The campus also offers an adult evening education program and a one stop shop for educational and health services. Students have shown greater engagement with school, higher rates of educational completion and an increased sense of belonging, both to the school and the local community.

YOUNG PEOPLE AND PARTNERSHIPS

School-community partnerships frequently invoke the needs of young people as a prime motive for their creation, yet young people are typically left out of the discussion about how partnerships are to be created or implemented. My PhD study, which is being undertaken at time of writing with the Australian Youth Research Centre at The University of Melbourne, illustrates the fact that this omission of young people persists despite a strong policy agenda that seeks to foster young people's civic and community participation (Black, 2010). This is an extension or facet of the policy push, which I have described earlier, that seeks to maximize the activity of citizenship at the level of the community.

In Australia, as in comparable systems, this stance has seen a proliferation of place-based initiatives designed to build the capacity of individuals and communities, the reallocation of responsibility for social agendas amongst the public and private sectors, and a corresponding growth in the role of non-state actors in domains previously seen as the responsibility of the state (Angus, 2009; Jupp, 2000). Increasingly, these statements describe and advocate a role for young people as an antidote to their perceived social exclusion and disengagement (Bessant, 2004). Recent examples include the guiding principles of the national Office for Youth, which state that the Australian Government "respects and understands the value and contributions young people offer as citizens of today, not just the leaders of tomorrow" (Office for Youth, 2010) and the National Strategy for Young Australians, which articulates the Government's vision that all young people "engage in community life and influence decisions that affect them" (Australian Government, 2009, p. 3).

The omission of young people from the discourse and practice of partnership also persists despite evidence that young people are keen to participate in their immediate community: 80 per cent of young Australians believe that being a good citizen entails participation in activities that are of benefit to the local community (Mellor & Kennedy,

2003). A growing body of research, including research commissioned by FYA, shows that young people are willing, even eager, to participate and make a difference in relation to a range of community issues (Arvanitakis & Marren, 2009; Collin, 2008; Horsley & Costley, 2008; Kimberley, 2010; Taylor, 2010; Wierenga, 2003). Young Australians are keen to contribute to the leadership of their schools (Walsh & Black, 2009). This is in marked contrast to young people in other settings. One Canadian study, for example, has found that even having a say in school decision-making is unimaginable for students (Raby, 2008). A New Zealand study produced parallel findings: of 66 students asked to describe how they might participate in their school, only one recognized that this could include participation in the school's decision-making processes (Taylor et al., 2008). Australian students believe that they could make a beneficial contribution to the operation of their schools, although they do not feel that their participation is well supported (Mellor & Kennedy, 2003). They want their schools to connect them to "the world 'outside' where public decisions are made" (Harris & Wyn, 2009, p. 340).

Bentley observed a number of years ago that "young people themselves are probably the greatest untapped resource in the process of educational transformation" (2002, p. 15). The evidence is that little has changed. If anything, opportunities for young people to participate in the process of educational change—including the creation of fruitful education partnerships—appear to

291

be diminishing rather than increasing (Mitra & Gross, 2009). Instead, the invitations and opportunities for young people to take an active and agential role in their school are both constrained and compromised. In particular, as Percy-Smith explains, many youth or student participation initiatives are limited in their scope, their influence and the impact that they are permitted to achieve (2010) ruMAD? (are you Making A Difference?), an initiative of Education Foundation, seeks to bring the vision and abilities of young people into the school-community partnership picture. This youth participation and leadership framework has been recognized by policymakers as an exemplar of student participation (Keamy et al., 2007; Manefield et al., 2007). When fully implemented, it is supported by the school as part of its core practice and forms part of an effort to turn the classroom and the school into genuine learning communities where students have an active role in decisions about school organization, curriculum, teaching and learning (Black et al., 2009).

ruMAD? operates through four phases. During the Understanding Phase, young people identify their vision for community or social change. They agree upon one issue that they wish to pursue and develop a detailed project proposal for action. During the Planning Phase, young people plan the implementation of this proposal, ensuring that the project is SMART (Specific, Measureable, Achievable, Realistic and Timely). They form connections with community organizations or individual partners that can assist them. These may be local agencies or wider social action groups already working in the field. During the Action Phase, young people implement the project. As part of this implementation, they are encouraged to gather evidence that indicates its impact and effectiveness. Finally, the Evaluation and Celebration Phase provides an opportunity to reflect on the process as well as the outcomes of their social change initiative and to mark its conclusion with a performance, a conference, a publication, an exhibition or a community event.

The story of one small rural school exemplifies the ruMAD? experience. Whitfield District Primary School serves an agricultural township northeast of Melbourne. Jessie's Creek, which runs through the town and alongside the school, had become an eyesore. It was overgrown with exotic weeds and used as a dump for rubbish and the community had abandoned attempts to regenerate it. Using the ruMAD? framework, students took up the challenge. They started by trying to clear and restore vegetation to the creek, but soon recognized that the task was too big to tackle alone and began to raise community awareness about the issue. After carrying out a biodiversity study to analyze the environmental values of the creek, students surveyed community attitudes and produced a brochure promoting the challenges and future potential of the site. They issued a press release and shared their findings with conservation groups, the local government council and the regional catchment management authority. The Authority responded by conducting a comprehensive assessment of the work required to bring about change. With the assistance of the Authority and its Water Watch program, students helped to conduct a trial of the effects of regeneration activities including extensive replanting. In this way, what began as a small, student endeavor became the focus of a large, formal and sustainable community collaboration. Further recognition came in the form of a national land-care award and generous funding from Commonwealth Environmental Fund and Australian Geographic.

A second example comes from south-western Victoria. As part of its operations, the local government conducts a youth council, a group of young people drawn from each of the five local schools. A longstanding concern of this council had been the consistently negative portrayal of young people in the local media. This poor image had some basis in fact: young people in the community were known to engage in antisocial or self-destructive behavior in the absence of safer and healthier leisure opportunities. Using the ruMAD? framework, the youth councilors undertook a strategy to change this community perception and address its underlying causes. A project was designed entitled *Ctrl-Alt-Delete: It's Time for Youth to Push the Switch*. Its intentions were to *control* community issues, *alter* perceptions by and of young people, and *delete* negative images of the local youth. Because the youth council wanted to promulgate this message to younger people in the area, they selected primary school students as the audience. The primary outcome of the project was a Youth Expo designed to inform young people about the range of leisure activities in the local area and to generate positive media coverage. The youth council secured the local sports stadium, engaged the support of local school principals and enlisted local sponsors and media. The Expo attracted over 800 people, including 600 students. The local radio station broadcast live to air from the Expo on the day and the youth council was inundated with letters of support and appreciation from the community. The less public outcomes of the project included the substantial increase in confidence and agency experienced by youth councilors themselves (Waters-Lynch, 2008).

CONCLUSION

Despite numerous reform efforts, there is a growing gap in the educational and life outcomes of young Australians. While the ultimate responsibility for solutions to this gap must rest with policymakers and school systems, there is a great deal that can be done at the local level. Fruitful partnerships that link schools, business and communities can do a great deal to improve the life opportunities and outcomes of young people. They can also do the important work of cultural change, fostering the creation of an education system that is built on collaboration rather than competition and encouraging the recognition that the future of young people is the responsibility of the whole community.

An independent organization like FYA has tremendous potential to reframe the discourse of schooling and carve out a new social role for schools as builders of social capital and communal wellbeing. The equitable and participatory cross-sectoral relationships facilitated by FYA are themselves models for a new social alliance between schools and other community institutions. These alliances have the potential to build significant capacity within Australian schooling by legitimizing the efforts and innovations of schools, sharing knowledge around the sector, brokering entry points into an often closed culture and acting as a catalyst for change. They also have the potential to affect a needed cultural shift wherein young people become recognized and integral players in education decision-making, not just at the level of their own school but at the community and systemic levels as well. This is, after all, the ultimate endpoint of any education partnership; young people are enabled and recognized as confident shapers of their own lives and the world in which they live.

EDITOR'S COMMENT

By limiting businesses donations through foundations changes the context so that business involvement is not essential for foundation success. The language of education has not become one of corporate responsibility. The range of programs has been limited and there is a strong attempt to encourage grass-root involvement.

Creative programs, such as ruMad,? show student involvement and interest is clear but Ms. Black's involvement in the reorganization that transformed the Education Foundation would be helpful. By changing the context and the scale of reform, partnerships have become a more definite basis for reform. Less open to corporate influences than America, Australia is more creative.

The involvement of students is strikingly different in this case from previous reports. It is difficult to imagine GWU involved in ruMad? or serving on community councils. The art projects also proceed without direct corporate support. It would be interesting to see how Roberta Lamb's music program could be developed in this context. The balance between corporate support, student creativity, and education seems close. However, support for poor students is missing. A more focused activist would attempt to achieve equality.

Chapter 10
Follow Your Star: A Rural Explosion

Ann Jones, former Superintendent,
Southwest District, Nova Scotia

The context in which partnerships are built is extremely important. Since partnerships connect communities of interest with school systems, they are, by definition, situational. Education must reflect community norms and assist in economic support and renewal in communities. When students are active partners in their cities, towns and villages, rural areas and the suburbs, they respect the context in which they live and they are appreciated and better understood.

Building partnerships in a rural area has a different set of dynamics than in an urban area. As a senior administrator in both urban and rural areas, I have experienced specific lessons about the approach to take, what people or organizations to include in the partnership, longevity, focus and how to influence the expected outcome in these very different situations.

AN URBAN PARTNERSHIP EXPERIENCE

Partnerships in urban areas tend to be with businesses, governmental organizations or non-governmental organizations that are able to make decisions locally.

Discussions are held face to face, meetings can be scheduled quickly and travelling to meetings and finding a suitable meeting location are not difficult. Urban partnerships have more direct access to decision making. Those working on partnerships at the table have the power to quickly move the partnership forward.

For example, in my position of Assistant Director with the Ottawa Board of Education we were working to link our schools in a wide area network. The Ottawa Board of Education amalgamated with the Carleton Board of Education into the Ottawa-Carleton District School Board (OCDSB), with over 70,000 students located in an urban center of almost one million people. Ottawa is a center for high technology, has colleges and universities, a well-developed community infrastructure, and a high interest in education. It is also small enough for the education, business and government communities to know who are the decision makers. Being the National Capital of Canada, there is direct access to federal government and national headquarters of non-governmental agencies.

With all of these advantages, a natural outcome was the building of fairly significant education/business/ community partnerships. Over a meeting at the Ottawa-Carleton Media Centre shared by all boards of education in the area, we identified the need to link all of our schools. Since the infrastructure of the Media Centre existed, senior decision makers had frequently worked with each other. In this context, the partnership had an easy and a natural beginning.

The next step was a search for partners. This partnership did not start out to be the very large and complicated project. As many good things do, it started with a casual conversation about mutual interests and some good ideas. This was followed by the most important statement needed for any successful venture, "Why don't we . . ." The idea was to connect all our schools in the Ottawa Board and to automate the libraries.

In the City of Ottawa and Carleton County, public and separate schools have either French or English as the language of instruction. There is a well-developed library system that connects the public library and the libraries of the University of Ottawa and Carleton University. There are high technology firms that need a venue to see if their products could support community and educational needs. The result was the Ottawa/Carleton Network for Education: World Consortium Project (ONEWorld).

Unique to an urban area, there already existed the Ottawa-Carleton Learning Foundation (OCLF) established to assist partnerships. The existence of the Foundation made finding the partners easy, gave us a neutral venue for meeting, and had facility for telephone and video conferencing. The Foundation also provided us with leadership. By assigning time of the executive director of the OCLF to ONEWorld, the partnership could maintain minutes, access to public relations professionals and writers. This infrastructure was essential to facilitating and maintaining the partnership.

ONEWorld partners included the two French language school boards, two Roman Catholic separate school boards and two public boards of education, Bell Canada, TV Ontario, Apple Canada, Ottawa/Carleton Media Centre, Exocom, Napean and Ottawa Public Libraries, Dymaxion Ltd., SchoolNet, and Knet First Nations. Each joined the partnership to enable schools to connect to each other, to the library and outside resources, to test the application of products to education, and to generally 'push the envelope' of network technology applications to education. The ONEWorld connected all six boards to curriculum materials, student information systems, student/teacher networks, administrative networks, and Multi-media on Demand.

The project did have a clear objective end; as partners were added, the objective took on a broader context but always had the focus of connecting the student with resources that were beyond what the school board could provide without this access to the wider community. Another important element that is part of the urban context of this partnership was access to decision makers who saw the potential, and who not only championed but also took part directly in the planning and implementation. These leaders could also make quick decisions and provide resources. Those involved were experienced in taking risks.

Since the beginning of the project the overall objective had not changed, but the players had. Successful partnerships need time to plan and even more time to implement. Education in the last two decades has become highly politicized. The result has been changes in governance of education, reduction in funding, amalgamation of boards and administration. These changes create an atmosphere that is not fertile ground for innovation or risk taking. With the instability of the leadership and structure of educational institutions, the necessary time and commitment was difficult to maintain. This is frustrating to educators and also to their potential partners. Each partner needs to be able to trust the commitment to the project. This is very difficult for the educational partner who is operating in an area of uncertainty.

For ONEWorld, the uncertainty about funding, the loss of key players, and the disruption of the amalgamation of the school boards caused the partnership to be suspended. During this time the overall objective, the connection of students to resources via technology, continued but at a much slower pace and without being able to take advantage of opportunities offered by the partners.

Partnerships need the time to develop and must be nurtured in a stable environment. More time is required to implement and evaluate the changes in them. Partnerships in urban areas can be started quickly because the resources are available, but like all partnerships, once established, need continued support to prosper. Changes in urban environment can make partnerships too difficult to direct.

RURAL PARTNERSHIPS

In rural areas, building partnerships between education and the community takes on a very different dynamic. In small communities and towns, schools are a focal point. There is often a great deal of support for education, including trust and respect for educators. Administrators and teachers are usually leaders in the community and in many cases, hold political office at the municipal or provincial level. School board members are often known, they know their communities and most believe that their board members act in the best interest of their communities. The leadership for building partnerships comes more from within the educational system, administrators, teachers and board members, than in urban areas.

Although large businesses impact on rural areas, the decisions they make are more remote. Partnerships must be built with local or regional managers who are very willing but are not given direct authority to act. This slows down the process and requires a commitment to the project to move it forward. Local business owners are an important part of the rural community and are essential partners.

In small towns, there are so many small businesses and entrepreneurs, they are difficult to contact. They are very diverse and are busy with their businesses which are more 'hands on.' Local service organizations such as Rotary, Lions, Women's Institutes, Churches, Garden Clubs and Exhibition Societies play an important role in rural communities. As a source of support in time, money and planning, they supplement small businesses.

Augmenting schools, businesses, and service clubs, in rural areas governmental agencies at all levels provide a great deal of the infrastructure and are an important source of allies. Provincial hospital boards and health authorities, housing authorities, family and children's services, justice, sport and recreation, town and municipal councils, and public libraries are natural partners to education. Since all have limited funding and large responsibilities, they are very receptive to cooperation with education. It may be a case of misery loves company, or lute necessity. At the federal level, particularly in rural areas, Human Resources Development Canada (HRDC) is a most important source of support, direct funding, and personnel resources. They have a mandate of human and community development and are linked to education through many federal programs. What they want is to ensure that monies produce results through their expertise and ability to access resources for a partnership.

Aside from all the formal organizations, rural partnerships are different. A partnership in a rural area depends on the informal leadership in the community. There are leaders in communities that hold no elected office, neither municipal councilors or business leaders, but people who get things done. These individuals are essential to a good educational partnership. They know how to make the necessary connections with service organizations, small and large businesses, other community leaders, and the community in general.

NOVA SCOTIA

When I moved from Ottawa to Nova Scotia in 1996, partnerships existed in every possible rural community. As the first Superintendent (CEO) of the Southwest Regional School Board (SWRSB), I was able to pursue these opportunities. The SWRSB is fairly typical of a large rural board with many diverse communities. The SWRSB was established in 1996 as an amalgamation of county school boards serving Digby, Yarmouth, Shelburne, Queens and Lunenburg Counties. The board has 19,000 students spread over 5,500 square kilometers with 65 schools that range from 10 students, K-5, on Big Tancook Island, accessible only by ferry, to a high school of 900 students in the Town of Bridgewater.

Students come to SWRSB from rural and small towns with diverse economies along the shore of the Gulf of Maine, the Bay of Fundy and the Atlantic Ocean. The area is supported by lobster, scallop and ground fishing and by inland areas where small farms and logging are the main occupations. The five counties that make up the SWRSB have a 450 million dollar fishing industry. This represents 70% of the total fishing income in Nova Scotia that, in turn, is economically the most lucrative fishing industry of any province in Canada (ITG Information Management, 2000).

Because the school board amalgamation caused disruption in the web of informal contacts so important in these places, SWRSB was seen as very remote from the communities and their individual schools. Links between the new board and the separate schools was essential. The SWRSB worked with communities and schools to be the first school board in Nova Scotia to fully implement and support School Advisory Committees (SACs). These SACs link school administration, teachers, parents and the community and are charged with the task of school improvement. Establishing SAC was essential to building and maintaining partnerships.

After establishing SACs, a series of partnerships or groups of partnerships was created. An initial project included community literacy and encouraging school competition. A significant group, Blacks in Nova Scotia, was the concern of a significant community. Community services for children and youths have been integrated. Individual teachers have organized projects, such as respect for war veterans. A huge partnership has been organized with three American states and another Canadian province for environmental education.

Each of these partnerships has grown from the identification of a community need, and connecting a group of dedicated students, educators, parents and community members who work towards a goal that really matters to them. Partnerships are human endeavors that connect people. My own personal interest in partnerships had been nourished in Ottawa. Community needs and my interests were cast into a shared set of goals. Rural partnerships became easier to maintain because their returns are more tangible and the programs areas more localized. People, resources and the environment are welded.

LEARNING COMMUNITY PILOT PROJECT

In 1998, a series of projects began in one of the communities in SWRSB. This community is on the Atlantic coast: Barrington, Barrington Passage and Clarks Harbour including Cape Sable Island. This is an area with two industries; lobster and ground fishing, and tourism. It is also a place with very active and innovative Municipal and Town Councils with strong leadership. One of the informal and important connections in this community is the Warden of the Municipality. He is the husband of the first Vice-Chair of the Board and former Chair of the Shelburne County Board. When the SWRSB first amalgamated, all board members in the six former boards remained on the board until the next election, October of 1997. For a full 16 months between the amalgamation and the next election there were 52 board members. As the board moved to 18 members, many of the former board members either did not run or were defeated. These former board members were leaders in their community who knew the school system and their communities and wanted to continue to be of service to students. The former Vice-Chair, Linda Stoddart, was one of these people.

After a talk over coffee at the local Tim Horton's with Linda, her husband, Warden Steven Stoddart, turned into a "Why don't we?" which became the Learning Community Pilot Project (LCPP) in Barrington, Barrington Passage and Clark's Harbour. Included in this conversation was Don Glover, the former Superintendent of the Shelburne Board and then Director of Learning Services with the SWRSB who is a long time resident in the area. This is a pattern that has repeated itself as partnerships with literacy groups in Yarmouth and anti-poverty groups in Bridgewater were built.

In these settings what is important is the attitude. When a person says, "Why don't we?" others have to say "Why not?" and "How can I help?" In a rural setting, over coffee, in a persons kitchen or boardroom, these confirming conversations are more likely to happen. The focus of the Learning Community Pilot Project (LCPP) was very tangible. They were to make sure that students graduate from high school with a high level of literacy and numeracy, including computer literacy. These new skills were to benefit the community, not just the individuals.

The next step for our informal group was to meet with the principals of the local junior high/secondary school, and the four elementary schools in a planning session. Principals in these rural communities are very important. They have deep roots in their communities; they are community leaders. Because the schools are small compared to urban centers, they also know the families of their students. We also spoke to current local school board members, teachers, school secretaries, bus drivers, and, with the help of Warden Stoddart, with municipal and town councils.

Some of those identified were formal leaders with titles; others were identified as people who were influential and were respected by the community. We also invited students. Not just those who were part of student government, but also those who were identified by their peers and by their teachers as students who influenced their peers. We had a list of over 50 people from all age groups and all occupations.

At the suggestion of one of the principals who said that the best work gets done in the kitchen, we invited them to dinner cooked by the cafeteria workers in one of our schools. Over 30 local leaders attended the dinner and those that couldn't, let us know that they supported this effort and were really sorry they would miss dinner. From this dinner the Learning Community Pilot Project was established.

We were able to focus influential members of the community, families, businesses, municipal, provincial and federal government agencies and educational institutions on the importance of learning. Because literacy and numeracy were critical for the success of the individual and the prosperity of the community, three committees were established: School-to-Work, Community Literacy and Support Services (CLASS), and Stay-In-School.

Each of these three committees had clear and realistic goals. I have found that people in rural communities are very realistic and pragmatic. While they have an overall vision of where they want to go, the steps needed to accomplish the goal need to be very concrete. They also want their children to stay in their communities, to be able to make a living at home. The students share this view. While urban parents and families focus on the job or profession, rural students and their parents focus on what they can do at home, in their communities. Even moving away to Halifax is seen as going away from home.

The School-to-Work Sub-Committee offered annual job fairs; to assist students in course selection they are working to produce for student use a database of credentials required for certain professions. Human Resources Development Canada (HRDC) and Access Nova Scotia partnered to place a job/career computer terminal at Barrington Muncipal High School (BMHS); the terminal was replaced by internet access once the school was connected. The students have appeared before the municipal councils of Barrington and Clark's Harbour to express their views about the need for diversification in employment in the area.

Activities of the School-to-Work Committee focus on local issues that affect their communities. Students working with the sub-committee approached Basin Productions to mount a theatrical production around issues raised by the Supreme Court decision on Native treaty rights for access to fish and forests. This is an important decision since lobster fishing is a million dollar industry in this community. This project was discussed with the Shelbourne Campus of Nova Scotia Community College as a partnership to produce a video.

Student differences or problems have been the focus of a partnership with Mental Health Services. This school-based project offers adolescent self-referral counseling services. This partnership has worked with the school board Coordinator of Race Relations, Cross Cultural Understanding and Human rights (RCH) to organize classroom visits/student workshops to address diversity (gender, socio-economic status, beliefs, etc.). The school and the Nova Scotia Community College are jointly implemented courses in Mi'kmaq Studies 10, Oceans 11, and Personal Development and Relationship 7/8.

The second committee, CLASS, has worked with parents and community members as well as students. The board used partnerships with Human Resources, Children's Aid Society, Mental Health and Nova Scotia Housing Authority (NSHA), to established locations for Family Community Support Centres within the community. One location was in a former school board office, in a newly renovated facility owned by the housing authority; later, it approached the board to use the former Barrington Elementary School. For ease of access to the community, these facilities are located across this coastal area, including Cape Sable Island. These centers offer parenting support classes, pre-school parent-child learning, homework clubs, anger management programs, adult upgrading, family literacy programs, Special Olympics programs, subsidized child care and school-based school age care, seniors programs, drug and alcohol dependency support and a Community Access Project.

The Stay-in-School committee implemented programs and courses including career programs, cooperative education, and work experience. Working with the Coordinator of Junior and Senior High Programs, it has offered courses through the Nova Scotia Community College, Shelburne Campus. This third committee, joining with the Stay-In-School Committee linked with the Open for Business Centre, an entrepreneurial support service, and planned a job terminal, with the support of HRDC, to be located in the school in the future.

The Stay-in-School Committee wanted to keep students in school. With a winter lobster season, November to May, students in the senior grades are attracted to the fishery where they can make upwards to $30,000 for the season. Parents are concerned that their children will give up their education for the money in the fishery and in their future. Because of their lack of a high school diploma and academic skill, these young adults are not going to be able to advance in the fishery. With high tech equipment on boats, and the entrepreneurial nature of being a captain of your own boat, the lack of formal education is a serious deterrent.

This project developed a half/half program which allows students to start four semester courses in the Fall, leave school in November to fish on a lobster boat during the season, and return to school in May to complete the four courses. Student time on a lobster boat could be given credit through Cooperative Education. Courses were planned with the general fishing community to establish courses at the Nova Scotia Community College to train for Master, Mate and Mechanics papers for the industry. Having this program in the community will show students that just 'hauling rope' on a lobster boat, while attractive when you are young, leaves you will little future in the industry.

The Learning Community Pilot Project was successful because it is grounded in the community. It has empowered community members and students to take an active role in the projects. They have also been supported by federal and provincial government agencies such as Human Resources and the Housing Authority. Because of these connections, this project has not been affected by changes in leadership at the board level or funding issues. It was successful because the community owns these programs and they have taken on an attitude of 'we're OK.' This project received a grant from the Walter and Duncan Gordon Foundation to determine the reasons for its success so that it could be replicated in other rural communities.

ORAL HISTORIES IN PETITE RIVIERE

"This is the best way to learn about history." It's much easier to write the next chapter of our Dr. Cameron story now that we have been to the house where he used to live." "The best part of the project was the presentation in the community hall . . . It didn't seem like school work at all" (Mary Jane Harkin, personal communication, June, 1999). These are some of the comments from students in Jessie Haché's elementary class.

In these rural areas, families have strong ties to their communities going back generations. Most live in the same area and live in a home that their parents, grandparents, great grandparents or even great-great-grandparents built. Rural communities are natural partners for student activities that focus on the history and cultural development of the community.

Each year students in Jessie's class at Petite Riviere School participate in an oral history project. They decided on a project, gathered data from a variety of sources including research at the provincial archives, conducted interviews with local seniors, and created a classroom museum so community members could bring information and artifacts into the school.

The project started in 1989 when this unique teacher read from a diary of a former Petite Riviere teacher, Inga Volger. The diary talked about life in the community in 1916 when she was 10 years old. This inspired the students to begin to tell their own family stories. They found out that Inga Volger was still alive with family members still in the community. The students wrote to her and her recollections became the first edition. Over the years, with direct support from the principal, school board and superintendent, the work of the grade 6 students continued. They have written a series of history books and companion storybooks about their local communities. The books are a part of the National Library of Canada's Collection and Provincial Archive's Collection.

These oral histories are a writing process for children. They spend many weeks writing interview questions and taping interviews with community members, as well as writing and editing the manuscripts. They make decisions about what to include in the writing and what artwork to use.

Once the publication is completed they have a community celebration. The night before, the children and their parents prepare an 'old meal' of local traditional foods, during which the children and the community members discuss the collected information. The final celebration is a public presentation in the community hall. The children engage in readings, plays, dances, and a presentation of their books to the community members who have been involved in their project.

This project illustrates what one person can do. An individual teacher responded to students in a unique teachable moment. Like many rural teachers, Jean Haché comes from the community where she teaches, and she has strong connections with the community unlike urban areas where almost everyone is CFA. Jean comments, "Students discovered the richness of their culture, their community, and their experiences through their writing. They feel special and they think of themselves as writers. They have goals and aspirations and they see themselves as successful" (Mary Jane Harkin, personal communication, June, 1999).

ENVIRONMENTAL EDUCATION

Aside from teachers in schools, other individuals bring about enormous partnerships that change schools. For example, John Terry had an interesting idea about the environment in this part of the Atlantic Ocean. Unlike Haché, Terry was a newcomer to the area, another CFA. He is an educator and a former professor at the Massachusetts Institute of Technology in the United States. He is also the editor of *New Designs for Youth Development*, a US publication. When Terry walked into the school board office, he had the idea of a service learning project focusing on the Gulf of Maine watershed. He knew of projects in Massachusetts and New Hampshire and felt that these projects could be linked with similar projects in the Southwest of Nova Scotia.

The Gulf of Maine is essential to the economic, physical and social well being of the population in Digby, Yarmouth and Shelburne Counties of the Southwest. The Gulf of Maine and its watershed, shared by Canada and the U.S., is one of the richest regions in terms of biomass in the world. To focus students on the importance of this area, boards and community groups in Nova Scotia, Maine, New Hampshire, New Brunswick and Massachusetts formed a partnership around the common interest of living around, and being supported, by the ecosystem of the Gulf of Maine called the Gulf of Maine Institute Without Walls (GMIWW).

The credo of the GMIWW is: Youth are our most Valuable Resource. They are the citizens, scientists, decision-makers and cultural transmitters of tomorrow. If we are to ensure a sustainable future for the Gulf of Maine region, we must engage in actions today that create and support networks of people who care about it as a rich and varied resource in perpetuity. Learning through doing, in apprenticeship and partnership with adults, is the most effective way to prepare youth to work forward securing this future (John Terry, email, December 12, 2000).

Students in Nova Scotia did environmental research on the Tusket River, Yarmouth shore and Cape Forchu, the Cocheco River Watch Project in New Hampshire, in Maine the Official KIDS Guide to the Marginal Way, a project in Massachusetts on the effects of acid rain on salt and plant life in the Muddy River system, with students in New Brunswick acting as the official masters of the GMIWW website.

The GMIWW now has five major projects, one in each of the three states and two provinces. Much of the time of the partners has been fundraising. After much work, many disappointments, the formal funding partners are: Tusket River Environmental Protection Agency (TREPA), Gulf of Maine Council, United States Environmental Protection Agency, Southwest Regional School Board, Canadian Maritime Millennium Initiative, Community businesses and agencies. The total budget for the 5 projects was almost $500,000. The Gulf of Maine Council, an international body of governmental and business interests, which is supported by the governments of Canada and the United States, sponsors this institute.

The project is supported by local service clubs such as Rotary and Lions and by small businesses who donated everything from hotdogs and milk to canoes. Though initially welcomed and encouraged by educators at the board level, the idea had rapidly captured the imagination of the entire community. Family members got involved along with members of the school board, municipal council, senior citizens, garden clubs, university departments and environmental groups. The GMIWW received a $108,000 millennium grant from the Government of Canada to have the first Summer Institute Without Walls. The Institute was held in July 2000, in Yarmouth, Nova Scotia. This was the first time students, teachers, university and community supporters, from all five jurisdictions could meet and share their work and findings. The institute allowed students to present their projects and to take part in cultural and environmental activities in the Yarmouth area.

Most importantly, students were on their land with those from another country, taking part in a project that connected their individual interests with those who live with them in a common environment. They rode in canoes in the Tusket River watershed, slogged through marches, clambered over the rock of Cape Forchu, and took part in a Sweet Grass Ceremony led by an Acadia Band First Nations elder. One student from inner city Boston, lying on the wet grass feeding a mallard duck from his hand said, "I didn't think these ducks actually existed." The Summer Institute included a trip to New Hampshire for students to be part of the Gulf of Maine Council's tenth anniversary celebration.

This project is successful because an individual brought a good idea and the small communities, provincial and state governments, federal governments and non-governmental agencies saw the potential. It would not have happened if there had not been a direct connection to the community. I am not sure this could have happened in an urban area. There are so many activities of this type in an urban area that it is hard to have one focus for so many agencies and levels of government. Because it happened in a rural area, it was unique and exciting. But, it would not have happened anywhere without a person with a vision. When people saw the value of the idea for their place and lives, being a CFA or NFH was an obstacle that could be overcome with perseverance and the support of key people.

CONCLUSION

These partnerships represent the variety of activities that link students with their rural communities. These projects are encouraged and supported by the board and administration at all levels. They are successful because they meet needs. The communities in the area in and around South West Nova Scotia value these projects and, as a result, are willing to support public education.

Would these partnerships be the same in an urban setting? Would they even be possible outside a rural context? I believe they are successful because they are rooted in their direct culture of rural people as it is lived. Evaluation of the projects is very personal, direct and honest. If a partnership does not directly impact the community, and is not relevant and socially responsible, there will not be community support. Successes in rural partnerships depend on individuals and are very personal. People will tell you what they believe is working and is not working, if the project is going in the right direction, and what needs to be done to improve it. What they respect is openness and honesty in return.

No matter how much they are needed, they must have an infra6+structure of support from organizations and individuals. Partnerships develop in a stable political environment. Leaders of communities, board, small and large business and governmental and non-governmental agencies must be free to take risks, must have secure sources of funding and be allowed to make decisions on the ground. With these elements, partnerships in either rural or urban areas flourish.

EDITOR'S COMMENT

As Ann Jones shows, strangers as well as long-time residents can work together and develop a variety of programs. Only the program built around the Gulf of Maine allows for a coalition to form around the issue of the environment. There are even more partnerships than this essay has covered. These partnerships allow the community to organize as it might. And individuals even develop their own partnerships. Rural communities can adapt rapidly to differences within them and can incorporate outsiders with their ideas and different perspectives.

However, there is not a polarity of opinions with the rural communities. Furthermore, divisions within the community are not recognized insofar as they have different ideals or values. If everyone identifies with the community, meets over the kitchen table, and forms committees, will they agree? The next group of authors does not think so. Ann Jones has, unlike them, is not arguing one position, nor is she attempting to achieve greater equality in her new home, Nova Scotia. She is just connecting the new rural partnerships with previous urban ones without attempting to change either.

Chapter 11
Finding Issue for Urban Organizing

Judy Duncan, John Anderson, Jill O'Reilly, Josh Stuart, Tatiana Jaunzems, and James Wardlaw, Association of Community Organizations for Reform Now (ACORN) Canada, and Heather Marshall, Toronto Environmental Alliance

In 2004, Toronto became home to the first ACORN field office in Canada after training for a year and a half in Seattle. In 2005, the Greater Vancouver office was opened and, in the spring of 2007, the Ottawa office began operations. A Hamilton office followed in December of 2008. Each of these programs is different and the campaign priorities in each city are identified by the members who live there. From the membership, leaders are trained and developed. Staff assist while leaders connect the local issues to the larger policy context. In New Westminster and Ottawa, campaigns have reached out and obtained support from many diverse groups for our living wage campaigns while in the original site of Toronto, allies have been developed for common campaigns on the environment.

FIGHTING FOR TENANTS

The Weston/Mount Dennis area in Toronto was visibly run down in August 2004 when (ACORN) launched its inaugural drive. Weston/Mount Dennis is dominated by a large number of high-rise buildings that are a mix of social housing and private rentals. Many of the buildings were in derelict condition, with obvious pest problems, including cockroaches and bed bugs, large, unfixed holes in both common areas and occupied units, mold spreading through ceilings and walls and elevators in high-rise buildings which were not functioning. Nothing was being done about these problems. Residents felt powerless to get the attention of their landlords.

ACORN Canada adopted a door knocking methodology that was largely the same—and highly successful—as that used by ACORN offices across the United States. Organizers have 15 to 25 minute conversations with local residents talking about local issues and the power of collective action. After each conversation, an organizer methodically asks people to join the local organization as a full member. Membership requires a bank draft of $10 per month. Individuals who decline full membership are asked to join as an associate or provisional member, which requires them to pay a small one time sum or nothing at all. Associate and provisional members are invited to join in the developing campaign, but do not receive the same voting rights as full members. Experience has shown ACORN that the people who join as full members are by far the most engaged in the organization; and value their ownership stake and voice in the organization.

The pay-for-membership model is sometimes criticized as exploiting low income people who are "too poor" to have to pay dues. However, ACORN encourages provisional membership for people who wish to be involved but are concerned about paying the monthly membership dues. More importantly, this approach avoids the condescending position that implies that low income people are not able to make decisions about their personal and limited spending pattern. Further, like the concept of unionism, an independent funding source from the membership base is the key to maintaining control of the campaign and objectives for the organization by its board, which is comprised of ACORN members.

During two months of working in the neighborhood, we talked to over 800 people in their homes about the community and larger issues that they identified and were concerned about. We also undertook hundreds of hours of house visits to interested people and worked the phone bank with nightly phone calls. At the end of these two months of door to door organizing, we finally felt there were enough engaged community members to hold a community organizing drive.

The organizing drive started with a series of three meetings, one each week, with the new members. In this way, the new group sprung to life. The group overwhelmingly voted to start their first campaign focusing upon improving apartment building conditions. The other two priorities that were identified for future action were police profiling and the need for more youth-based community programs.

The group quickly identified that the Toronto Municipal Code established apartment building standards. For example, the Municipal Code has an explicit standard related to pest control:

> 629-9. Pest control. All properties shall at all times be kept free of rodents, vermin, insects and other pests and from conditions which may encourage infestations by pests.

However, the reality that ACORN members live is that this standard is not met in either private or publicly owned buildings. The Municipal Licensing and Standards office with the City of Toronto has no effective way of enforcing the Municipal Code. The process of issuing work orders and the penalties related to them do not create a penalty costly enough to give landlords an incentive to maintain their buildings.

The three introductory meetings were followed by a fourth and final planning meeting at which members created an action plan. The members decided to do a Cockroach Derby press event, to take place outside one of the worst buildings in the neighborhood, 1775 & 1765Weston Road. The members and newly emerging leaders invited all media outlets, Municipal Licensing and Standards, the absentee landlord, and all levels of politicians. Staff and members started working on turnout while members collected cockroaches.

In late October 2004, ACORN Canada held its first event. About 30 members, some with cockroaches to physically demonstrate the conditions in which they live, showed up for the Cockroach Derby. The media, Municipal Licensing and Standards officials and some local politicians attended and the event was a success. The media picked up the event. The City of Toronto agreed to move all of its rent supported tenants out of the building. The consensus was that the buildings were far below the standards outlined in the municipal code. The landlord did not attend the consensus meeting. For a short time after the event, the landlord, Vincenzo Barrasso, responded to the negative press and boosted maintenance, such as painting obvious places or fixing broken locks on the front door, but these efforts were not sustained.

As a result of city's special investigations audit team, work orders were issued for some 490 units. While the landlord took responsibility for some of the repairs, some things were never fixed. ACORN continued organizing and doing press events. Actions included "The Prison of 1202," which focused on ACORN member Sharol Jason, who is in a wheel chair, and how she was trapped in her apartment for six weeks due to an inoperative elevator. Living on the twelfth floor, she had no way of getting up and down in her building while the elevator awaited repair. The press tracked the story and was at the building about once a week for 3 months. Headlines included: "Tenants Lived in Hell", "Highrise Hostage", "Home not so Sweet" and "Building Tension." These headlines tell the stories of members who lived in the two buildings.

Although ACORN Canada and the members had initial success with its actions, it had a more difficult time maintaining pressure on the landlord to continue to respond to work orders and tenant issues after the City left the building; ACORN was no longer organizing a press event at the building every two weeks. The landlord stopped investing any money in bringing the building up to standard. Over time, the building started to slip back to its original state.

Then, ACORN decided to use the Ontario Rental Housing Tribunal to force their landlord to bring the building up to the standards outlined in the Municipal Code. However, due to the pro-landlord bias of the legislation and procedural requirements for proceedings before the Board, this approach turned out to be extremely cumbersome. Because of the requirements to act against their delinquent landlord, ACORN had interested tenants fill out the complaint form required by the Tribunal. This activity alone took hundred of hours by ACORN staff, leaders and members in the building to organize. ACORN paid the filing fee required by the Tribunal for the forms from the 105 people who chose to file collectively. The filing fee alone was $45 per building plus $5 per additional tenant. When the case went before an adjudicator, we realized a legal aide lawyer would be needed to address 105 complaints.

York Community Services Legal Clinic (YCL) picked up the case. One of the lead filing tenants was on Ontario Disability, which enabled him to qualify for legal aid. Hundreds of hours were spent by YCL, ACORN staff and ACORN leaders to continue to put together this case and the hearing before the Tribunal. In March of 2005, Elizabeth Beckett, a member of the Tribunal, issued an interim order ruling in favour of the 105 tenants. Subsequently, in her final order, Beckett separated the rent abatements into two time periods based on the evidence of disrepair that she heard. Tenants received a 20 per cent refund on rent paid from March 1, 2004 to Feb. 28, 2005 and a 10 per cent rebate from March 1, 2005 to Dec. 31, 2005. As the average monthly rent costs about $900, a tenant would receive a total of $3,060 in return. Some tenants were compensated an additional $100 to $600 for the inconvenience caused to them due to damages in the common areas such as the elevators. Victory! This equaled over $321,300 dollars in savings to tenants.

However, the lengthy process and ongoing frustration with the landlord and the state of their homes had taken its toll on tenants. By the time the tenants were able to claim the rent abatements, about thirty percent of the tenants who participated in the action had moved out. Rent abatement was of no benefit to them at that point and the landlord received a windfall. To this day, the buildings are still in massive disrepair and most of the people who had the means to move out did so long ago. Approximately ninety-five percent of the 105 tenants who brought the action against the landlord before the Tribunal have now moved out. As soon as the City, ACORN or the press stopped investing energy into enforcement of basic building standards, the landlord stopped doing any repairs. The complaint based system has no long-term incentives to maintain standards and is completely ineffective with a landlord, who resists compliance with work orders. It is cheaper for the landlord to ignore the Municipal Code as a standard operating practice and deal with the consequences repeatedly, than it is for the landlord to maintain a building in a state of good repair. Tenants be damned.

However, ACORN established itself as a leading voice for tenant rights and members were well engaged in tenant issues, which affected them directly. By 2006, ACORN staff had done two other organizing drives in other communities in Toronto, Scarborough Centre and Chalk Farm at Jane and Wilson, both of which resulted in ACORN members deciding to tackle massive disrepair in apartment buildings. In short, these decaying high rises with absentee slumlords were numerous across the city of Toronto in the lower income neighborhoods.

THE LANDLORD LICENSING PROGRAM

The ACORN leaders across Toronto communities decided it made no sense to try to fix the buildings one at a time. They started researching potential legislative fixes to this enforcement catastrophe on a broader scale. As a result, Toronto ACORN leadership decided to put together a Landlord Licensing and Rent Escrow Campaign. Landlord licensing programs exist in other cities like Los Angeles. These programs require landlords to maintain a license for their buildings. Where building conditions fall below basic requirements, it triggers tenant use of a rent escrow account. Rent escrow programs allow tenants to pay their rent into a rent escrow account, typically held by a city, where a unit is in disrepair for a given period of time. The city can then draw on that money to fix outstanding work orders and the tenant is protected from eviction due to non-payment of rent. Landlords are pressured by the loss of rental income to address the outstanding complaints. The city can post signs in the lobby if an apartment building is below code so that tenants become more aware of their rights and the vehicles that they have available to assert those rights.

ACORN lobbying was successful in winning the support of City Councilor Anthony Perruza, who introduced a motion at City Council directing staff to research and implement a landlord licensing system. The City staff report returned with the recommendation from Municipal Licensing and Standard to boost the already existing audit program with a target of four buildings in each ward across Toronto. The recommendation, adopted by Toronto Council, was a huge organizational victory but was a very small step forward. The audit program focuses on common areas and has made minimal progress for the tenants in the actual units.

Although 100 million dollars may have been spent on the program, the program has not been consistent. The city may have not come out with a full landlord licensing program because the landlord lobby was too strong. This program would have put the city in a conflict because the largest landlord in the city. which is also far below the code is Toronto Community Housing, a crown corporation that houses thousands of low income tenants.

MAKE IT SOMETHING:
THE LIVING WAGE LAW

Working people on Canada's West Coast in British Columbia (BC) have more reason to be mad about low wages that anyone else in Canada or the USA. The lowest minimum wage in the country coupled with the highest cost of living sounds bad enough, but get this: in 2001, when the last part of the former socialist government's gradual minimum wage increase came into effect, the new Liberal Government managed to make this province have the only two-tiered wage law in Canada—making the old bottom floor $8 while digging a new one down to $6 for 'entry level workers.' That meant the last legislation regarding wages was a decrease in the minimum wage of twenty-five percent. Even George W. Bush, the extreme former U, S President, raised the Federal Minimum Wage to $7.25 before leaving office. In the Bring Cash Province of BC, a New Canadian Immigrant has to work 3 and a half months full-time in order to get $8 Canadian per hour. Needless to say, the issue of wages in BC is what organizers call burning hot.

Considering these demoralizing factors, any outside political hack could assume that the progressive forces in BC have been clobbered in the last 10 years. That's obvious. What is more subtle is that within the progressive brain trust there is even significant debate of whether or not to continue fighting the BC Federation of Labour's "Make it Ten!" the Minimum Wage Campaign. Many have taken up believing that $10 is too low, and that a Living Wage is where we need to be focusing as if the two were from different planets. ACORN members, on the other hand, know that the two go together like a Canadian and a hockey puck and that you could use a Living Wage campaign to benefit the Minimum Wage Campaign. Victories are victories, plain and simple and any organizer worth a dime knows that some victory was needed in BC badly to motivate the manically depressed progressive troops. BC ACORN is represented on the *Living Wage for Families* Advisory Council, had done some events and petitioning with the BC Federation of Labour on their well branded "Make it Ten" campaign in previous years, and had a constituency that was bearing the full load of low wages. We knew that these three things combined could be turned into a winning campaign with positive spinoffs if fought in the right place.

If the law won in one city, other cities would more likely follow and the illogical and perverse economic arguments used by the Liberal Government NOT to raise the minimum wage would then become publicly highlighted and help leverage a long awaited increase. New Westminster BC, is the oldest city in Western Canada, has been solidly working class since settlement in the late 1800's. It is located in the middle of Canada's third largest metropolitan area, and, for the most part, has voted for the New Democratic Party since the 1950's. Its electorate brought in a city council with a labour backed majority in 2008. It has a small population of 60,000 with a solid base of ACORN members, an obvious choice to be the first City targeted by anyone west of Waterloo Ontario for a Living Wage Campaign. It was very winnable and could lead to juicy political repercussions.

BC ACORN leaders began holding campaign planning meetings in the summer of 2009 for a Living Wage in New West. New Westminster Leaders David Tate, Sheldon Schroeder, Peter Gardner, Noel Ouellette, Lois Golonko, and Pearl Nunns were leading the way and driving the program. Points of discussion in these meetings were a game plan to get the word out effectively and what the actual Living Wage number ought to be. BC ACORN also was working on the advisory panel of the *Living Wage for Working Families Campaign*, which is a project supported by First Call: BC Child & Youth Advocacy Coalition, the BC Canadian Center for Policy Alternatives (CCPA) and a number of labour unions. In this working group, the BC CCPA argued convincingly and incredibly thoroughly that a Living Wage should be set on the basis of a family of four not on individual need. ACORN members, not being the ones to be convinced of such ideas, thought that $16.74 was needed but understood that in the end the number could possibly be impractical if we could not get the progressive forces on New West Council to go for it the whole program.

ACORN members targeted a couple of the most progressive councilors we had known from earlier tenant and public safety campaigns and asked them for their support in a family living wage campaign. ACORN leaders asked them to champion the cause by being the inside voice on council—a role that was necessary and crucial. The march to $16.74 was on! New Westminster ACORN's Campaign for a Living Wage was launched on a Saturday in October of 2009 to much fanfare in the middle of a giant downpour that seemed very fitting for BC—if not photogenic due to the umbrellas. Half of city council was at the launch due to the annual Citizen Ceremony at New Westminster City hall taking place one hour before our launch. The vast majority of people at the launch were either ACORN members or people who turned out due to our door knocking in New West. The media presence was noticeable. ACORN Leaders David Tate and Pearl Nunns were the ACORN Canada spokespeople taking turns with the politicians in front of the cameras and microphone. Councilor Jamie McEvoy, the crucial city councilperson that was vital to the success to the campaign, spoke loudly through a bull horn about getting City Hall "to boldly go where no city has gone before".

It was 48 hours later on a Monday at City Hall in New Westminster that David Tate and Scheldon Scroeder—with the backing of a respectable contingent of New West ACORN members—officially made a presentation to council. Quickly they laid out the arguments for a living wage by law, showed the labour, business and organizational support the campaign that ACORN had through our Coalition with *Living Wage for Families.* Dave asked the council to start thinking about it and, as planned, our councilor ally, Jaimie McEvoy, was able to get council to pass a motion to have city staff write a report about the feasibility of New Westminster enacting Canada's first Living Wage By Law. After that weekend we all knew it was on and that this was very winnable.

Our campaign focused around the direct engagement of the residents of New West. This was important because of New West's elite's belief that ACORN leaders and members were outsiders (aliens from the USA!) even though most of the same people recognized our members as lifelong residents of the city! We knew it was going to be crucial not to get signatures from all of our chapters, but only from residents of New West which has complications in a city that ends at a busy street and when the membership loved petitioning at the mall or skytrain station. That wouldn't work. A classic door to door

ACORN style Associate Member Canvass was the only way to do it.

The associates' canvass made it possible for us to get our message out to the public, drive up the level of supporters and, by signing up cash associate ACORN members along the way, we were able to collect the money that would sustain the canvass. In all, we knocked on over one half of the doors in the city—signing up hundreds of new dues members and collecting over 1500 names and numbers on a supporter form. Support for the campaign was strong and our membership numbers grew to the extent that a second chapter in Queensborough was needed. Queensborough is a working family area that is separated by part of the Fraser river. Win or lose, ACORN was winning this campaign as new members came to support us. We knew that from the start.

After the canvass, which ended in early 2010, until the City of New Westminster's Human Resource department finished the report concerning the financial implications of the Living Wage members, leaders and staff waited anxiously. Allies on council were telling us "not to pressure" council too much, and our allies in the coalition were doing a great job of giving advice to New West's Human Resources department on how to write a report.

This was all relaxed and was the reality for winning on the West Coast, but organizationally, a campaign principle of building momentum is status quo and "Down Time" in an active campaign is counterintuitive. How were we to keep the issue relevant without doing any direct action which is by far the quickest and most effective way of building our membership? We decided to hold a public forum that would emphasize the importance of the Family Living Wage of $16.74 and raise the profile of the campaign. We did it up!

On the poster and on stage was the Director of the BC CCPA, Seth Klien, the before mentioned New Westminster councilor, Jaimie McEvoy and *Living Wage for Families* organizer, Michael McCarthy Flynn. They joined Preeti Misra and David Tate from BC ACORN at the Food and Commercial Workers' union hall for our Living Wage Forum. Turnout was good for the event but overall it gave us a reason to go over the lists that we had built during the canvass to see who was missing and what else could be done. If campaigns are won through backroom deals, no community capacity is built. Democracy is built by engaging the community in decision making—this is a core principle of ACORN organizing.

Other organizations attended the forum including union members and, people from local non profits, the local branch manager from the credit union VanCity, as well as prominent provincial and federal politicians. The all supported New Westminster Chair David Tate in passing the microphone around to hear the astute arguments of Seth Klein and to the more passionate and humorous voices of Preeti and Jaimie. It was also good to see various people from town who don't really like ACORN or good wages show up, state their arguments and beliefs only to be consistently out debated by the panel. Solidarity Forever!

By the time the vote was immanent after the Forum people were involved since they had come there for ACORN's large free tax service. The meeting built up to a buzz of excitement. Staff and leaders were excited and talked about the merits of the Living Wage. Everyone learned again how community members getting together really can make a difference! Over 1000 people came into our free income tax site and left with their taxes done and got the direct messaging that ACORN was on the move and that this living wage thing was big and for real.

THE CAMPAIGN IN THE NATION'S CAPITAL

Ottawa ACORN members kicked off their campaign in May, 2009 but a lot of work was done before the initial launch. In December, 2008, members from across Ottawa held a city wide meeting to decide priorities for the coming year. Members decided that the top three priorities for the campaign should be wages, housing and education. Since wages and incomes were a clear priority, leaders of the organization met in January, 2009 to decide what kind of income related campaign could be run. Raising the minimum wage was discussed thoroughly at the meeting. Toronto ACORN developed publicity about the provincial government's plan to raise the minimum wage to $10 an hour and Ottawa ACORN took part with its sister city as part of its own first year of action. Both offices worked with unions to force the government to raise the minimum wage higher. Instead of $10 an hour, the provincial government chose to raise the minimum wage to $10.25 over four years while raising their own salaries by 30%.

ACORN members decided that instead of focusing on the provincial minimum wage, they would focus on a municipal campaign. The leaders of the Ottawa office decided to push for something higher than simply a minimum, a living wage. Members and organizers referred to municipal campaigns run by US ACORN, data compiled through their living wage resource centre, and to living wage research done in Canadian contexts for the Ottawa campaign. The Canadian Centre for Policy Alternatives for instance conducted research about what a living wage would look like for Toronto. Also, Vibrant Communities, using much of the precedent from US ACORN offices, was trying to get the city of Calgary to adopt a living wage by-law. However, after reaching out to many non-profits organizations and unions, Ottawa ACORN could not find any research on what living wages would look like in the city of Ottawa.

Members picked parameters for the campaign at a meeting held in March 2009. They wanted to focus on Ottawa, aim to fight for a wage of between $13-$15 per hour, focus on getting a bylaw enacted and also hone in on where public dollars were being spent. The premise of the campaign became that public dollars shouldn't subsidize poverty wages. The Ottawa board waded through research and went to the leadership with the data. Fighting for universal living wage in the city would be hard, especially with the current political climate on Ottawa city council. So why not narrow the scope to focus solely on how people were being paid with public dollars? Other campaigns had been won in the US doing this very thing. Narrowing the scope meant focusing on who the municipal government does business with, including contractors who gain tenders as a cleaning company, firms or companies receiving economic development assistance, and anyone receiving grants or funding from the city. After a consensus on who was the target for a living wage, we had to justify making the living wage around $13 to $15 an hour and also find out how many people would be affected by the campaign.

With the help of student interns, we figured out that the Low Income Cut Off (LICO) justified the amount our members wanted to fight for. LICO, although criticized by some critics on the far left such as not the best index to measure the true cost of living, calculates the cost of housing, food and clothing/essentials in a given region based on population. This index was used by the city of Calgary to generate their living wage and by the city of Waterloo. After taxes, the base living wage was $13.25 per hour without benefits and $12.20 per hour with benefits. In June 2009, LICO was reassessed, therefore making the real amount $13.50 per hour.

The big question our members, allies, and targets then began to ask before we officially launched our campaign in May was: who and how many will this affect. After asking many city HR staff and policy staff, we were told that approximately 477 people are not in the city union, but are on contract and that their wages were unknown. We then asked for the list of businesses receiving contracts from the city since the living wage campaign would affect these workers (and also our members, cleaners, parking attendants, security guards for parking lots, etc). However, (after asking just about every councilor and attempting to contact city staff) no one could provide a list of businesses who receive contracts or funds from the city. We had student interns go through the city minutes from 2008-2009 and pull all the contractors mentioned in the minutes to compile a list of businesses who would be targeted in the campaign. Some of those businesses probably paid living wages and some we knew for certain did not, since our members were working for these contractors. So we still had only an approximate answer to release.

What we did know was that the city had no solid record of where they did business and that the city of Ottawa recently enacted the Ethical Procurement Policy (www.ottawa.ca), which says the city doesn't do business with sweatshop or involved in child labor. Both of these elements became justifications when speaking with councilors, especially naysayers. Our members could say, "hey our city doesn't know who they are doing business with therefore we at least need to get living wage on the table for the city staff to investigate.' Also, the city has committed to being ethical, so living wage is a logical next step. This helped us win the support of the councilors on the fence about living wage itself. But who would support placing it on the agenda for the June 2009 Community and Protective Services committee? City councilors on this committee, Peggy Feltmate and Alex Cullen, agreed to bring it forward. Members and organizers began setting up meetings with city councilors on the committee and outside the committee to find out who we could count on and who needed work.

The press event and campaign launched in May 2009. Leaders Michelle Walrond and Kathleen Fortin hosted the agenda and members chose guest speakers who from federal as well as provincial level supported the program. Non-profits, such as Canada Without Poverty, came to the meeting as well as unlikely supporters such as Councilor Marianne Wilkeson, whose record is proven fiscally conservative but socially liberal. Our organization received great coverage from the media and interest from other non profits across Canada such as Vibrant Communities Calgary and Opportunities in Waterloo.

Gradually, staff and members have gained a list of supporters. We set up meetings with allies such as labor, non-profits and the business community. In June 2009, Councilor Cullen and Councilor Feltmate introduced our living wage campaign at the Community and Protective Services committee, where councilor Georges Bedard moved to include it as part of the city's proposed, Poverty Reduction Strategy which was still in its infant-stages.

Unprepared for this to happen, our members finished speaking and watched this debate unfold as councilors voted to incorporate a living wage as part of the strategy. And it was done.

Was this the best route to go? Many poverty reduction strategies in North America do not include wages and income as part of their goals. But our board and members went with what unfolded. The next step was to meet with all the people appointed to the Poverty Reduction Strategy Committee appointed by the city's Community and Protective Services Committee. Members of the Poverty Reduction Strategy Committee include: the Community Foundation of Ottawa, the United Way, Entraide Budgetaire, a business representative, a representative from the Health and Community Resource Centre, two city of Ottawa staff, Ottawa Inuit Children's Centre, and Ottawa Community Immigrant Services Organization. Leaders and organizers worked to set up meetings with everyone except for two (who were in support anyway) in order to make sure there was a clear understanding about our campaign. In September 2009, the leaders made a presentation to the committee which was well received. After this, the committee held two public consultations. Our office mobilized many of our low income members and time was spent ensuring that our living wage campaign was well understood so as to give it more support.

In November 2009, the Poverty Reduction Strategy was supposed to be presented to the Community and

Protective Services Committee, but the city moved the date to December 3 009. The meeting was subsequently moved again, which we found out only a week before, to January 21 2010. In order to change councilors' minds from being undecided to supporters of the strategy, our members and organizers started a living wage canvass in target wards in May and 'at councilors voted with us since we had run a canvass in their ward. The council, Rick Cherielli, who voted against our campaign did not have a canvass in his ward. Councilor Cherielli's arguments on the right, against our campaign were that it is not the city's jurisdiction and that it would raise property taxes. When the motion went to council on Feb 10 2010, councilors on the right again raised these same concerns. But we passed a major hurdle which was winning council's support for the living wage in principal in a vote called by the mayor. 14 councilors voted to research, report and make a decision on living wage in the spring of 2010. 7 councilors voted against even the idea of researching and reporting back to councilors on point 14 of the Poverty Reduction Strategy (living wage). More councilors were actually against the provision in the Poverty Reduction Strategy around improving the Ontario Disability Support Program (ODSP), where 13 voted for the provision and 8 against.

Feb 10 marks a huge hurdle in our campaign. Despite the conservative Mayor's efforts to squash our campaign at council, (he made people declare a vote on our living wage point and on the ODSP provision), it still passed.

We also discovered that some councilors had definitely increased their commitment to the campaign and to working with our membership. So far, our campaign has received over 60 media hits, many of them positive. Although some negative pieces in the Ottawa Citizen by columnist Randall Denly likened our fight for $13.50 to communism. One of our members, Michelle Walrond, who has taken a leadership role in the campaign, always says to right wing supporters: "We are only fighting for a small bite of the elephant and $13.50 is still a poverty wage." Disturbingly, Walrond noted that every time she told councilors this line they seemed to sigh relief, that working people would still be poor, that they cannot get rich off of our campaign.

Support came from some important business leaders, such as the Chamber of Commerce since a member, Nadia Willard, appeared on Talk Ottawa, a local call-in-show. In October, on television, Nadia invited, the Chamber to support the campaign and since then we have sent them our documents and asked for meetings. We have yet to hear back from the Chamber of Commerce, but in the Ottawa EMC East on Jan. 23rd, the director of the Chamber of Commerce, Erin Kelly, stated they wanted to work with Ottawa ACORN and they also support the principal of a living wage. Our leaders and members were very pleased to hear that we have support from the business community. In Calgary, the Chamber of Commerce was a vocal supporter of the living wage. We asked the Chamber director in Calgary to send their comments of support to Ottawa's Chamber, so this helped us to move the local Chamber closer to us. Many of those who haven't made a decision claim that this is the province's responsibility and that we should run campaigns again them. As we have done in the past, members will continue to pressure the provincial government to increase the minimum wage. But we have essentially run this campaign and won an increase over a four year period.

We received immediate support from many of our allies, but a few were critical of the rate per hour that our members picked saying that it was too low. Our members, of course, wanted to fight for a higher rate, but at the end of the day, we chose something that was winnable. Critics from the right think $13.50 is far too high despite research linked to the Low Income Cut Off provided by Statistics Canada. Some supporters on the left also didn't think our campaign should apply to non-profit organizations. But our board and leadership have decided to push for this provision. If an organization, like the United Way can pay a living wage without core government or corporate funding, everyone can too. Those on the left wanted our campaign to cover far more, such as an across the board wage increase for everyone in Ottawa, workplace safety provisions, and benefits.

Members feel relieved but, at the same time, now they know that the real battle is, before city staff reports to councils. Our members want to see what a living wage would look like in the city of Ottawa and hear spokespersons for it. However, in 2012 councillors supporting this proposal were defeated and the committee considering the reform was disbanded.

COMMUNITY ORGANIZING GOES GREEN

Have you ever wondered what would happen if a prominent local environmental organization partnered with a low and moderate income member based community group? In the last two years, the Toronto Environmental Alliance and ACORN Canada have successfully worked together on two new grassroots initiative in Toronto that simultaneously green the city, reduce poverty and build community capacity and leadership.

For over 20 years the Toronto Environmental Alliance (TEA) has been successfully advocating for environmental change in Toronto. TEA's mission is to address local issues through community engagement and fight for a healthier and greener city for all Torontonians. Some key areas of advocacy work include reducing pesticide use and toxic pollution from factories, recycling and composting, public transit, and local food. All of these environmental issues are connected to the health and well being of everyone who lives and works in Toronto. TEA's efforts in these areas have always been through a social equity lens, ensuring that any environmental changes we make in Toronto will improve the well being of all residents.

As in most cities and with most environmental movements, those who do not own their homes and those living in poverty are almost always left out. Without the appropriate networks, experience, or profile finding outreach and engagement in low to moderate-income high-rise buildings was a major challenge for TEA.

Enter ACORN. Now in their 6th year, Ontario ACORN has been organizing and maintaining community based groups of low and moderate income families in neighborhoods across Toronto and Ottawa to advocate around issues of shared mutual concern. Toronto ACORN members have taken action and won victories on issues as diverse as a higher minimum wage, regulation of payday lenders, and better housing for tenants. A different approach emerged when, in 2008, when TEA approached ACORN Canada about an project they were organizing called Low Income Tenant Energy Savers (LITES). With financial support from the Government of Ontario, the LITES project was to work with tenants and landlords to promote energy conservation in high-rise apartment buildings in Toronto and Ottawa, reducing greenhouse gas emissions and energy costs in the process. Over the course of a year, tenants living in the 2 high-rise buildings were identified by Toronto and Ottawa ACORN's organizing staff, then trained and hired to become tenant leads on the local project.

Low and moderate income families face many unique challenges not faced by affluent communities that constrain their ability to collectively reduce their environmental footprint. First, they often do not own their home infrastructure (eg. major appliances, windows, doors, insulation), which has such a big impact on their energy consumption. Second, many families are "low income" and therefore don't have the financial means to engage in actions that reduce their environmental footprint.

Ontario ACORN, with over five years of experience doing community organizing, worked to train the community leaders on basic door-to-door engagement techniques for outreach. This was paired with TEA's expertise on community-led energy conservation strategies to endow these community leaders with the knowledge, skills and resources to carry out the projects successfully.

These community leaders became the key community based organizers and educators on the project, engaging their neighbors on the importance of saving energy and enabling them to participate by providing energy saving tips, tools and one-on-one assistance. Together the project was able to offset at least 45 tones of CO_2 and engage over 400 tenant households per city in the energy conservation program, called PLANET (Preserving Lawrence Avenue's Natural Energy Today). Both TEA and ACORN are organizations that fight for systemic and legislative change at all levels of government around social, economic, and environmental issues that impact specific populations. Both organizations also run well developed active campaigns in Toronto that have meaningful, albeit sometimes controversial, social and political implications, making them unusual candidates to set up and manage purely educational, community development projects like LITES. One might ask to what benefit would both organization direct trained staff and organizational resources in such a direction, and one would be posing a very good question.

ACORN saw LITES less as a way to encourage low income residents to reduce energy but more as a vehicle to build extensive lists of people who might later on become ACORN members. The scope and length of the project allowed ACORN to build meaningful relationships, develop leaders, and identify local issues that would help tie folks into broader ACORN campaigns once the Province's deliverables had been satisfied.

Before LITES, ACORN had not used environmental conservation issues as way to draw new people into the organization in any notable fashion, and its lack of experience in transitioning people from being engaged in one highly focused 'feel good" activity to participating at a deeper level. Serious social and political campaigns did not contribute to building up ACORN's membership. Regardless, ACORN's participation in LITES was not organizationally fruitless. This longer-term and indirect approach to organizing communities around ACORN campaigns was experimental for Ontario ACORN and provided staff with some basic skills and tools and ideas they would need to be more successful in similar types of projects down the line. If we can secure funding to do outreach, we *have to* find a way to make it work for ACORN.

The second project that we partnered on is ongoing and is called Live Green Toronto. This is an initiative funded and led by the City of Toronto, under the leadership of Mayor David Miller with the goal of engaging residents across Toronto to take actions to improve the environment by reducing greenhouse gas emissions in their homes and communities. In an effort to make the Live Green Toronto initiative more accessible and relevant to everyone living here, the City tendered a Request for Proposal for the provision of community outreach services.

Toronto ACORN and TEA made the case that in order to engage low—to moderate-income tenants on 'living green' across Toronto, a special model and extensive networks of organized citizens would be required. Together we are able to provide just that. Toronto ACORN deploys a door to door canvass in targeted neighborhoods to identify residents interested in doing environmental initiatives. The canvass is supported by our existing membership and leadership in the neighborhood who share environmental concerns. TEA is then able to step in and help with information and resource gathering and finding connections between day-to-day concerns and doable actions that contribute to meaningful environmental change.

In the first 12 months alone, 1306 community members in four different neighborhoods across Toronto were engaged and 31 community meetings and events were held with a total of 591 participants. In addition, 1,200 trees have been planted and one container garden site established. With TEA's help, ACORN has been able to find relevant local groups to partner with on specialize local 'greening' projects such as clean up days, community gardening and garden tours, tree planting, recycling, and more. These projects are not just reducing greenhouse gas emissions. They are making the neighborhoods cleaner and greener, and the communities stronger and healthier.

In past years TEA helped design and implement similar energy conservation projects in Toronto Community Housing buildings, but the LITES project was the first of its kind for low-income tenants living in privately-owned rental housing. While TEA had anticipated the hard work of engaging tenants in energy conservation when there were many of other priorities in their buildings like broken appliances and infestations, there were other new challenges they hadn't experienced before. TEA was faced with the challenge of engaging tenants who were not directly paying for utility costs and landlords with whom they had no previous relationship. These landlords also had no real business plans, or dedicated funds, to work toward energy conservation. Not only does ACORN have an extensive network of tenants who are ACORN members in high-rise buildings across Ontario cities, they also have working relationships and the 'ear' of all major high-rise landlords. They have built trust among tenants and a repertoire among landlords for getting things done in buildings as a result of years of organizing for improved rental housing.

In the Toronto ACORN side of the arrangement we were also able to utilize these two partnerships to another important organizational goal: to help overcome capacity shortfalls and maintain existing chapter activity. When organizing a precariously housed and employed constituency, a drop off in organized neighborhood activity has the effect of greatly reducing the ability of organization to continue to grow the organization. One of the fundamental principles of acorn's unique organizing model is: *If you're not growing you're dying.* The Live Green Initiative enables us to bring new individuals into the organization and keep the level of activity higher than would otherwise be possible. The continued activity has shown to greatly increase the organizations ability to maintain a coherent community level group through times when resources are scarce or staff capacity is limited for other reasons.

Half way through the second year of a potentially five year program we are trying to build the capacity of the local live-green working groups even further. Traditionally the Live Green program relied heavily on ACORN members that had become leaders by participating in Toronto ACORN's leadership development programs over the last 6 years. However, the second year of Live Green is focusing on plugging the new Live green members that have had little exposure to ACORN's classic work into ACORN's leadership development program. This will even further build the capacity of the leadership of the program.

From its very inception, the Live Green project was more attractive from a community organizing perspective than LITES because its work plan involves a significantly greater focus on community meetings and collective "green" community actions a method to create change as opposed to attempting to influence individual, isolated behaviors. This means people with laundry lists of social and economic issues are regularly coming together in the same place at the same time to talk about improving their communities. These groups have exciting political potential and ACORN is gradually learning from, and experimenting with, different ways to harness it and direct it towards other municipal, provincial, and federal campaigns.

At the doors, Toronto ACORN also chose to talk to folks about environmental issues *as* social justice issues, a distinct difference from the approach we used to engage people during the LITES project. Individuals at the door are given the opportunity and are encouraged to talk about *any* issues important to them, and our organizers are trained to tie those issues, whatever they may be, to the environment. For instance, a single mother who works two jobs to feed her children will likely be interested in a local food security initiative in which she can have a voice. This approach has allowed ACORN to better identify potential ACORN members and actually build the community organization in a meaningful way through a city funded environmental project.

We hope the results and learning from these experiences will help build confidence and momentum in other communities, and lead to similar initiatives across Canada or beyond. No community should be left behind in an effort to improve the environment, or society, especially when the benefits of taking action can directly improve the living standards and quality of life for the residents who need it most.

EDITOR'S COMMENT

The perspective of ACORN organizers on the environment is different from the views of our Northern teacher, vocational trades organizer, credit union manager or school superintendent. More importantly, these ACORN organizers are bringing groups together for a number of different campaigns. They are building allies for the future. For advocates, there are no enemies, just future supporters. Action is primary; surveys are to persuade councils to change their votes. Ideology is important insofar as issues of concern to the Left are focused, discussed, and acted upon.

Similar to other chapters in this part of the book, this international organizing combines opposites that make for a dynamic organization. The environment and social justice are different aims that can only partially be reconciled. Political opposition brings about an increasingly diverse set of allies, such as the chamber of commerce joining unions to support the Living Wage Campaign. Coalitions become political when change agents move beyond local partnerships. The preoccupation with action means unfortunately for an editor that advocates are not concerned with their writing; it is an achievement to obtain writing from them at all. With all his grammar mistakes, James Wardlaw, in particular, explodes with feeling and appeals to ACORN members. All of the advocates reveal their imaginations and dedications to greater social justice for everyone in our society.

Chapter 12

After Partnerships

The authors let us consider that partnerships, much like a cocktail party, allow for the scope of a conversation to expand with the addition of each new voice. A multi-layered conversation reveals new opportunities and of course challenges. But based on the experiences of the contributors, the plunge into the right conversations with the right guests is worth the exploration. To take it further—partnerships may be one of the last great frontiers—a passport to explore the "white space" or unchartered land that exists between two organizations that otherwise has not been uncovered. It's a place ripe for opportunity for those who embrace leadership, vision, collaboration, growth and risk (Colleen Janssen Hood, Commix Consulting, n.d.).

The evolution of this book has been constant and dramatic. As the path has become clearer, several contributors have been omitted, including Mrs. Hood. The previous work by the author had been on local partnerships involving arts groups, businesses, and non-profit organizations (Mitchell, 2003 & 2006).

This book was to present the personal experiences of those involved in partnerships. Most partnerships for schools, for example, are with individuals, not companies or organizations. The first essay is then an account of forming a partnership with parents and students in the North by one teacher.

Close to the original starting point, rural educators were drawn into my orbit while I served as Coordinator of the Rural Principals Program at the University of Calgary. Tim Goddard, a former principal in the North, who was a teacher in the program for rural principals, suggested Nancy MacIntouch. Another rural writer, Ann Jones, was a speaker in the Rural Education Congress at the University of Saskatchewan and she became a contributor to this book as well as a previous one (Mitchell, 2002).

The second author Amanda Tattersall represents a different position, political change in broader societies: Australia, Canada, and the United States. Her work was brought to my attention by Wade Rathke, the founder of Associations for Community Reform Now (ACORN). Mr. Rathke had been influenced by father H. L. Mitchell, who founded the Southern Tenant Farmers Union (Mitchell, 2007). Mr. Rathke, in Chapter 8, along with organizers for ACORN, in Chapter 11, contributed chapters that focus on issues of changing social conditions and challenging the existing power structure.

These radicals have challenged the very definition of partnership or rather have provided an alternative structure to partnerships, coalitions. Mrs. Hood says "partnerships are unique, relationship-based and seek mutually beneficial human-based outcomes (Ibid)." Policy changes are more than outcomes and the change in terms of reference in societies is not unique. Coalitions, unlike partnerships, can be hierarchical within society and between societies, not just grass-roots alliances in one settings.

Both partnerships and coalitions require visions as Black argues in Chapter 9, but Tattersall in Chapter 2 is very clear that organizations, such as teacher unions must pursue educational improvements, not just membership benefits, in order to be effective. Mrs. Hood, Ms. Black, and many of the other contributors have participated in my previous books on partnerships (Mitchell, Klinck & Burger, 2004). Mrs. Hood agrees with Ms. Black' definition and have gone on to indicate key indicators of local partnership success:

> ***Effective Communication and Stakeholder Relations,*** *such as the coordination of varied programs in Chapter 3;*

> ***Leadership or the passion for it as shown by the organizer of the vocational program in*** *Chapter 4;*

> ***Clarity of purpose and goal exemplified by the music program in*** *Chapter 5;*

> ***Accountability & Outcome, as shown by***
> *the audit conducted by First Calgary in Chapter*
> *6 and the multiple evaluations of enviroworks*
> *conducted in Chapter 4;*

> ***Organizational   Adaptability   &***
> ***Commitment to Collaboration, such as the***
> ***boundary spanners discussed in*** *Chapter 7;*
> *and*

> ***Sustainable Funding/Resources is best***
> ***based upon multiple partnerships, not just***
> ***corporations as shown in*** *Chapter* 9.

Mrs. Hood's 2004 survey of funders in Calgary supported the last result. Financial commitment by both partners is essential to sustaining the partnerships.

An equally impressive set of measures is emerging from the work on coalitions. In Chapter 2, Tattersall argues that fewer partners are better and brokers are necessary for the local organization. In Chapter 8, Rathke shows how international and national organizations supplement grass-roots ones. In Chapter 9, Black shows how empowerment of students leads to creative projects, such as ruMAD. In Chapter 10, Jones reveals how a summer program can leak outsiders and insiders as the local people develop confidence from international attention. In Chapter 1l, allies can be built from the

Chamber of Commerce by poverty groups; there are no permanent opponents.

The best connection between partnership and coalition theories is suggested by the work on Lynn Bradshaw. Reflecting, perhaps, her own change from an administrative position to an academic role in the partnership she discusses, Dr. Bradshaw states: "Visioning continues throughout the life of a collaborative effort. As the participants and the context for the partnership change, stakeholders continue to clarify and refine the vision." (Bradshaw, 2002. p. 180) She further shows scouts play a critical role in adapting to change: Mrs. Hood comments, "They are described as key individuals at the boundaries who link resources, craft solutions, and weave together available programs and resources into a long-term vision." (Hood, n. d.). Bradshaw believes successful implementation depends upon collective ability to manage change.

Creativity may depend upon both partnership and coalition approaches being combined. It is in such dynamic approaches that the contributions of individuals and individual partnership can suggest new paths. Individuals can be a part of shareholder networks, particularly as scouts or boundary spanners. Contributions of individuals can be measured by results, changes in frames of references or what is discussed, and strength of the shareholder partner organizations.

Furthermore, creative solutions emerge from the combination of opposites shown repeatedly in the discussion of international relationship, such as insiders and outsiders in Chapter 10 or environmental and social justice goals in Chapter 11. Individual creativity among teachers and students is shown in Chapters 9 and 10. The options for policy can also be multiple as Rathke discusses in Chapter 8. Organizers and advocates for changes reveal these contrary pulls and pushes, which writers who assume a professional stance hide.

BIBLIOGRAPY

Abdal-Haqq, I. (1996). An information provider's perspective on the professional development movement. *Contemporary Education*, 67(4), 237-239.

Ad Hoc Private Sector Group (1998). Building better partnerships-statement from the *ad hoc* private sector group at the Jakarta Conference. *Health Promotion International*, 13(3), 191-2.

Alberta Science and Research Authority. (1998). *A strategy for information and communications technology in Alberta* [On-line]. Avaailable: http:www.gov.ab.ca/sra/publicdocs/ ict/index.html.

Allen, S. (1997). Building harmonious relationships. *Teaching Music,* 5 (2), 33-34, 52.

Alltrichet, H., & Somekh, B. (1993). *Teachers investigate their work*. New York: Routledge.

Andrews, A. (1990). Interdisciplinary and interorganizational collaboration. In A. Minahan (Ed.), *Encylopaedia of social work*. Silver Springs, MD: National Association of Social Workers.

Angus, L. (2006). Educational leadership and the imperative of including student voices, student interests, and students' lives in the mainstream. *International Journal of Leadership in Education*, 9(4), 369-379.

Angus, L. (2009). Problematizing neighborhood renewal: community, school effectiveness and disadvantage. *Critical Studies in Education*, 50(1), 37-50.

Annesley, B., Horne, M. & Cottam, H. (2001). *Learning buildings.* London: SchoolWorks.

Annie E. Casey Foundation. (1999). *Kids count data book: State profiles of child well-being.* Baltimore, MD: Author.

Appreciative Inquiry Commons (n. d.). *Outstanding cases: A Chicago case of intergenerational appreciative inquiry* [On-line]. Available: wysiwyg://75 /http:// appreciativeinquiry.cwru. edu/intro/bestcases.

Arvanitakis, J., & Marren, S. (2009). *Putting the politics back into politics: Young people and democracy in Australia.* Discussion paper. Sydney: The Whitlam Institute.

Associated Press (2002, July 10). Foundations yank funding to Pittsburgh schools. *CNN News* [On-line]. Available:wysiiwyg:// http://fyi.cnn.com/ 20002/fyi/ . . . ws/07/10/ pittsburgh.schools. ap/index.html.

Australian Government. (2009). *Towards a national strategy for young Australians: A discussion paper.* Canberra: Department of Education, Employment and Workplace Relations.

Babineau, N. (1998). Partners in the arts: The orchestra as community resource. *Connect, Combine, Communicate: Revitalizing the Arts in Canadian Schools, Summary of Proceedings, the National Symposium on Arts Education, Cape Breton, August 1997,* Brian A. Roberts, Ed. Sydney: The University College of Cape Breton Press.

Babineau, N. (2000). Enriching the curriculum—enriching the community: Canadian partnerships for arts education. *Music of the Spheres Conference Proceedings*, 12-28.

Bainer, D. (1997). A comparison of four models of group efforts and their implications for establishing educational partnerships. *Journal of Research in Rural Education*, 13(3), 143-152.

Bainer, D. (1998 October). *Why partnerships endure.* Paper presented at the National Symposium of Partnerships in Education organized by the National Association of Partners in Education, Los Angeles.

Bainer, D., Barron, P., & Cantrell, D. (1998 Summer). *Scienceing with watersheds, environmental education and partnerships (SWEEP): Instructor's guide to implementation.* Mansfield, OH: SWEEP Project, Ohio State at Mansfield.

Baker, L. (1994, April). *The politics of collaboration: How an educational partnership works.* Paper presented at the Annual Meeting of the American Educational Research Association, New Orleans, LA.

Bank of America (1995, April 1). *The Orr school network a community-based educational partnership 1989-1995.* Chicago: Bank of America.

Bardach, E. (1996). Turf barriers to interagency collaboration. In D. Kettl, & H. Nilward *The state of public management.* Baltimore: Johns Hopkins University Press.

Barnett, B., Hall, G., Berg, J., & Camarena, M. (1999). A typology of partnerships for promoting innovation. *Journal of School Leadership*, 9(6), 484-510.

Battiste, M. and Barman, J. (Eds). (1995). *First Nations education in Canada: The circle unfolds.* Vancouver: University of British Columbia Press.

Bednarz, D. (1983). Quantity and quality in evaluation research: A divergent view. Revised version of paper presented at the Joint Meeting of the Evaluation Network and the Evaluation Research Society, Chicago.

Belsie, L. (2001, September 13). 'Look for what's right.' *Christian Science Monitor* [On-line]. Available: http://www. csmonitor.com/2001/0913/p15sl-lihc.html.

Bentley, T. (2002). *Learning beyond the classroom*. Melbourne: Centre for Strategic Education.

Berliner, B. (1997). *What it takes to work together: The promise of educational partnerships*. (Knowledge Brief No. 14). San Francisco, CA: WestEd.

Bessant, J. (2004). Mixed messages: Youth participation and democratic practice. *Australian Journal of Political Science*, 39(2), 387-404.

Birch, D. (2001). *Partnerships from a business perspective*. Paper for the Enterprise and Career Education Foundation Research Forum, Sydney, 14-15 May, 2001.

Black, R. (2004). Thinking community as a social investment in Australia. In Mitchell, S., Klinck, P., & Burger, J. (Eds). *Worldwide partnerships for schools with voluntary organizations, foundations, universities, companies, and community councils* (pp. 223-252). Lewiston, NY: Edwin Mellen.

Black, R. (2007). *Crossing the bridge: Overcoming entrenched disadvantage through student-centered learning*. Melbourne: Education Foundation.

Black, R. (Black 2008a). *Beyond the classroom: Building new school networks*. Melbourne: ACER Press.

Black, R. (2008b). *New school ties: Networks for success*. Melbourne: Department of Education and Early Childhood Development.

Black, R. (2009). *Boardroom to Classroom: The role of the corporate and philanthropic sectors in school education.* Melbourne: Department of Education and Early Childhood Development.

Black, R. (2010). Promise or practice? Student participation in low-socioeconomic communities. *Youth Studies Australia*, 29(2), 9-15.

Black, R., Lemon, B., & Walsh, L. (2010). Literature review and background research for the National Collaboration Project: Extended Service School Model. A report for the Department of Education, Western Australia.

Black, R., Stokes, H., Turnbull, M., & Levy, J. (2009). Civic participation through the curriculum. *Youth Studies Australia*, 28(3), 13-20.

Black, R., & Walsh, L. (2009). *Corporate Australia and schools: Forming business class alliances and networks.* Melbourne: Centre for Strategic Education.

Black, R. (Forthcoming). Civic Participation for Community Capacity Building. In D. Bottrell & S. Goodwin (Eds.), *Schools, communities and social inclusion.* Melbourne: Palgrave Macmillan.

Bloom, M. (1993). *Evaluating business-education collaboration: Values assessment process.* Toronto: Conference Board of Canada.

Blum, J., (2000, May 26). Scores are up in D.C. Schools, *Washington Post*, B1, B5.

Bollman, R. (Ed.). (1993). *Rural and small town Canada.* Toronto: Thompson.

Book, C. (1996). Professional development schools. In J. Sikula, T. Buttery, & E. Guyton (Eds.), *Handbook of research in teacher education* (2nd ed., pp 194-210). New York: McMillan.

Boston, B. (1996, August). Report card: A new study identifies successful partnerships in music education. *Symphony,* 47(4), 46-48, 50, 82-86.

Bourdieu, P. (1986). The forms of capital. In J. Richardson (Ed.), *Handbook of theory and research for the sociology of education* (pp. 241-258). New York: Greenwood Press.

Bourdieu, P. and Passeron, J. (1996). *Reproduction in Education, Society and Culture.* Second Edition. London: Sage.

Bradshaw, L. (1999). Principals as boundary spanners: Working collaboratively to solve problems. *NASSP Bulletin, 83,* 611, 38-47.

Bradshaw, L. (2000). Improving communication across school boundaries. *The Delta Kappa Gamma Bulletin, 64* (6), 5-11.

Bradshaw, L. (2000, May). The changing role of principals in school partnerships. *NASSP Bulletin, 84,* 616, 86-96.

Britt, L. (Ed.). (1985/86). *School and business partnerships.* Bloomington, IN: Phi Delta Kappa.

Brody, H. (2000). *The other side of Eden: Hunters, farmers and the shaping of the world.* Toronto: Douglas &McIntyre. Vancouver: University of British Columbia Press.

Brousseau, C. (1999, February 6). Harmonious Partnership. *Kingston Whig Standard,* Companion section, pp. 1, 3.

Brown, D (1995). *School with heart: Voluntarism and public education.* Vancouver: Faculty of Education, University of British Columbia.

Brownlea, A. (1987). Participation: myths, realities and prognosis. *Social Science and Medicine,* 25(6), 605-614.

Bullough, R. (1982). Professional schizophrenia: Teacher education in confusion. *Contemporary Education,* 53(4), 207-211.

Bullough, R. Hobbs, S., Kauchak, D., Crow, N., & Stokes, D. (1997). Long-term PDS development in research universities and the clinicalization of teacher education. *Journal of Teacher Education*, 48(2), 85-95.

Buse. K. & Walt, G. (2000a). Global public-private partnerships: Part I—a new development in health? *Bulletin of the World Health Organization*, 78(4), 549-561.

Buse, K. & Walt, G. (2000b). Global public-private partnerships: part II—what are the health issues for global governance? *Bulletin of the World Health Organization,* 78(5), 699-709.

Business Council of Australia (2007). Restoring our Edge in Education: Making Australia's Education System its Next Competitive Advantage. Melbourne: Business Council of Australia.

Butterfoss, F., Goodman, R., & Wandersman, A. (1996). Community coalitions for prevention and health promotion: Factors predicting satisfaction, participation, and planning. *Health Education Quarterly*, 23(1), 65-79.

Button, K., Ponticell, J. & Johnson, M. (1996). Enabling school-university collaborative research: Lessons learned in professional development schools. *Journal of Teacher Education*, 47(1), 16-20.

Calhoun, E., & Glickman, C. (1993, April). *Issues and dilemmas of action research in the league of professional schools.* Paper presented at the annual meeting of the American Educational Research Association, Atlanta, GA.

Canadian Chamber of Commerce (1992). *Focus 2000: Business-education partnerships, your planing guide.* Don Mills, ON: CCH Canadian.

Carley, M., Chapman, M., Hastings, A,. Kirk, K. & Young. R. (2000). Urban regeneration through partnership: a study in nine urban regions in England, Scotland and Wales. York: Joseph Rowntree Foundation.

Carrington, S. (1999). Inclusion needs a different school culture. *International Journal of Inclusive Education, 3*(3), 257-268.

Carrington, D. (2003). *How trust and foundations can be more than grantmakers.* Melbourne: Asia Pacific Centre for Philanthropy and Social Investment.

Centre for Corporate Public Affairs. (2007). *Corporate Community Investment in Australia.* Melbourne: Centre for Corporate Public Affairs.

Centre for TeleLearning and Rural Education. (2000, July 10). *Research projects* [On-line]. Available: http://www.tellearn. mun.ca/fresearc.html.

Chalker, D. (Ed.) (1999). *Leadership for rural schools.* Lancaster, PA: Technomic.

Chavis, D., & Wandersman, A. (1990). Sense of community in the urban environment: a catalyst for participation and community development. *American Journal of Community Psychology*, 18(1), 55-81.

Cibulka, J. G., & Kritek, W. J. (Eds.). (1996). Coordination among schools, families, and communities. Albany: State University of New York Press.

Christensen, C. (1997). *The innovator's dilemma: When new technologies cause great firms to fail.* Boston: Harvard Business School Press.

Christen, F., Eldredge, F., Ibom, K., Johnston, M. & Thomas, M. (1996). Collaboration in support of change. *Theory into Practice*, 35(3), 187-195.

Clark, C., Dyson, A., Millward, A., and Robson, S. (1999). Theories of inclusion, theories of schools: Deconstructing and reconstructing the 'inclusive school'. *British Educational Research Journal, 25*(2), 157-177.

Clark, C., & Peterson, P.L. (1986). Teachers' thought processes. In M.C. Wittrock (Ed.), *Handbook of research on teaching* (pp. 255-296). New York: Macmillan.

Clark, R. (1988). School-university relationships: An interpretative review. In Sironik, K. & Goodlad, J. (Eds.) *School-university partnerships in action* (pp. 32-65). New York: Teachers College, Columbia University.

Clifford, P., Friesen, S., and Jacobsen, M. (1998, June). An expanded view of literacy: Hypermedia in the middle school. *Proceedings of the Ed-Media and Ed-Telecom 98: World Conference of Educational Multimedia and Hypermedia & World Conference on Educational Telecommunications*, Freiburg, Germany.

Cobb, C., & Quaglia, R. (1994, April). *Moving beyond school-business partnerships and creating relationships.* Paper presented at the annual meeting of the American Educational Research Association, New Orleans, LA.

Cohen, A. & Kible, B. (1993). *The basics of open-systems evaluation: A resource paper.* Pacific Chapel Hill, NC: Institute for Research and Evaluation.

College Board (2000, January 9). *AP—Subjects* [On-line]. Available: http://www. collegeboard.org/ap/subjects.html.

Collin, P. (2008). *Young people imaging a new democracy: Literature review*. Sydney: Whitlam Institute.

Connell, J. (2010). *Expanding Our Horizons: An Exploration of the Implementation of the International Baccalaureate Programme in Prince Edward Island*. Unpublished master of education thesis, University of Prince Edward Island.

Cooperrider, D. & Whitney, D. (n.d.). *A positive revolution in change: Appreciative inquiry* (Draft) [On-line]. Available: wysiwyg://82/http:// appreciativeinquiry. cwru.edu.

Coopers & Lybrand L.L.P. (1996). *State of North Carolina Smart Start performance audit: Final report*. Raleigh, NC: Joint Legislative Commission on Governmental Operations, North Carolina General Assembly.

Copenhagen Centre (1999). *New employment partnerships in Europe*. Copenhagen: Copenhagen Centre.

Cordiero, P., & Kolek, M. (1996). Introduction: Connecting school communities through educational partnerships. In P. Cordiero (Ed.), *Boundary crossings: Educational partnerships and school leadership* (pp. 1-14). San Francisco: Jossey-Bass.

Corporate Council on Education. (1998). *Employability skills profile: The critical skills of the Canadian workforce*. Toronto: Conference Board of Canada.

Corporate-Higher Education Forum (1987). *From patrons to partners*. Montreal: Corporate-Higher Education Forum.

Council for Aid to Education (1994). *Business/education organizations: roles and opportunities to work together*. New York: Council for Aid to Education.

Covallis School District 509J, Oregon State University & Hewlett Packard (n.d.). *Science Education Partnterships* [On-line]. Available:http://www.septs.org. whatis.htm.

Cramphorn, J. (1999). *The role of partnerships in economic regeneration and development: International perspectives.* Luton, England: University of Warwick.

Crow, G. (1998). Implications for leadership in collaborative schools. In D. Pounder (Ed.), *Restructuring schools for colloboration: Promises and pitfalls* (pp. 135-153). Albany: State University of New York Press.

Crowson, R. L., & Boyd, W. L. (1995). Integration of services for children. In L. C. Rigsby, M. C. Reynolds, & M. C. Wang, (Eds.), *School-community connections: Exploring issues for research and practice* (pp. 121-141). San Francisco: Jossey-Bass Publishers.

Crowson, R. L., & Boyd, W. L. (1996). Structures and strategies: Toward an understanding of alternative models for coordinated children's services. In J. Cibulka & W. Kritek (Eds.), *Coordination among schools, families, and communities* (pp. 137-169). Albany: State University of New York Press.

Cutietta, R. A. (1997). Industry and schools as partners. *Teaching Music,* 5(2). 40-41.

DareArts Foundation (2001). *Annual Report.* Caledon East, On: DareArts.

David, A. (1992). *Public-private partnerships: The private sector and innovation in education* [On-line]. Available: http://www. rppi.org/education/ps142.html.

David, T. (1995). *Community development at work: A case of obscurity in accomplishment.* London: CDF Publications.

Davies, C. (2000a, April 15). Getting health professionals to work together: There's more to collaboration than simply working side by side. *British Medical Journal*, 320 (15 April), 1021-1022.

Davis, M. (2002, June 19). New Ed. Dept. office reaches out to the faithful. *Education Week*, 21(41), pp. 15, 28.

Deal, T., & Peterson, K. (1999). *Shaping school culture: The heart of leadership*. San Francisco: Jossey-Bass.

Denham, C. H. (1996). A report from the national center for social work and education collaboration. In K. Hooper-Briar & H. A. Lawson, (Eds.), *Expanding partnerships for vulnerable children, youth and families* (pp. 107-112). Alexandria, VA: Council on Social Work Education.

Department of Education, Employment and Training, (2000a). Ministerial review of post compulsory education and training pathways in Victoria. Melbourne.

Department of Education, Employment and Training, (2000b). Public education: the next generation. Report of the Ministerial Working Party. Melbourne

Department of Education and Training (2005). Schools as Community Facilities: Policy Framework and Guidelines. Melbourne: Department of Education and Training.

Deushle, K. (1982). Community-oriented primary care: Lessons learned in three decades. *Journal of Community Health*, 8, 13-22.

DiPeso, J. (n. d.). Religion and the environment [On-line]. Available: http://www.lightparty.com/Economic /ReligionAnd Environment.html.

Dixon, N. (2002, June 21). Chicago seeks soldiers for schools. *Washington Post*. On-line: wysiwyg://9/http: //www.washing tonpost.com.

Down East Partnership for Children. (2000). *Five year strategic plan: 2000-2005*. Rocky Mount, NC: Author.

Dryfoos, J. (1994). *Full-service schools: A revolution in health and social services for children, youth, and families*. San Francisco: Jossey-Bass Publishers.

Dusseldorp, J. (1999). Australia's youth: from risk to opportunity. Practices and potential of community partnerships. Education and Industry in Partnership vol. 6, no. 2, December 1999. Melbourne: Victorian Industry Education Partnerships.

Edgar, D. (2001). The patchwork nation: Rethinking government, rebuilding community. Sydney: Harper Collins Publishers.

Edwards, B., Goodwin, M., Pemberton, S., & Woods, M. (2002). *Partnership working in rural regeneration*. Bristol: The Policy Press

Edwards, H. (1999, February). *The evolution of the Permanent Liason Committee*. Yarmouth, NS: Southwest Regional School Board.

Eisenberg, E. M. (1995). A communication perspective on interorganizational cooperation and inner-city education. In L. Rigsby, M. Reynolds, & M. Wang, (Eds.), *School-community connections: Exploring issues for research and practice* (pp. 101-119). San Francisco: Jossey-Bass Publishers.

El Ansari, W. (1998e, Winter). Partnerships and new ways of learning: a second opinion. *NHS Magazine.* 15, 21.

El Ansari, W. & Phillips, C. (1998, June). Partnerships in health? A case study of an urban community partnership in

South Africa. *Proceedings of the Ninth International Congress on Women's Health Issues*, pp. 1-13.

El Ansari, W. (2004). Incentives for partnerships and subsequent difficulties.

In Mitchell, S., Klinck, P., & Burger, J. (Eds.) *Worldwide partnerships for schools with voluntary organizations, foundations, universities, companies, and community councils* (pp. 191-222). Lewiston, NY: Edwin Mellen.

Eldridge Report (2001). Footprints to the future. Summary report from the Prime Minister's Youth Pathways Action Plan Taskforce. Canberra: Office of the Prime Minister.

Eng, E., Salmon, M., & Mullan F. (1992). Community empowerment: The critical base for primary health care. *Family & Community Health*, 15(April): 1-12.

Epstein, A. (2002, January 30). Bush's Un-American and immoral call for "national service." *MediaLink Ann Rand Institute* [On-line]. Available: http://www.aynrand.org/medialink.

Epstein, J., Coates, L., Salinas, K., Sanders, M., & Simon, B. S. (1997). *School, family, and community partnerships: Your handbook for action*. Thousand Oaks, CA: Corwin Press.

Epstein, J., & Associates, (2009). *School, family, and community partnerships: Your handbook for action* (3rd ed.). Thousand Oaks, CA: Corwin.

European Foundation for the Improvement of Living and Working Conditions (1998). *Management-union partnerships are rare in Ireland* [On-line]. Available: wysiwyg://5/http://www.eiro.eurofound.ie/1998/07/featur3e/ IE9807120F.html.

Feeney, A., Feeney, D., Norton, M., Simons, R., Wyatt, D. & Zappala, G. (2002). Bridging the gap between the 'haves' and the 'have nots'. Report of the National Education and Employment Forum. Brisbane: World Education Fellowship Australian Council.

Fetterman, D. (1996). Empowerment evaluation: An introduction to theory and practice. In D. Fetterman, S. Kaftarian, & A. Wandersman (Eds.), *Empowerment evaluation: Knowledge and tools for self-assessment & accountability* (pp. 3-46). Thousand Oaks, CA: SAGE Publications, Inc.

Finch, F. (1977). Collaborative behavior in work settings. *Journal of Applied Behavioral Science, 13*, 292-302.

Fisher, R. (2010) (Ed.). *The People Shall Rule: ACORN Community Organiizing and the Struggle for Economic Justice.* Nashville, TN: Vanderbilt.

Fizzard, G. (1992) Distance Education. *Our Children Our Future: Commissioned Studies.* St. John's, NF: Queen's Printer.

Foote, C., Battaglia, C., & Vermette, P. (1999). A partnership for the future of secondary education in Niagara Falls, N. Y. Paper presented to American Educational Research Association.

Foss, K. (2002, July 12). Living together a popular first step, data show. *Globe and Mail*, p. 1, 10.

Fowler, J. (1991). *A guide for building an alliance for science, mathematics and technology education.* College Park, MD: Triangle Coalition for Science and Technology Education.

Freedman, M. (1994). *Seniors in national and community service.* Philadelphia: Public/Private Ventures.

Freethought Today (2000, April). Church-school "partnerships" decried [On-line]. Available: htt:// www.ffrf.org.fttoday/ april2000/partnerships.html.

Friere, P. & Macedo, D. *Literacy*. New York: Bergin and Garvey, 1987.

Fuhrman, S. (1999). The new accountability. *CPRE Policy Briefs, RB-27*-January 1999. Philadelphia: Consortium for Policy Research in Education.

Fullan, M. & Stiegelbauer, S. (1991). *The new meaning of educational change*. New York: Teachers College Press.

Fullan, M. (1998). The three stories of educational reform: Inside; inside/out; outside/in. Online paper at http://home. oise.utoronto.ca/~mfullan/articles.html.

Gardner, J. (1990). *On learning*. New York: Free Press.

Gary, T. (2002) An extract from Commonly used strategies for change, relationship to donors and considerations (expanded from a chart by Stephanie Clohesy). Author.

Gaskell, J., Binkley, N., Nicoll, C., & McLaughlin, K. (1995). *The arts as an equal partner: The story of Langley Fine Arts School*. Toronto: Canadian Education Association.

Gaudet, J. (2008). *A case study of inclusive education service delivery in Prince Edward Island's Eastern School District*. Unpublished master of education thesis, University of Prince Edward Island.

Gay, G. (2002). Culturally responsive teaching in special education for ethnically diverse students: Setting the stage. *Qualitative Studies in Education, 15*(6), 613-629

Giamartino, G. & Wandersman, A. (1983). Organisational climate correlates of viable urban organisations. *American Journal of Community Psychology*, 11(5), 529-41.

Gillies, P. (1998). Effectiveness of alliances and partnerships for health promotion. *Health Promotion International*, 13(2), 9-120.

Ginsberg, R., Davies, T. & Quick, D. (2004). A North American public-private higher education partnership. In Mitchell, S., Klinck, P., & Burger, J. (Eds) *Worldwide pPartnerships for schools with voluntary organizations, foundations, universities, companies, and community councils* (pp. 3-32). Lewiston, NY: Edwin Mellen.

Gladstone, B., & Jacobsen, M. (1999). Educational partnerships in Rocky View School Division, Part 1. *International Electronic Journal of Leadership in Learning*, 3(1). [On-line]. Available: http://www.acs.ucalgary.ca/~iejll/volume3/gladstone.html.

Glassick, C., Huber, M. & Maeroff, G. (1997). *Scholarship assessed: Evaluation of the professoriate.* San Francisco: Jossey-Bass.

Glickman, C., Hayes, R. & Hensley, F. (1992). Site-based facilitation of empowered schools: Complexities and issues for staff developers. *Journal of Staff Development*, 13(2), 22-26.

Gottlieb, N., Brink, S., & Gingiss P. (1993). Correlates of coalition effectiveness the Smoke Free Class of 2000 Program. *Health Education Research: Theory & Practice*, 8(3), 375-84.

Government of Ontario. (1998) *Ontario Curriculum, Grades 1-8: The Arts* [On-line].Available: http://www.edu.gov.on.ca/eng/document/curricul/arts/arts.html.

Governor's Office, State of Texas. (1998). *Report of the Governor's science and technology council.* Austin, TX.

Gray, B. (1985). Conditions facilitating interorganizational collaboration. *Human Relations*, 38, 911-936.

Gray, B. (1989). *Collaborating. Finding Common Ground for Multiparty Problems.* San Francisco: Jossey-Bass.

Gray, B., & Wood, D. (1991). Collaborative alliances: Moving from practice to theory. *Journal of Applies Behavioral Science, 27* (1), 3-22.

Gray, B. (1995). Obstacles to success in educational collaborations. In L. Rigsby, M. Reynolds, & M. Wang, (Eds.), *School-community connections: Exploring issues for research and practice* (pp. 71-99). San Francisco: Jossey-Bass Publishers.

Green, J., & Vogan, N. (1991). *Music education in Canada: A historical account.* Toronto: University of Toronto Press.

Green, N. (1978, May 23). *Evaluation in the matter of the complaints by Janice Edith Miller, et al., and the Board of Trustees, Digby Regional High School.* Digby, Nova Scotia: Court of Nova Scotia.

Haas, T., & Nachtigal P. (1998). *Place value.* Charleston, WV. Clearinghouse on Rural Education and Small Schools.

Hamilton, W. (1999). Back from the brink: An administrator's perspective. *Teaching Music*, 6(4), 38-39, 59.

Hargreaves, A. (1994). *Teachers' work and culture in the postmodern age.* New York: Teachers College Press.

Hargreaves, D. (1994). The mosaic of learning: schools and teachers for the next century. London: Demos.

Harper, G., & Carver, L. (1999). "Out-of-the-mainstream" youth as partners in collaborative research: Exploring the benefits and challenges. *Health Education and Behavior*, 26(2), 250-255.

Harris, A., & Wyn, J. (2009). Young people's politics and the micro-territories of the local. *Australian Journal of Political Science*, 44(2), 327-344.

Harris, S. (1990). *Two-way Aboriginal schooling: Education and cultural survival.* Canberra: Aboriginal Studies Press.

Heim, J. (1999, January 11). Top job goes unfilled in many large school districts. *Education Daily*, 32(5), 1, 3.

Heller. K. (1990, Summer). Limitations and barriers to citizen particpation. *The Community Psychologist*, 4-5.

Herzberg, F. (1966). *Work and the nature of man.* New York: John Wiley.

Hildebrandt, E. (1994). A model for Community Involvement In Health (CIH) program development. *Social Science and Medicine*, 39(2), 247-254.

Hill, L. (2000). What does it take to change minds? Preservice teachers and conceptual change. *Journal of Teacher Education*, 51(1), 50-62.

Hillman, K. & Rothman, S. (2007). The movement of non-metropolitan youth towards the cities. Longitudinal Surveys of Australian Youth Research Report Number 27. Melbourne: Australian Council for Educational Research.

Hofstede G. (1980) *Culture's consequences: International differences in work-related values.* Beverly Hills, California: Sage.

Hood, C. (n.d.) Chapter 12: Conclusions.

Hood, L. & Rubin, M. (2004). *Priorities for Allocating Corporate Resources to Improve Education.* Urbana: University of Illinois.

Hooper-Briar, K., & Lawson, H. (1996). *Expanding partnerships for vulnerable children, youth, and families.* Alexandria, VA: Council on Social Work Education.

Hooper-Briar, K., & Lawson, H. (1996). *Expanding partnerships for vulnerable children, youth, and families.* Alexandria, VA: Council on Social Work Education.

Hord, S. (1981). *Working together: Cooperation and collaboration.* Austin, TX: Research and Development Center for Teacher Education, University of Texas.

Hord, S. (1986). A synthesis of research on organizational collaboration. *Educational Leadership*, 53(5), 22-26.

Horsley, M., & Costley, D. (2008). *Young people imaging a new democraccy: Young people's voicxes.* Sydney: Whitlam Institute.

Howard-Pitney, B. (1990). Community development is alive and well in community health promotion. *The Community Psychologist* Summer:4-5.

Howey, K.R. (1990). Changes in teacher education: Needed leadership and new networks. *Journal of Teacher Education*, 41(1), 3-9.

Huberman, M. (1999). The mind is its own place: The influence of sustained interactivity with practitioners on educational researchers. *Harvard Educational Review, 69*(3), 289-319.

Huffman-Joley, G. (1996). Professional development schools revisited. *Contemporary Education*, 67(4), 169-170.

Humana City Institute (2001). *Ten years of Imagine Chicago* [On-line]. Available: http://www.humancity.org.

Huskins, B. (1999, November). Teaching the parents; Educating the kids. *Leadership Calgary Newsletter* [On-line]. Available; htt:://www.volunteer calgary . . . leadershipCalgary/archives/9922newletter.html.

Ihejirika, M. (2000, March). Imagine Chicago, Depaul 6 museums, 7 schools—Bingo! *Catalyst* [On-line]. Available: http://catalyst-chicago.org/03-00/0300imagine.html.

Imagine Chicago (2001). *About Imagine Chicago* [On-line]. Available: http://imaginechicago.org/about-us.html.

Immerwehn, J., Johnson, J., & Kernan-Schloss, A. (1992). *Cross talk: the public, the experts, and competitiveness*. Washington, D.C.: Business-Higher Education Forum.

Israel, B., Schulz, A., Parker, E., Becker, A. (1998). Review of community based research: Assessing partnership approaches to improve public health. *Annual Review of Public Health*, 19, 173-202.

ITG Information Management (2000, February 10). *Need and feasibility of developing a fisheries training school in Southwest Nova Scotia*. Nova Scotia: Southwest Shore Development Authority.

John-Steiner, V., Weber, J. R., & Minnis, M. (1998). The challenge of studying collaboration. *American Education Research Journal, 35*(4), 773-783.

Johns, S., Kilpatrick, S., Falk, I. & Mulford, B. (2000a). *Leadership from within rural community revitalisation and school-community partnership*. Launceston: Centre for Research and Learning in Regional Australia.

Jordan, A. (2007). *Introduction to inclusive education*. Toronto: John Wiley and Sons.

Jordan, C., Orozco, E. & Averett, A. (2001). *Emerging issues in school, family and community connections*. Texas: Southwest Educational Development Laboratory.

Jupp, B. (2000). Working together: Creating a better environment for crosssector partnernerships. London: Demos.

Kagan, D. (1992). Professional growth among preservice and beginning teachers. *Review of Educational Research*, 62(2). 129-169.

Katz, R., & Tushman, M. (1979). Communication patterns, project performance, and task characteristics: An empirical evaluation and integration in an R & D setting. *Organizational Behavior and Human Performance, 23*, 139-162.

Keamy, R. Nicholas, H., Mahar, S. & Herrick, K. (2007). Personalising education; from research to policy and practice. Paper No 11. Melbourne: Melbourne: Department of Education and Early Childhood Development.

Keating, J. (2009). *A new federalism in Australian education: A proposal for a national reform agenda*. Melbourne: The Foundation for Young Australians.

Kegler, M., Steckler, A., McLeroy, K., & Malek, S. (1998) Factors that contribute to effective community health promotion coalitions: A study of 10 Project ASSISST coalitions in North Carolina. *Health Education and Behavior*, 45(3), 338-353.

Kelly, P. (2000). The mutual benefits of business and society in Australia. Keynote address, Second National Conference on Corporate Citizenship, Melbourne, 16-17 November, 2000.

Kenyon, P (1998). *20 clues for creating and maintaining a vibrant community*. York: Centre for Small Town Development.

Kilpatrick, S., Johns, S., Mulford, B., Falk, I. & Prescott, L. (2002). *More than an education: Leadership for rural school community partnerships*. Rural Industries Research and Development Corporation.

Kimberley, M. (2010). *What works Australia: Inclusive approaches with young people*. Melbourne: The Foundation for Young Australians.

King, T. (1988). *Here come the anthros*. Paper presented at the 88th Annual Meeting of the American Anthropological Association, Washington, D.C. As quoted in Battiste and Barman (1995).

Kisil, M. & Chaves, M. (1994). Linking the university with the community and its health system. *Medical Education Research*, 7, 31-46.

Kjaergaard, C. & Westphalen, S. (Eds.) (2001). *From collective bargaining to social partnerships: New roles of the social partners in Europe*. Copenhagen: Copenhagen Centre.

Knapp. M. (1995). How shall we study comprehensive, collaborative services for children and families? *Educational Researcher*, 24(4), 6-13.

Knott, J. (1995, March). *Building sustainable partnerships*. Paper prepared for the W.K. Kellogg Foundation conference. "Building Partnerships: An Agenda for Health Around the World," Miami.

Kreuter, M., & Lenzin, N. (1998). *Are consortia/collaboratives effective in changing health status and health systems? A critical review of the literature*. Atlanta, GA: Health 2000.

Kreuter, M., Lezin, N., & Young, L. (2000). Evaluating Community-Based Collaborative Mechanisms: Implications for Practioners. *Health Promotion Practice*, 1(1), 49-63.

Kristensen, J. (2001). Corporate social responsibility and new social partnerships. In Kjaergaard, C. & Wesphalen, S. (Eds.) *From collective bargaining to social partnerships; New roles of social partners in Europe* (pp. 21-37). Copenhagen: Copenhagen Centre.

Lamb, R. (2002). Community support for music: Symphony education partnership. In Mitchell, S. *Effective educational partnerships* (pp. 137-155). Westport, CT: Preger.

Larcombe, G. (2002). Emerging local employment opportunities for young people: Innovative employment & learning pathways. Sydney: Dusseldorp Skills Forum.

Larson, E. (1999). The impact of physician-nurse interaction on patient care. *Holistic Nurse*, 13, 38-47.

Larson, G. (1997). *American canvas*. Washington, D. C. National Endowment for the Arts.

Lasker, R., & Committee on Medicine and Public Health (1997). *Medicine and public health: The power of collaboration*. Chicago: Health Administration Press.

Latham, M. (2001). Reinventing collectivism: the new social democracy. Paper for Centre for Applied Economic Research Conference, Sydney, 12 July 2001.

Lauer, P., Apthorp, H., Vangsnes, D., Schieve, D., & Van Buhler, R. (1999). *McREL collaborative research initiative interim progress report*. Aurora, CO: Mid-continent Research for Education and Learning.

Learner, N. (2000, March 7). A good school principal is hard to find, study says. *Education Daily 33*(43), 1-2.

Lebrecht, N. (1991). *The maestro myth: Great conductors in pursuit of power*. London: Simon & Schuster.

Lechner, S. (1999, September 17). Common ground: Different backgrounds help GW, Howard University AmeriCorp volunteers effect change. *Hatchet*, D.C. Diary, 4, 6.

Levine, M. (1998). *Designing standards that work for professional development schools*. Washington, DC: National Council for Accreditation of Teacher Education. (ERIC Document Reproduction Service No. 426 052)

Lieberman, A. (1992). School/university collaborations: A view from the inside. *Phi Delta Kappan*, 75(2), pp. 147-156.

Limestone District School Board (LDSB). (2000, August 2). *Focus programs: Choices for secondary students* [On-line]. Available: http://www.limestone.edu.on.ca/ctypgm.

Lindsay, G., & Edwards G. (1988, August/September). Creating effective health coalitions. *Health Education*, 19, 35-6.

Lippert, C. (1999, February). Back from the brink: A teacher's perspective. *Teaching Music* 6(4), 34-36.

Logan, K. (1997). Changing roles: Artists and educators. *American String Teacher* vol. 47 no. 1, Winter 1997 (85, 87-88).

Lortie, D. (1975). *Schoolteacher: A sociological study*. Chicago: University of Chicago Press.

Ludowyke, J. (2001). Leading reform and the art of bodysurfing. Paper for Leading Learning Statewide Conference, Melbourne, 16 November 2001.

Luellman, D. (2000, June). Public private partnerships: Selling off the future of public education. *Labour News* (Alberta Federation of Labour) [On-line]. Available:http://www.telusplanet.net/public/afl/LabourNews/june00-14-html.

Madan, T. (1987). Community involvement in health policy: socio-structural and dynamic aspects of health beliefs. *Social Science and Medicine*, 25(6), 615-20.

Manefield, J., Collins, R., Moore, J., Mahar, S., & Warne, C. (2007). *Student voice; a historical perspective and new directions*. Melbourne: Department of Education and Early Childhood Development.

Mannes, M. (1996). Foreword. In K. Hooper-Briar & H. Lawson, (Eds.), *Expanding partnerships for vulnerable children, youth, and families* (pp. x-x1). Alexandria, VA: Council on Social Work Education.

Marginson, S. (2001). Global schooling and social capital: the contribution of education and training to successful outcomes for individuals and to economic development in a knowledge economy. Keynote address for National Education Summit, Melbourne, 28 September 2001.

Mawhinney, H. (1996). Institutional effects of strategic efforts at community enrichment. In Cibulka, J. & Kritek, W. (Eds.), *Coordination among schools, families, and communities* (pp. 223-243). Albany: State University of New York Press.

McClure, P. (2000). Participation support for a more equitable society. Canberra: Department of Families and Community Services.

McCullum, P. C. (2000). 6 points of a partnership. *Journal of Staff Development*, 21(2), 39.

McKay, L., Soothill, K., & Webb, C. (1995). Troubled times: the context for Interprofessional collaboration. In K. Soothill, L. Mackay, & C. Webb C., (Eds). *Interprofessional relations in health care*. London, Edward Arnold.

McKersie, W. (1999). Local philanthropy matter. In E. Lagemann (Ed.). *Philanthropic Foundartions: New scholarship new possibilities* (pp. 329-358). Bloomington, IN: Indiana University Press.

McLaughlin, M. (1990). "The Rand change agent study revisited: Macro perspectives and micro realities. *Educational Researcher 19* (9), 11-16.

Melaville, A., & Blank, M. (1993). *Together we can: A guide for crafting a profamily system of education and human services.* Washington, DC: U.S. Government Printing Office.

Mellor, S., & Kennedy, K. (2003). Australian students' democratic values and attitudes towards participation: Indicators from the IEA civic education study. *International Journal of Educational Research*, 39(6), 525-537.

Mitchell, S. (1971). *A woman's profession, a man's research.* Edmonton, AB: Alberta Association of Registered Nurses.

Mitchell, S. (1990). *Innovation and reform.* York, ON: Captus.

Mitchell. S. (1995). *Sociology of Educating.* York, On: Captus.

Mitchell, S. (1996). *Tidal waves of school reform.* Westport, CT: Praeger.

Mitchell, S. (1998 and 2007). *Reforming educators: Teachers, experts, and advocates.* Westport, CT: Praeger and Calgary, AB: Author.

Mitchell, S. (2000a, April). Rural visions. Paper presented at the Seventh Annual Conference on Educational Access, University of Arkansas, Pine Bluff.

Mitchell, S. (2000b). *Partnerships in creative activities among schools, artists, and professional organizations.* Lewiston, NY.: Edwin Mellen.

Mitchell, S. (2001a). The Practice of Partnership. Paper delivered for Faculty of Education, Queens University.

Mitchell, S. (2001b). Partnerships and charter schools: Contrasts in Canadian Reform. *Encounters on Education.* Vol. 4, 91-103.

Mitchell, S. (2002). *Effective partnerships: Experts, Advocates, and scouts.* Westport:CT: Praeger.

Mitchell, S., Klinck, P. & Burger, J. (2004). *Worldwide partnership for schools, with voluntary organization, foundations, universities, companies, and community councils.* Lewiston, N. Y: Edwin Mellen.

Mitchell, S. (2007). *A leader among sharecroppers, migrants, and farm workers: H. L. Mitchell and friends.* Mitchell: Calgary.

Mitra, D. & Gross, S. (2009). 'Increasing student voice in high school reform: Building partnerships, improving outcomes'. Educational Management Administration & Leadership, 37(4), 522-543.

Mizrahi, T. & Rosenthal, B. (1992). Managing dynamic tensions in social change coalitions. In *Community organization and social administration: Advances, Trends, and emerging principles.* Haworth Press.

Morgan, C.,& Murgatroyd, S. (1994). *Total quality management in the public sector.* London: Open University Press.

Morgan, G. (1997). *Images of organization.* Thousand Oaks, CA: Sage.

Mortensen, I. (2001, March). *First local report Hiiumaa, Estonia.* Copenhagen: Copenhagen Centre.

Mountain Institute (1998). Sacred mountains and environmental conservation: A practitioner's workshop. Spruce Knob Mountain Center, WV: Authors.

Moyneux, P. & Wooley, M. (2004). Partnership for multigrade and bilingual education in Vietnam. In Mitchell, S., Klinck, P., & Burger, J. (Eds). *Worldwide partnerships for schools with voluntary organizations, foundations, universities, companies, and community councils (pp. 253-283)*. Lewiston, NY: Edwin Mellen

Mullan, F. (1982). Community-oriented primary care: an agenda for the 80s. *New England Journal of Medicine*, 307(1), 1078-1079.

Murnighan, J. (1978). Models of coalition behavior: game theoretic, social psychological, and political perspectives. *Psychological Bulletin*, 85(5), 1130-53.

MENC (Music Educators National Conference). (1996). MENC News: MENC, NY Philharmonic begin collaboration. *Teaching Music*, 4(3), 15.

Myers, D. (1996). *Beyond tradition: Partnerships among orchestras, schools, and communities* (NEA Coop. Agreement DCA95-12). Atlanta, GA: Georgia State University.

Myers, D. (2000, July). Preparing performing musicians and teachers as collaborators in music education. *Music of the Spheres Conference Proceedings*, 290-302.

Myers, D., & Young, M. (1996). MENC teacher's guide to Live From Lincoln Center, New York Philharmonic: An educational guide to the PBS broadcast, January 15, 1997.

NAB. (2010). Schools First 2009 Public Report. Retrieved 27 July 2010, http://www. choolsfirst.edu.au/sf-toolkit/index.phps.

National Association for Music Education (n. d.). Oscar Mayer contest prize winners announced [On-line]. Available: wysiwyg://5/http://www.menc.org.

National Association of Partners in Education (2001). *Partnerships 2000: A decade of growth and change*. Alexandria, VA: National Association of Partners in Education.

National Business and Education Center (NBEC) (1999). *Operating principles for business-edcation partnerships*. Toronto: Conference Board of Canada.

National Institute for Clinical Excellence (NICE). (1999). *A guide to our work*. London: NICE.

Neighbors Project (2000). *Capital city initiative to serve Shaw and Columbia Heights*. Washington, D. C.: Authors.

Nelson, J. & Zadek, S. (2000). *Partnership alchemy: New social partnerships in Europe*. Copenhagen: Copenhagen Centre.

Nierman, G. (1993, Spring). Perspectives of collaboration versus cooperation. *Journal of Music Teacher Education*, 25-28.

Nieto, S. (1996). *Affirming diversity: The sociopolitical context of multicultural education*. Boston: Longman Publishers.

North Carolina Child Advocacy Institute (1995). *Children's index: A profile of leading indicators of the health and well-being of North Carolina's children*. Raleigh, NC: Authors.

North Carolina Council of Churches (2002). Partnerships between schools and religious communities [On-line]. Available: http://www.nccouncilof churches. org/ Sabbath/ Partnerships.html

Nystrand, R. (1991). *Professional development schools: Toward a new relationship for schools and universities, trends and issues*. Washington, DC: Office of Educational Research and Improvement. (ERIC Document Reproduction Service No. 330 690)

O'Donoghue, F. (1998). *The hunger for professional learning in Nunavut schools*. Doctoral thesis, submitted in conformity with the requirements for the degree of Doctor of Education. Ontario Institute for Studies in Education, of the University of Toronto.

Office for Youth. 2010). Retrieved 27 February 2010 from http://www.deewr.gov.au/Youth/ fficeForYouth/Pages/default.aspx.

On our terms: The state of Inuit culture and society. (2001). Inuit Nunavut Social Development Council.

Orchestras Canada. (2000, May). International Education Models. Paper delivered at Orchestras Canada World Conference

Osguthorpe, R., Harris, R. Harris, M., & Black, S. (Eds.). *Partner Schools.* San Francisco, CA: Jossey-Bass.

Osguthorpe, R., & Patterson, R. (1998). *Balancing the tensions of change.* Thousand Oaks, CA: Corwin Press.

Palmer, P. (1998). *The courage to teach.* San Francisco, CA: Jossey-Bass.

Panet-Raymond, J. (1992). Partnership: myth or reality? *Community Development Journal,* 27(2), 156-165.

Pasch, S., & Pugach, M. (1990). Collaborative planning for urban professional development schools. *Contemporary Education,* 61(3), 135-143.

Patel L. (1993). *Children and women in South Africa: A situation analysis.* Johannesburg: Auckland House.

Percy-Smith, B. (2010). 'Councils, consultations and community: rethinking the spaces for children and young people's participation'. Children's Geographies, 8(2), 107-122.

Pfeffer, J., & Sutton, R. (2000). *The knowing doing gap: How smart companies turn knowledge into action.* Boston: Harvard Business School Press.

Pollack, M. (2002). Student service in a nation's capital: Neighbors Project. In Mitchell, S. (Ed.) *Effective educational partnerships* (pp. 121-135). Westport, CT: Praeger.

Popay, J., & Williams, G. (1996). Public Health Research and Lay Knowledge. *Social Science and Medicine*, 42(5) 759-768.

Porter, S. (1995). *Nursing's relationship with medicine.* Avershot, UK: Avebury.

Preparing North Carolina for 21st Century Schools (2000). *Programs leading North Carolina's preparation for 21st Century Schools* [On-line]. Available: http://www.ga. unc. edu/21stcentury schools/programs.

Prestby, J., Wandersman, A., Florin, P., Rich, R., & Chavis, D. (1990). Benefits, costs, incentive management and participation in voluntary organisations: A means to understanding and promoting empowerment. *American Journal of Community Psychology*, 18(1), 117-149.

Price Waterhouse. (1996). *EMC technology forecast for 1996.* New York: Author.

Prime Minister's Youth Pathways Action Plan Taskforce (2001). Footprints to the Future. Canberra: Department of Education, Science and Technology.

Putnam, R. (1993). *Making democracy work.* Princeton, NJ.: Princeton University Press.

Putnam, R. (2000). Bowling alone. the collapse and revival of American community. New York: Simon and Schuster.

Putnam, R. (2004). Education, Diversity, Social Cohesion and "Social Capital". Paper presented at Meeting of OECD Education Ministers, Dublin, 18-19 March 2004.

Raby, R. (2008). Frustrated, resigned, outspoken: Students' engagement with school rules and some implications for participatory citizenship. *International Journal of Children's Rights*, 16, 77-98.

Rathke, W. (2009). *Citizen Wealth: Winning the Campaign to Save Working Families.* San Francisco:, Berrett-Koehler.

Raysmith, H. (2001). Building better communities: The way to go. Melbourne: Victorian Local Governance Association.

Reed, R.,& Cedja, B. (1987). *Attributes and preconditions of collaboration between and among schools, institutions of higher education, and state education agencies.* Elmhurst, IL: North Central Regional Laboratory.

Remer, J. (1996). *Beyond enrichment: Building effective arts partnerships with schools and your community.* New York: American Council for the Arts.

Renzaglia, A., Hutchins, M., & Lee, S. (1997). The impact of teacher education on the beliefs, attitudes, and dispositions of preservice special educators. *Teacher Education and Special Education*, 20(4), 360-377.

Rich, R. (1986). Neighborhood-based participation in the planning process: In Taylor, R. (Ed.), *handbook of Community Pscyhology.* New York: Plenum.

Richards, R. (circa 1995) *Building partnerships: the vision and the critical elements.* Partnership Quarterly Report, MUCPP Management Committee: South Africa.

Richards, R. (Ed.). (1996). *Building partnerships.* Jossey-Bass: San Francisco.

Richardson, V. (1996). The role of attitudes and beliefs in learning to teach. In J. Sikula (Ed.), *Handbook of research on teacher education* (pp. 102-119). New York: Macmillan.

Richardson-Koebler, V. (1988). Barriers to the effective supervision of student teaching: A field study. *Journal of Teacher Education*, 38(2), 28-34.

Rider, P. (2009). *Charlottetown: A history*. Charlottetown: Prince Edward Island Museum and Heritage Foundations.

Rifkin, S. (1981). The role of the public in the planning, management and evaluation of health activities and programmes, including self-care. *Social Science and Medicine*, 15(1), 377-386.

Rifkin, S. (1986). Health planning and community participation. *World Health Forum*, 7, 156-162.

Rifkin, S. (1987). Primary health care, community participation and the urban poor: a review of the problems and solutions. *Asia-Pacific Journal of Public Health*, 1(2), 57-63.

Rigden, D. (1991). *Business/school partnerships: A path to effective restructuring*. New York: Council for Aid to Education.

Rigden, D. (1992). *Business and the schools: a guide to effective programs*. New York: Council for Aid to Education.

Riggs, Frank (1987). *Report of the Small Schools Study Project*. St. John's, NF: Queen's Printer, 1987.

Rigney, P. (2001). *Social dialogue and lifelong learning in Ireland* [On-line]. Available: www.etfr.eu.int/ letfwnnsfl/pages/downloadmalmo.2001.

Rigsby, L., Reynolds, M., & Wang, M. C. (Eds.). (1995). *School-community connections: Exploring issues for research and practice*. San Francisco: Jossey-Bass.

Robertson, H. (1998). *No more teachers, no more books: The commercialization of Canada's schools*. Toronto: McClelland and Stewart.

Robinson, L. & Keating, J. (2005). Networks and governance: the case of LLENs in Victoria. ARC Linkage Project Occasional Paper No 3. The University of Melbourne.

Robinson, M. (1998). A collaboration model for school and community music education. *Arts Policy Review*, l00(2), 32-39

Rodgers, B. (1999). Back from the brink: The community's perspective. *Teaching Music*, 6(4), 40-41, 62.

Rogers, T., Howard-Pitney, B., Fieghery, E., Altman, D., Endres, J., & Roeseler, A. (1993). Characteristics and participation perceptions of tobacco control coalitions in California. *Health Education Research: Theory & Practice*, 8(3), 345-357.

Rose, F. (200^). *Coalitions across the cultural divide*. Ithaca, NY: Cornell University Press.

Rowe, I. (1989). School concerts by the TSO, 1925-1957. Master's thesis, University of Western Ontario, 1989.

Sagor, R. (1997). Collaborative action research for educational change. In A. Hargreaves (Ed.), *Rethinking educational change with heart and mind* (pp. 169-191). Alexandria, VA: Association for Supervision and Curriculum Development.

Samuels, C. (2010, July 23). Study: Effective principals embrace collective leadership. *Education Week*, 29(37), 1 & 3.

Sarason, S., & Lorentz, E. (1998). *Crossing boundaries: Collaboration, coordination, and the redefinition of resources*. San Francisco: Jossey-Bass.

Scannell, D. (1996). Evaluating professional development schools: The challenge of an imperative. *Contemporary Education*, 67(4), 241-243.

Schmidt, H., Neufeld, V., Zohair, M., & Ogunbode, T. (1991). Network of community-oriented educational institutions for the health sciences. *Academic Medicine*, 66(5), 259-263.

Schoor, L. (1988). *Within our reach*. New York: Doubleday Anchor.

Schverak, A., Coltharp, C., & Cooner, D. (1998). Using content analysis to evaluate the success of a professional development school. *Educational Forum*, 62(2), 172-177.

Scott, D. (2002). Report to Annual General Meeting, Philanthropy Australia. Melbourne, 24 April, 2002.

Seifer, S. & Maurana, C. (1998). Health professions education, civic responsibility and the overall health of communities-campus partnerships. *Journal of Interprofessional Care*, 12(3), 253-257.

Seitsinger, R. (1996). Nurturing partnerships between schools and families. In P. A. Cordeiro (Ed.), *Boundary crossings: Educational partnerships and school leadership* (pp. 15-29). San Francisco: Jossey-Bass Inc.

Sharp, J. (1990). Workforce. In *Disturbing the Peace: Texas Performance Review*. Washington, D.C.: National Alliance of Business.

Shelley, A., & Washburn, S. (2000). Our NCATE report card: A partnership for excellence. *The Educational Forum*, 64(2), 156-164.

Shelton, J. (2001). Consequential learning: Outcomes from connecting learning to place. Keynote address for Education Foundation Summit, Melbourne, 18 October 2001.

Short, C. (1998). The Cultural Metamorphosis of Cree Education. M. A. Thesis. University of Calgary.

Sills, B., Barron, P. & Heath, P. (1993, June). School reform through partnerships. In *Report of the Synergy Conference: Industry's role in the reform of mathematics, science and technology education* (pp. 68-71). Leesburg, VA: Triangle Coalition.

Sironek, K. & Goodlad, J. (1988). *School-university partnerships in action*. New York: Teachers College, Columbia University

Sirotnik, K. (1988). The meaning and conduct of inquiry in school-university partnerships. In K. Sirotnik & J. I. Goodlad (Eds.), *School-university partnerships in action* (pp. 205-225). New York: Teachers College Press.

Sizer, T. (1992). *Horace's school: Redesigning the American high school*. Boston, MA: Mariner Books.

Sloan, E. (1996). Strategies for fostering partnerships between educators and health and human services professionals. In P. Cordeiro (Ed.), *Boundary crossings: Educational partnerships and school leadership* (pp. 41-55). San Francisco: Jossey-Bass Inc.

Sparks, D. (1995). A paradigm shift in staff development. *The Eric Review, 3*(3), 2-4.

Sparks, D. (2000). Partnerships need purpose. *Journal of Staff Development, 21*(2), 3.

Spaull, A. (1998). Public education in Australia: An historical essay. In Reid, A. (Ed.), Going public: education policy and public education in Australia (pp. 3-8). Adelaide: Australian Curriculum Studies Association.

Spierings, J. (2001). Regional and local government initiatives to support youth pathways: lessons from innovative communities. Paper for Australian Council for Educational Research Conference, Melbourne, October 2001.

Stacey, M. (1994). The power of lay knowledge. A personal view. In J. Popay & G. Williams (Eds.) *Researching the people's health*. London: Routledge.

Stairs, A. (1995). Learning processes and teaching roles in native education: Cultural base and cultural brokerage. Battiste, M. and Barman, J. Eds. First Nations education in Canada: The circle unfolds. (pp. 139-153). Vancouver: University of British Columbia.

Statham, D. (2000). Guest editorial: Partnership between health and social care. *Health and Social Care in the Community*, 8(2), 87-89.

Statistics Canada. *The 2006 Canada census*. <www. statscan.gc.ca.>

Stewart-Weeks, M. (1998). Promoting social capital. Sydney: Unpublished working paper.

Stokes, H. & Tyler, D. (2001). Planning the future: the evaluation of phase one in the Pathways Project in Victoria. Melbourne: Department of Education, Employment and Training.

Strawn, J. (1998). *Beyond job search or basic education: Rethinking the role of skills in welfare reform*. Washington, DC: Center for Law and Social Policy

Suggett, D., Goodsir, B., & Pryor, S. (2000). *Corporate community involvement: Establiishing a business case*. Melbourne: Centre for Corporate Public Affairs and Business Council of Australia.

Swanwick, K. (1988). *Music, mind and education*. London: Routledge.

Tambling, P. (1999). Opera, education and the role of arts organisations. *British Journal of Music Education*, 16(2), 139-156.

Tattersall, A. (2009). *Power in Coalitions*. Ithaca, NY: Cornell.

Taylor, F. (2010). *What works Australia: Young* People Active in Communities. Melbourne: The Foundation for Young Australians.

Taylor, N., Smith, A. & Gollop, M. (2008). New Zealand children and young people's perspectives on citizenship. *International Journal of Children's Rights*, 16, 195-210.

Taylor, P. (1996). Supporting community involvement: the organisational challenges. In P. Burton & L. Harrison (Eds.) *Identifying local health needs. New community based approaches.* Bristol: The Policy Press.

Teitel, L. (1996). Getting down to cases. *Contemporary Education*, 67(4), 200-206.

Teitel, L. (1997). Changing teacher education through professional development school partnership: A five-year follow-up study. *Teachers College Record*, 99(2), 311-334.

Teitel, L. (1998). Separations, divorces, an open marriages in professional development partnerships. *Journal of Teacher Education*, 49(2), 85-96.

Townsend, T. (1999). Leading in times of rapid change. Keynote address for annual conference, Australian Secondary Principals' Association, Canberra, September 28, 1999.

Tushman, M., & Scanlan, T. (1981). Boundary spanning individuals: Their role in information transfer and their antecedents. *Academy of Management Journal*, 24, 289-305.

Vinh, T. (1994, August 30). Twin counties again seek smart start. *The Evening Telegram*, p. A1.

Volunteering Australia. (2006). *Corporate volunteering survey.* Melbourne.

Voss, K., & Sherman, R. (2000). Breaking the iron law of oligarchy: Union revitalization in the American labor movement. *American Journal of Sociology*, 106(2), 303-349.

W.K. Kellogg Foundation (WKKF) (1992). *Community Partnerships: Redirecting Health Professions Education Toward Primary Health Care.* Battle Creek, Michigan: W.K.Kellogg Foundation.

Walsh, L., & Black, R. (2009). *Students in the lead: Increasing participation by young people in a distributed leadership framework.* Melbourne: Centre for Strategic Education.

Wandersman, A. (1981). A framework of participation in community organisations. *Journal of Applied Behavioural Science*, 17(1), 27-58.

Waters-Lynch, J. (2008). 'Young people driving networks'. In Black, R., Beyond the *Classroom: Building new school networks.* Melbourne: ACER Press.

Watt, A., & Rodmell, S. (1988). Community involvement in health promotion: progress or panacea? *Health Promotion*, 2(4), 359-367.

Weigold, P. (1999). Changing arts practice. Unpublished paper

Wierenga, A. (2003). *Sharing a new story: Young people in decision-making.* Melbourne: The Foundation for Young Australians and Australian Youth Research Centre.

Wettenhall, G. & Alexander, K. (2000). Building partnerships between councils and their communities. Melbourne: Stegley Foundation and Victorian Local Governance Association.

Wichienwong, W. (1988). *The relationship of administrators' involvement in the evaluation process and evaluation attitudes.* Unpublished doctoral dissertation, Ohio State University, Columbus.

Williams, L., Konrad, J., & Larson, H. (1992). *A guide for planning a volunteer program for science, mathematics and technology education.* College Park, MD: Triangle Coalition for Science and Technology Education.

Williamson, C. (1999). The challenge of lay partnership. *British Medical Journal*, 319, 721-722.

Winitzky, N., Stoddart, T., & O'Keefe, P. (1992). Great expectations: Emergent professional development schools. *Journal of Teacher Education*, 43(1), 3-18.

Wise, A., & Leibbrand, J. (2000). Standards and teacher quality: Entering the new millennium. *Phi Delta Kappan*, 81(8), 612-621.

Wiseman, D. & Cooner, D. (1996). Discovering the power of collaboration: The impact of a school-university partnership on teaching. In C. D. Schmitz, (Ed.), *Teacher education and practice* (pp. 18-28). Austin, TX: Texas Association of Colleges for Teacher Education.

Wolcott, H. (1977). *Teachers vs. technocrats.* Eugene, OR: Center for Educational Policy and Management, University of Oregon.

Wood, D., & Gray, B. (1991). Toward a comprehensive theory of collaboration. *Journal of Applied Behavioral Science*, 27(2), 139-162.

Wood, J. (2000). Innovative teachers hindered by the "green-eyed monster." *Harvard Education Letter*, 16(4), 7-8.

Wright, B. (1994). Composition analysis. *Mid-Western Educational Researcher*, 7(2), 29-36, 38.

Wright, B. (1996, Summer). Pack to chain to team? *Rasch Measurement Transactions*, 10, 501.

Zakus, J. & Lysack, C. (1998). Revisiting community participation. *Health Policy and Planning*, 13(1), 1-12.

Zadek, S., Hojensgard, N., & Raynard, P. (2001). *Perspectives on the new economy of corporate citizenship*. Copenhagen: Copenhagen Centre.

Zalkind, H. (1996). *Down East Partnership for Children (DEPC) organizational development program*. Rocky Mount, ND: Down East Partnership for Children.

Zimmerman, M., & Rappaport, J. (1988) Citizen participation, perceived control, and psychological empowerment. *American Journal of Community Psychology*, 16(5), 725-750.

Zimmerman, M. (1990). Taking aim on empowerment research: on the distinction between individual and psychological conceptions. *American Journal of Community Psychology*, 18(1), 169-177.

Zuckerman, H. & Kaluzny, A. (1990). *Managing beyond vertical and horizontal integration: Strategic Alliances as an emerging organizational form*. Unpublished manuscript.

Zuckerman, H., Kaluzny, A., & Ricketts, T. (1995). Alliances in health care: What we know, what we think we know, and what we should know. *Health Care Management Review*, 20(1), 54-64.

Index

A

Abstract teaching versus
holistic learning 9-10,
17-19, 22-23, 28

Are you Making a Difference
(ruMad) 277, 292-295,
297

Association for Community
Organizations for Reform
Now (ACORN) 245-274,
322-356

Auluq, Nunuvut 12, 17,
20-21, 25, 29-30

Australia 275, 278, 286,
288, 294-295 196-197,
251-264

Australian Council for
Educational Research
(ACER) 287

B

Barrington Muncipal High
School (BMHS) 309, 311

Between Generations 143-144

Boundary role *x*, 202-245;
boundary spanners 91-92,
208, 209, 220-223, 231,
233-240

British Columbia 331-337

C

Calgary 124-126, 339, 345

Canadian Business for Social
Responsibility (CBSR)
150-151

Canada 250, 256-258, 262,
263, 267, 270, 271

Canadian Centre for Policy
Alternatives (CCPA) xi,
86-87, 333-335, 337, 339

Chicago Grassroots
Collaborative, 43, 44,
46, 258, 259

Child Care Resources and
Referral, Family Resource
And Exchange (CCR&R)
216, 220

Cockroach Derby 325-32716

Collaborative   11, 29, 41
    53, 72-73, 85, 203-206,
    229-232
Come From Away (CFA)   25,
    315, 319
Community and Protective
    Service Committee
    343-344
Community Literacy and
    Support Service(CLASS)
    309, 311
Community partners   48-50,
    52, 71, 79, 85, 247
Community Organization
    Practioners of Kenya
    (COPA-K) 272-273
Corporate Christmas
    Calendar   145-146
Corporate Citizenship
    79-80, 124 127, 129,
    131, 134, 156

D

Dominican Republic   251-253
Down East Partnership for
    Children (DEPC)   201,
    204, 209, 215, 217, 230,
    241, 273-274

E

Education Foundation
    275-276
Envision Financial   145-146,
    153
Environmental education   89,
    93, 105-107, 110, 63-82,
    207-210, 231-237, 318
Enviroworks   93-122

F

Family resource centers   216,
    220, 228
First Calgary Foundations
    124-126, 134-138,
    144-145, 148, 156
Focus program   99, 101
Foundations   244, 256, 274,
    313
Foundation for Young
    Australians (FYA)
    271-274, 277, 281, 287,
    291, 296

G

George Washington
    University (GWU) 2-3,
    51, 54, 55, 57, 77-81, 84
Gulf of Maine Institute
    Without Walls (GMIWW)
    316-318, 321

H

Heritage Park (12 Days of
    Christmas) 146-147
Human Resources
    Development Canada
    101, 102, 304, 310, 313

I

Imagine cities   xiv, 149,157
Incubation space   226
Inclusive education   26-27
India   264, 268, 272
Inuit   1, 5-20
Inuktitut   10, 11, 15-16

K

Kenya   257-270
Key success factors   358-359
Kingston, Ontario   95-96,
    101, 103 107, 110-121,
    162-163
Kingston Area Recycling
    Corporation (KARC)   106
Kingston General Hospital
    (KGH)   107
Kingston Symphony
    Association (KSA)   161,
    163, 168 169, 179, 181,
    184, 188

L

Landlord Licensing and
    Rent Escrow Campaign
    329-330
Learning Community Pilot
    Project (LCPP)   306,307,
    328, 313
Limestone District School
    Board (LDSB)   93,96,
    99-103, 110, 112-113,
    115, 119,161,165

Living Wage Law   331-335, 338-349

Local Industry Focusing on the Environment (LIFE)   89

London Benchmarking Group (LBG)   148-149

Low Income Cut Off (LICO)   340, 346

Low Income Tenant Energy Savers (LITES)   349-355

M

Mexico   255

Music program   xix, 161, 164, 178-179, 187-188,191-192;

N

new elements   196-199

National Australian Bank (NAB) 287

New South Wales (NSW) Teachers Federation   31, 34, 36

New Zealand study   291

Neighbor Project   43, 48, 52-88

Nova Scotia   305, 306. 321

Nova Scotia Community College   311, 313

Nova Scotia Housing Authority (NSHA)   311, 313

O

One Day Arts School   140-143

Ontario Health Coalition   48

Ontario Ministry of Education and Training   162, 166-167

Ontario Disability Support Program (ODSP)   344

Ontario Health Inquiry   43, 48

Oral history   313-315

Ottawa   28, 224-231

Ottawa Board of Education   299-301

Ottawa-Carleton Learning Foundation (OCLF)   300

Ottawa /Carleton Network for Education: World Consortium Project (ONEWorld)   300-302

P

Parent partnerships   1, 33

Partners in Education (PIE)
ii, v, viii, 123-159

Partnership definition   x, 8,
38, 89, 128-129, 161,
202, 229-244

Peru   252-255, 264-268,
280, 284, 356-362

Petite Riverie   313-315207

Poverty Reduction Strategy
343-344

Public Education Fund   32

Public Education Alliance   34

Q

Queen Elizabeth Collegiate
And Vocational Institute
(QECVI)   97, 101,
121-102

Queens University   101
105.113, 117, 119 161,
164,168, 195, 199

R

Race Relations, Cross Cultural
Understanding and
Human Rights (RCH)
3119

Rural partnership   302-305

S

School Advisory Committees
(SAC))   306

School Based Enterprises
(SBE)   81

Service clubs   304

School Business Community
Partnership Brokers   291

School-to-Work committee
309, 310, 312

Smart school funding
211-213, 214, 218-219,
224

Social Economy Research
Group   30

Southwest Regional School
Board (SWRSB)   305-306

Stay-in-school committee
205-207

Student partnerships   17-19

Symphony Educational
   Partnership (SEP)
      167-179, 181-187, 193,
      195, 201, 207
SEP six principles   183-186
Syndey, Australia   21, 345

T

Theatre Junction   125,
   136-138, 155
Toronto Environmental
   Alliance   (TEA) 347-352
Toronto Muncipal Code
   325-326

U

United Nations   116-118

V

Vibrant Communities   342
Vincent Inquiry   100
Volunteering   82-83, 132,
   135, 286-287

Y

York Community Services
   Legal (YCL)   327

W

Walmart   44, 48
WordFest   125, 139-140